# FROM BROKEN TO BLESSED

By

Dustin Bryan

Copyright © 2025 by Dustin Bryan

All Rights Reserved.
No part of this publication may be reproduced in any form or by any means, including scanning, photocopying, or otherwise without prior written permission of the copyright holder.

First Printing, 2025

# Contents

Foreword ................................................................................. 1

Introduction ............................................................................ 5

Chapter 1: The Scars We Carry, The Stories We Rewrite ............. 7

Chapter 2: The Cost of Defiance ............................................... 31

Chapter 3: The Weight of a Father's Return .............................. 43

Chapter 4: Through Chaos and Compassion ............................. 59

Chapter 5: From Chaos to Redemption ..................................... 85

Chapter 6: The Silent Witnesses and A Promise Made ............. 103

Chapter 7: The Weight of Her Words: The Power of Mine ....... 113

Chapter 8: The Highs, Lows, and Lessons of Poker .................. 129

Chapter 9: Forged in the Cold ................................................ 151

Chapter 10: Beyond Fear: The Courage to Grow ..................... 159

Chapter 11: Grace Over Anger ................................................ 179

Chapter 12: From Dreams to Despair: A Promise to Myself .... 193

Chapter 13: Becoming the Man I Prayed to Be ....................... 229

Acknowledgments .................................................................. 245

# FOREWORD

This book represents a journey—my journey. It's a story of resilience, faith, failure, and redemption. Writing these words, I can't help but think back to the little boy I used to be—the one who prayed to God for a different life. He was hungry, afraid, and uncertain about what tomorrow would bring, but he was hopeful. That hope, though fragile at times, carried me through some of the darkest seasons of my life and shaped the man I've become.

When I began this book, I didn't set out to write a simple memoir. My intention was never to recount my story but to testify to the power of perseverance and faith. Life has knocked me down more times than I care to admit, and I've made my share of mistakes along the way. But through it all, one truth has remained constant: growth is possible. Transformation is possible. Grace is always within reach, even in our darkest moments.

This book reflects the highs and lows of my life. It captures the innocence of childhood dreams and the painful reality of growing up in a world where love often felt conditional. It traces my journey from a young man chasing financial success, believing it would fix everything, to a husband, father, and believer in something far more significant than myself.

## FROM **B**ROKEN TO **B**LESSED

I've worn many hats—son, truck driver, poker player, business owner, husband, father, and servant. Each role has taught me lessons, many of them hard-earned. I've experienced the thrill of success, the devastation of failure, and the peace of surrendering to God's plan. Every chapter in this book represents a turning point in my life, a moment when I faced a challenge and had to decide whether to rise or fall.

What you'll find in these pages is not a perfect story, but a real one. It's a story about chasing dreams and falling short, rising from the ashes of failure, and discovering that success isn't defined by a paycheck or a title but by the strength of your character and the depth of your love. It's about learning to see setbacks as stepping stones and finding purpose in the seemingly impossible struggles.

I've also come to understand that success isn't just about what you build for yourself—it's about what you leave behind for others. This book is for my wife, Rachel, and my children, Gabriel and Iona, who remind me daily that family is the most precious gift. It's for the little boy I used to be, who dared to dream of a better life, and for the man I am today, who strives to live with integrity, love, and faith.

But most importantly, this book is for you—the reader. Whether standing on the edge of your next great leap or crawling through a valley of hardship, I want you to know that you are not alone. If there's one thing my life has taught me, there's always hope. There's always a way forward, even when it feels impossible. The man or woman you prayed to become is within reach—one step, one prayer, and one act of faith at a time.

As you turn these pages, I hope you'll see that life's most significant lessons often come wrapped in adversity. I hope you'll find encouragement in the rawness of my story and feel inspired to reflect on your journey with a renewed sense of purpose. I pray this book will remind you that failure isn't the end—it's an opportunity to rise, grow, and rebuild stronger than ever.

If I could leave you with one thought, it would be this: life isn't happening to you—it's happening for you. Every challenge, triumph, and moment of uncertainty shapes you into the person you were meant to become. Embrace it. Lean into it. And never stop fighting for the life you were created to live.

This is my story. I hope it helps you reflect on and shape your own.

With gratitude and faith,
Dustin Bryan

# INTRODUCTION

As a child, I closed my eyes and imagined a different life. In my mind, I was sitting at a dinner table in a house filled with love, surrounded by the warmth of a family that cared for one another. The smell of a home-cooked meal would drift through the air, and laughter would echo from the walls. I wasn't hungry, lonely, or scared—I was loved. Those moments in my imagination were my escape from a reality where I often felt invisible and unwanted. I wasn't just hungry for food; I was hungry for connection, belonging, and love that felt far out of reach.

Have you ever met someone who blames their parents or their past for the person they've become and their life? I know people who grew up in the system, living in residential homes, and they still blame their childhood for where they are today. Some are in their thirties now and haven't been in the system for over a decade. But I was determined not to be a product of my environment. I refused to let my circumstances define me or use them as a crutch. Rising above where I came from has always been my mission, and I've worked hard to turn my struggles into strength.

Life didn't give me much to hold on to in my early years. My constant companions were the chaos in my home, the fear that seemed to linger in every corner, and the overwhelming feeling of being unworthy of love. But even in the darkest moments, I held onto that dream. I didn't know it then, but those dreams were more than just fantasies—they were glimpses of what could be. They were the seeds of a promise I would one day make to myself: to build a life full of love and purpose that would silence the pain of my past.

This book is the story of how I kept that promise. It's about the struggles I faced, the lessons I learned, and the faith that carried me through when nothing else could. It's a journey from brokenness to blessing, longing to belonging, and despair to hope. This is not a story of perfection—it's a story of transformation, of taking the ashes of a painful childhood and turning them into something beautiful.

To anyone who has ever felt unseen, unloved, or unworthy, I want you to know this: you are not alone. I hope this story reminds you that change is always possible. Your dreams matter, and so does your promise to yourself. I'm living proof that even the most broken beginnings can lead to the most blessed endings.

# Chapter 1: The Scars We Carry, The Stories We Rewrite

Thin curtains let in the morning light, casting shadows on the naked strangers sprawled on my living room floor. The room resembled the aftermath of a silent war—bodies were scattered everywhere, draped over furniture, and stretched across the carpet like discarded mannequins. A man lay face down on the coffee table, his arm hanging limply over the edge, fingers brushing against an overturned ashtray. Nearby, a woman was curled into a fetal position, her damp hair clinging to her face as if she'd just emerged from a restless dream.

Soft snores punctuated the quiet, and the uneven rise and fall of chests created an irregular rhythm. Others lay still, their bodies twisted into unnatural poses like marionettes abandoned mid-performance. On the couch, a man slouched upright, his head thrown back and mouth frozen mid-sentence. Another leaned against the wall, bare legs splayed out, hands resting at his sides with palms upturned, as though in surrender. The stillness felt heavy, the silence charged with an unspoken tension I couldn't yet name.

Before I could fully process the scene, a strange cocktail of odors overwhelmed me. The air was dense and sour, carrying the pungent stench of sweat and the sharp tang of spilled beer that had seeped into the carpet. Cigarette smoke drifted lazily toward the open window. Its faint sweetness lingered like a ghost. But there was something else—a bitter, earthy scent that didn't belong. Years later, I would know it as marijuana. In that moment, though, it was just another thread in the stale air, leaving my throat dry and my stomach churning.

Empty beer cans and liquor bottles, strewn across the floor like fallen soldiers, bore silent witness to the previous night's revelry. Half-eaten meals sat abandoned on the kitchen table, their contents now stiff and inedible. A streak of white powder marred the glass surface of a nightstand as if someone had tried to wipe it clean but had given up halfway. In the corner, the record player sat still. Its needle pressed against the spinning vinyl, emitting a faint, scratchy hum. It was the only sound, aside from the occasional snore.

I was tiny, barely more than a baby, able to do nothing but crawl. My knees pressed into the worn carpet as I navigated the maze of bodies, my small hands encountering the cold, sticky remnants of spilled drinks. Each movement felt constrained like I was crossing invisible boundaries with every hesitant step. When my hand brushed against a man's bare arm, a shiver raced down my spine. I recoiled instantly, as if I had broken some unspoken rule. His face was buried in a torn pillow. His shallow breaths were warm and clammy against my skin. I felt a discomfort I couldn't explain. I instinctively recoiled from it.

Sunlight filtered through the window, illuminating the air in a soft haze. Floating dust particles danced in the beams, resembling tiny stars in the stale, heavy atmosphere. Their strange beauty mesmerized me, and I reached out to touch one. But the faint stir of movement nearby stopped me. I froze, holding my breath, my wide eyes locked onto the shifting figure. He fidgeted for a moment, then settled into stillness again, leaving me alone in the eerie quiet.

The silence wasn't peaceful; it was oppressive. A heavy, lingering quiet that felt louder than the chaos that had preceded it. It vibrated in the air, pressing down on me in a way I couldn't name. My stomach churned, though I didn't know why. The room's atmosphere seemed to seep into my skin, as tangible as the dampness of the carpet beneath my hands. It wasn't fear—it was something deeper, a strange unease that settled into my tiny frame and refused to let go.

The sight before me left me bewildered. The word "wrong" hadn't yet formed in my mind, but an unsettling feeling lodged deep in my chest refused to fade. These people, scattered across my world like discarded items, felt intrusive—unwelcome. Yet a quiet voice inside whispered that perhaps it was me who didn't belong, that I needed to adapt to their chaos. Seeking solace, I longed to find my mother, a reassuring anchor in the storm swirling around me.

My first memory wasn't just about crawling—it was about trying to exist in a world that already felt strange and fragile. Even then, I moved cautiously, instinctively aware not to disturb the delicate stillness. That carefulness stayed with me, a quiet echo reverberating through my childhood.

## Mother's Partying and the Unstable Environment

This wasn't a one-time occurrence. My mother, Julie, loved to entertain, but our home often felt more like a public venue than a sanctuary for a child. Her friends would sunbathe topless in the backyard, roll marijuana on the coffee table, or snort lines of powder off the countertops. Whenever they hesitated, glancing in my direction, my mother would wave off their concerns with a breezy, "Don't worry, he's too young to remember."

But I remember.

Their laughter was unnaturally loud. It felt like they were trying to drown out something dark beneath the surface. The chaos they left behind—empty bottles, crumpled bills, and ashtrays full of butts—etched itself into my memory. Despite the crowd, I felt profoundly alone. It was a world without rules, without security, and without the safety a child should have.

I was forced to grow up before I was ready. Those chaotic mornings were only the beginning. Soon, I would learn that curiosity had sharp edges—and that navigating this world came at a price.

## The Curling Iron Accident: A Scar from Neglect

My earliest lessons often came through suffering. As a toddler, too young to walk, I pulled a curling iron off the bathroom sink. Crawling on the floor, curious and unaware, I had yanked the cord. The iron crashed onto my leg, searing my soft, fragile skin.

The memory has softened over time, but fragments remain vivid: the excruciating pain and my dad's panicked reaction. He scooped me up, his face pale with fear, and carried me to the kitchen. Without hesitation, he plunged my burned leg into a bucket of ice water and then sped to the hospital. The doctors said his quick thinking saved my leg from permanent damage.

The physical scar faded over the years, but the emotional wound lingered. It took me a long time to fully grasp the lesson of that moment: even the smallest lapses can leave lasting marks. Negligence—whether from inattention or chaos—leaves scars. Some are visible, others are hidden. But, they are all deep.

Even at that young age, a quiet question lingered in my mind: Why wasn't anyone watching me? I didn't have the words to articulate it then, but that curling iron left more than a scar on my skin. It left a tiny crack in my trust, a subtle but unshakable doubt that would shadow me for years.

The accident exposed how deeply chaos and neglect had seeped into our lives. It was a preview of what was to come. It echoed louder in the years after my parents' divorce, as chaos deepened and trust grew rarer.

## The Phone Call That Ended It All: My Parents' Divorce

I struggled to understand the concept of family. On the surface, it seemed like a word meant to embody safety, belonging, and love. Yet, for me, it was a storm—a chaotic mix of tension, contradictions, and unresolved pain. My parents' marriage was turbulent, and their eventual divorce set a tone for my childhood that no child should ever grow accustomed to.

I was two years old when it all fell apart. My father, Don, was stationed four hours away at Fort Knox, Kentucky, and the miles between them mirrored the growing gulf in their relationship. The cracks in their fragile bond widened until it crumbled, leaving only silence in its place.

One afternoon, my mother picked up the phone and called him. Her voice was sharp, each word slicing through the thin thread that held their marriage together.

"If you're not here in the next four hours," she growled, her tone unwavering and unforgiving, "I want a divorce."

It wasn't a plea to reconcile or an invitation to fight for the relationship. It was an ultimatum—blunt, final, and designed to provoke a response.

But my father didn't shout. He didn't argue or beg. He didn't rush to the car, fueled by desperation to repair what was broken. Instead, he simply took her at her word.

Later that same day, the knock at the door came—not from my father, but from an attorney. My mother swung the door open, perhaps expecting some sign of contrition or explanation. Instead, the attorney handed her divorce papers.

Small acts of anger seeped into our daily lives like tiny, persistent leaks, slowly poisoning the atmosphere. At dinner, my mother would mutter bitterly about how my dad had left us behind. Her words would grow sharp, like knives slicing at his character if the conversation veered toward him.

"Your father doesn't care about us," she'd whisper, her voice cracking under the weight of unshed tears glistening in her eyes. I heard this refrain so often that it became an unrelenting background noise—impossible to escape or ignore.

My dad, however, never fought back. He kept his anger locked away, even when he had every right to defend himself. Not once did he speak ill of her in front of us. Instead, he absorbed her bitterness in silence as if unwilling to add fuel to the fire. But his silence wasn't passive—it was heavy, charged with the weight of all the things he left unsaid.

I often wondered if his silence was a shield, an effort to spare us from the ugliness of their conflicts. Or perhaps he believed his actions could somehow bridge the divide, choosing deeds over words.

Looking back now, I see their divorce as far more complicated than I could grasp at the time. My mother's anger wasn't just anger—it was hurt, raw, and unresolved. My father's silence wasn't indifference—it was a struggle, an effort to navigate his own pain without adding to ours.

They were two broken people, weighed down by their own baggage, pain, and inability to communicate. Their marriage wasn't a battle between a hero and a villain but a tragic clash of wounded souls. Their unresolved wounds dragged down our family's fragile foundation. We were left to navigate the wreckage.

Their divorce wasn't just the end of a marriage—it was a seismic event that shook the very foundation of my childhood. It wasn't merely about the physical separation but the emotional fractures that rippled through every corner of my life. My mom's bitterness seeped into our world, darkening holidays, mealtime conversations, and any mention of my father. On the other side, my father's silence loomed, echoing her rage that left me stranded between two clashing narratives.

As a child, I lacked the tools to understand everything. All I knew was that something essential was missing. My guides were at odds, their opposing views leaving me caught in the middle, struggling to reconcile the irreconcilable. My mom's anger clouded my view of my dad. Like creeping vines, her words wrapped around my thoughts before I could question them. And then there was the silence—the hollow absence of my father. Rare visits and his emotional distance made him feel more like a ghost than a parent. I remember wanting to ask him why he left, why he didn't fight harder, why he didn't fix things. But even as a child, I could sense the weight of his silence, and I didn't know how to break it.

The void between them left me searching for something I couldn't name. I didn't just want their love; I craved their understanding, their explanations, and the reassurance that I wasn't somehow to blame. But no one said those words. No one told me, "It's not your fault." I carried that question with me. I tried to fill the gap by piecing together their stories. I wanted to know where I fit amidst the wreckage.

The shaky, cracked foundation of their divorce foreshadowed the years to come. It wasn't a single event but a wound that refused to heal, a haunting presence that shaped my understanding of family, trust, and self-worth. Looking back now, I can see the complexity of their pain, failings, and humanity. But as a child, all I could see was the brokenness.

## Lesson: The Complexity of Family Dynamics

My parents' divorce profoundly shaped my childhood, its impact echoing through my thoughts as I grew up. It wasn't a clean break, like severing a rope—it was more like shattering a mirror. The pieces never fit back together the way they once did, and no matter how hard you try to look through them, the cracks distort the reflection.

When my parents divorced, my dad left our home for good. It felt like a door slamming shut, leaving an eerie silence in its wake. His absence became permanent, replacing not only the arguments and tension but also his flawed presence. He was gone, leaving only an empty space where he used to sleep and a faint whisper of his voice in my memory. He wasn't there to share in our daily lives. Though the divorce took him physically from our home, something much heavier took him away from me and my brother David.

The absence didn't happen all at once. It came in stages, each one carving a deeper void. At first, the divorce created distance—a physical and emotional barrier between us. But as if that weren't enough, something else drove my dad even farther away. Though I didn't understand it then, I could feel its weight in how my mom spoke about him. Her voice was angry. But there was something deeper. A hurt hung in the air, making the room heavier each time Don's name was mentioned.

My mom's voice cut through the quiet, her sharp words amplifying the silence he left behind. "He's not here because he doesn't care!" she snapped, slamming a dish into the sink. "All he ever thinks about is himself." Her bitterness took root early, wrapping around her words and twisting them into accusations I couldn't yet rebut. I believed her—how could I not? He wasn't there to offer his side of the story, and the ache of his absence made her version of events feel true.

But there were cracks in her narrative, subtle hints that the story was more complicated than she let on. I overheard whispers not meant for my ears. They spoke of past actions and betrayals my mother blamed on him. At first, I tried to ignore them, burying those words deep in my mind so I wouldn't have to face their implications. Yet, the more I tried to suppress them, the heavier they grew, sitting in my chest like a weight I couldn't shake.

Then there was his absence—from our home and the country. Deployment had taken him far from us to places I couldn't picture, doing things I couldn't yet comprehend. His leaving wasn't just a consequence of the divorce. It stemmed from something far more complex, an entanglement of duty, circumstance, and pain I was too young to understand.

Growing up in the shadow of those absences taught me an early, bitter truth: family is never simple. Families are messy, tangled, and layered with complexities that defy a single narrative. It wasn't just that my dad wasn't there—it was the reasons he wasn't there, the layers of conflict and unresolved hurt that had unraveled their marriage.

There was no clear villain or victim, no simple explanation of what had happened between them. They were just two flawed people navigating the wreckage of their relationship as best they could. And sometimes, no matter how hard you try, your best isn't enough.

My younger self couldn't grasp the complexity of it all. My mom's words painted a vivid picture of betrayal, abandonment, and anger. To her, the divorce proved his selfishness. His deployment was another chapter in the story of his choices. They always seemed to prioritize something, anything, over us. She needed that story to make sense of her pain, and for a time, I accepted it without question.

But even then, I could feel the gaps in her version of events—the unspoken truths she wouldn't, or couldn't, share. Those gaps loomed like vast, shadowy voids, growing more profound in the night's stillness. I'd lie awake staring at the ceiling, the weight of unanswered questions pressing down on me. Why had things turned out this way? What had driven my parents to this point? My dad wasn't there to explain, and my mom's sharp words, laced with pain, filled the silence with a narrative I didn't know how to challenge.

I thought about how her voice would rise when she spoke about him, the edge that never softened, and I wondered what lay behind it. I replayed snippets of overheard conversations. Her tone shifted at times, and then the words stopped as if the subject was too painful to continue. I tried to piece together the puzzle of my family, but the pieces didn't fit—at least not in a way that made sense to me.

Their fight wasn't confined to the years they spent together or the arguments we witnessed. It seeped into the air we breathed, reshaping how I saw the world, love, and trust. It wasn't just their marriage that fractured, it was my sense of stability and the belief that family should mean safety, warmth, and belonging.

I carried that quiet ache with me for years, a weight I couldn't name or understand. It shaped me and left invisible marks on how I navigated relationships and the world around me. I didn't know it then, but those gaps—those unanswered questions—would follow me far beyond the walls of my childhood home.

As I grew older, I saw the humanity in both of them. My mom wasn't just bitter—she was hurting, grappling with a life that hadn't turned out the way she had hoped. My dad was, more than anything, absent. He had troubles. His burdens made it impossible for him to be the father I needed. They were two flawed people whose pain spilled into our lives, leaving behind scars I couldn't understand until much later.

Their pain didn't make mine disappear, but understanding it shifted my perspective. It taught me that family dynamics are never black and white. They're layered—woven with love and resentment, hope and disappointment, joy and heartbreak. Sometimes, the path to peace lies in acknowledging all of it: the good, the bad, and everything in between.

Reaching that conclusion wasn't easy. It was like peeling back the layers of an onion, each one revealing deeper truths and more complexity. The more I tried to understand their pain, the more I realized their struggles weren't just about them—they had shaped me, too. Their wounds had left marks I'd carried for years, ones I'd have to work to heal.

Healing didn't come all at once. It didn't erase the hurt, but it began with understanding—with allowing myself to see their humanity and flaws without judgment. That understanding didn't make everything okay, but it gave me the tools to move forward. It helped me see my family for what it truly was: a tangled, messy story of two people who tried their best but fell short.

And in that mess, I found something unexpected: compassion. Compassion for them, for their pain, and for myself. It didn't undo the past, but it allowed me to grow beyond it—to embrace the complexity of our shared story and find peace within it.

## A House Divided by Day and Night

We lived under the perpetual weight of our mother's unpredictable and corrosive energy. It wasn't a home; it was a battleground, and her temper was the ticking time bomb that kept us on edge. When it detonated, there was no refuge. Her rage came like thunderclaps. Slamming doors rattled the walls. Her cutting voice cut the air like lightning. Words became weapons, and her favorite was hurled with venom that lingered: "Retards!" It wasn't just an insult; it was a splinter lodged in our minds, impossible to dislodge, no matter how hard we tried to convince ourselves it didn't hurt.

Mornings were the worst. The house became a minefield, and every step felt like a risk. Julie's heavy footsteps stomped through the halls, her mood dark and oppressive. We learned to tiptoe and become shadows, hoping to avoid her wrath. Sarcasm dripped from her words like acid, her tone turning even the mundane into something hostile. Then there was her bitter anthem. It was sung with a sneer that made our stomachs tighten: "Happy fucking doo-dah day, doo-dah, doo-dah..." What might have been a joyful jingle became a cruel mockery. It reminded us that happiness was a luxury we couldn't afford in her presence.

Anger followed her out of sleep like a shadow she couldn't shake, creeping into the light of day. It was suffocating, a taut and volatile tension that felt poised to erupt at the slightest provocation—a landmine waiting for a misstep. Even the sound of her footsteps could twist my stomach into knots. Each heavy thud warned of the storm brewing just around the corner. On those days, her fury filled the house like smoke, making it hard to breathe or think. My brothers and I exchanged wary glances, silent negotiations over who might take the blame if she decided today was the day to lash out.

The walls themselves seemed to shudder under the force of her rage. On one occasion, she slammed the door so hard that the vibrations buzzed beneath my skin, a physical echo of her fury. Her voice tore through the house—razor-sharp and unrelenting, her words clinging to me like burrs I couldn't shake. "One day, I'm going to leave, and you'll all be alone!" she screamed, her voice cracking with an emotion that felt like grief but burned like anger.

For a fleeting moment, I wondered if she meant it. And then, I said the words that stayed with me far longer than I'd care to admit: "Maybe it would be better if you did." The shadow of that exchange loomed over every fragile hope I dared to have, every belief in what a family could or should be.

That day, my brother David and I decided we'd had enough. Armed with a skateboard and bike, we rode down windy back roads towards our grandparents' home. We didn't have a plan, just an unspoken understanding that anywhere else had to be better than where we were.

As we pedaled away, the air felt fresher and lighter. The weight that clung to us in that house seemed to lift, if only for a moment. I still wonder how long it took her to realize we were gone. Did she feel relief? Panic? Or was it simply another storm that passed through her day, leaving nothing in its wake but silence?

### The Nighttime Transformation

As night fell, she became someone else entirely. The bitter, stormy woman we knew by day disappeared when her friends arrived. In her place was someone vibrant, someone alive. Her loud, uninhibited laugh echoed through the house as music blared from the stereo. The smell of liquor mixed with the sharp bite of cigarette smoke clinging to the air like a second skin.

I watched from the shadows, a silent spectator to her transformation. Cigarettes and drinks in hand, she danced with abandon. Her loose, carefree movements contrasted with the rigid anger of her daytime hours. In those moments, she seemed happy, but it wasn't a happiness we were part of. She chased the party, the escape, the illusion of freedom. Every drink and every line of cocaine she snorted off the coffee table fueled it.

Her fleeting moments of compassion left me questioning and conflicted. When she laughed, and her eyes sparkled, it was easy to forget the volatile woman who dominated our days. But those moments weren't for us. They belonged to the people she surrounded herself with who helped her forget the life she despised.

As I lay in bed, trying to sleep, the bass thudded through the walls—a second heartbeat reverberating in the house. Each note made the mattress hum beneath me, a relentless vibration I couldn't escape. Laughter erupted from the next room, wild and sharp, ricocheting off the walls. I squeezed my eyes shut, desperate to block out the sound. But the voices spilled through the thin walls. Slurred shouting tangled with the occasional crash of something breaking.

The air reeked of stale beer and cigarette smoke, creeping under the door and saturating my tiny room with its sour, acrid tang. It grew heavier with the earthy, skunky scent of weed, entwined with the sharp, chemical bite of something harsher—something I couldn't name. I buried my face in the pillow, desperate to escape it. But the smell clung to the fabric as if it had been ground into the fibers. It was inescapable and oppressive.

Shadows flickered on the ceiling above me, erratic and mocking as they leaked through the crack beneath the door. The lights in the other room flashed in chaotic bursts, spinning like a cruel carnival ride. I pressed my eyes shut. But the noise grew louder, pounding in my ears. It was a chaotic symphony of blaring music and drunken cackles that shattered the stillness of the night.

I curled into myself, clutching my blanket as though it could block out the noise and the cold draft creeping through the window. The more I tried to drown it out, the more the world conspired against me. Every sound and smell grew louder. It felt like the universe existed to remind me of my smallness and powerlessness.

Her nighttime revelry didn't just stay in the living room—it spilled into every corner of the house, into every crack of my being. It seeped into the boundaries—or the absence of them—that defined our fragile and fractured relationship.

## Blurring the Lines

When I was twelve, the line between parent and child dissolved. I smoked weed with her, the harsh smoke burning its way down my throat as I struggled to match her reckless abandon. "See? It's not a big deal," she'd say, exhaling a cloud of smoke with a laugh. "You're tougher than your father ever was."

I wanted her approval so desperately that I ignored the small voice inside me, whispering that this wasn't right. I silenced it, convincing myself that if this was what it took to feel close to her, I would endure it.

Sometimes, when the liquor flowed and her bitterness bubbled up, she'd say: "You know, I didn't get to have a real life because of you kids. If it weren't for you, maybe I'd have been happy."

I told myself she didn't mean it. I told myself it was just the alcohol talking. But the words lingered long after the night ended, gnawing at the part of me that still wanted to believe she cared.

Her laughter in those moments felt like a rare treasure—something I could never quite hold on to. But even as I cherished it, I could feel its hollowness settle deep in my chest. We drank together too, passing bottles of cheap liquor back and forth like we were equals. The condensation on the bottle's neck chilled my hands, but I pretended not to notice the burn as it seared my throat.

She leaned back, laughing at something one of her friends had said. I wasn't listening. Instead, I was watching her—the woman who was supposed to protect me—and wondering when she decided I didn't need a mother anymore. A sharp pang cut through me, but I shoved it down, forcing a smile as the smoke filled my lungs. Her approval felt worth any cost.

But deep down, I knew the truth: the person she wanted me to be—the drinking buddy, the confidant—wasn't me. Worse, I feared I could never go back to being the child she had never really wanted.

There were no boundaries, no separation. Instead of guiding me, Julie encouraged us to numb ourselves together. "It's fine," she'd say, brushing away any concern like it didn't matter. She even encouraged sex, often saying, don't get anyone pregnant. Wrap it up.

Everything was blurry during those nights. In those moments, Julie wasn't my mom—she was a drinking buddy, a partner in self-destruction. It felt wrong, but I didn't know any better. I wanted her approval, her attention, so I accepted it, even though I knew this was the only way I could get it.

Her laughter during those nights felt like a rare gift, a brief escape from the constant anger and bitterness. But deep down, I knew it wasn't real. The version of her that came alive at night was as fleeting as the high she chased. By morning, she was gone again, replaced by the woman who slammed doors and called us names.

## The Absence of Structure

I grew up without rules, boundaries, or a safety net—an upbringing that was both unmoored and precarious. There was no curfew, no expectation to attend school, no guidance to steer us toward anything better. Our lives drifted, day by day, without direction or purpose.

Jesse never graduated high school, a fact that still haunts me. It feels like a failure—not just his, but mine. Now, he's in prison for six years on drug charges, and I can't help but wonder if his story might have ended differently with the right guidance.

I wasn't much better. By eighteen, I had two felonies and eight misdemeanors under my belt. I told myself it was because I was tough, because I knew how to survive. But deep down, I was lost—angry, hopeless, desperate for something I couldn't even name, like a shadow always just out of reach.

Our mom's strange behavior shaped us. During the day, she was explosively angry. At night, she desperately escaped. I could only understand this with time. Her anger instilled fear. Her detachment fostered neglect. And her struggle to love herself left her unable to give us the love we so desperately needed.

Without structure, our lives were adrift. In that chaos, I sought something deeper—a sense of belonging, something to ground me in the world.

## Life Without Luxury

Our mom raised us to appreciate the simple things, as we never had the luxuries that others took for granted. Clothes shopping wasn't about keeping up with the latest trends; it was about making the most of thrift store finds. There was a store that ran a deal where you could fill a bag with as many items as possible for a fixed price. Mom took full advantage, loading up 50-gallon trash bags with clothes.

Restaurants were an entirely foreign concept to us—not because we didn't know they existed, but because they seemed as far out of reach as something on another planet. Eating out was a luxury for other families—the ones who seemed to live lives pulled straight from a sitcom. That was a dream that never came true for us. Instead, we made do with what we had, finding small joys wherever we could.

We were constantly at the mercy of our old TV antenna, perched stubbornly on our console television, dictating our entertainment choices. Every evening, the ritual began with one of us—me or David—standing behind the set, adjusting the rabbit ears this way and that, wrapping tin foil around the ends to capture a signal strong enough for a halfway decent picture. The screen flickered, ghostly images dancing in and out of focus while static crackled in the background. Occasionally, we'd hit the jackpot—a slightly clearer image of a cartoon or a rerun of an old show. But even then, the picture was never sharp, and the sound was full of distortion, voices warped by the relentless interference.

"Slide it over to the left!" Jesse would call from the couch, his small frame leaning forward, squinting at the screen. I'd oblige, nudging the antenna until the picture sharpened.

"Wait, that's too far!" he'd bark again. I'd bite my tongue, muttering under my breath as I searched for the elusive sweet spot. It felt like chasing a mirage—knowing the clear image we were striving for would vanish the moment we let go.

Even when the picture was at its best, the experience was far from perfect. Static lined the edges of the screen, and characters moved with a jerky, almost ghostly quality. But the flickering light still offered a brief respite from our chaotic lives. The cartoons became more than just entertainment. They were an escape, opening a window to a world where problems were solved in twenty-two minutes, the good guys always won, and laughter was constant.

Those brief moments of clarity felt like tiny victories, proving that focus and clarity could exist even in a life full of static.

## A Rare Escape

Our maternal grandparents' house was the only place where we could watch television uninterrupted. It felt like another world where the TV worked without constant adjustments, and the static that defined our home life didn't exist. On those rare visits, we gathered around their television with wide eyes as if witnessing magic. The colors were vibrant, the sound crisp, and the stories felt larger than life.

Our favorite was Teenage Mutant Ninja Turtles. Every fight scene had us cross-legged on the floor, leaning forward in anticipation. We burst with joy when the Turtles triumphed. Watching Leonardo, Donatello, Michelangelo, and Raphael fight off bad guys with camaraderie and humor felt like stepping into a universe where anything was possible. Their laughter echoed through the room, and for a moment, I was with them—part of their world, their family. A family that fought for each other always came back together, no matter how dark things got. I clung to that warmth, aware of how fleeting it was.

But when the credits rolled, I felt it all slip away, leaving behind the same cold ache I carried home. The static of my life roared back to fill the silence, and I realized what hurt most wasn't the chaos—it was knowing there was something better I'd never have.

## A Hunger for Stability

Each fleeting escape deepened my longing for a joyful life. I wished for laughter to be a constant companion, not a rare treasure. At home, joy was always temporary, overshadowed by the storm clouds of our mother's temper or the weight of our collective struggles.

It wasn't just the lack of material possessions that left me feeling insecure—it was the absence of warmth and stability. I longed for the childhood I saw on TV, where parents guided and protected their kids. Siblings argued over trivial things but always had each other's backs.

Though it may seem silly now, the Turtles embodied everything I craved: loyalty and love, not blood, forming the bond of family. They faced their challenges, but they did so together, their connection unbreakable. Even when everything seemed to fall apart, there was always a sense of safety in their world. No matter how dark things got, they would always have each other.

## The Reality of Chaos

I knew a hard truth awaited me at home. The static-filled television wasn't just a quirk of our evenings; it was a metaphor for our lives. Everything felt fractured and incomplete as if we were always reaching for something just beyond our grasp.

Our home wasn't a sanctuary but a place where survival took precedence over comfort. Even simple meals, like SpaghettiOs or grilled cheese, brought immense gratitude because they meant we had food. If the lights stayed on for the month, it felt like a quiet victory. Comfort and stability were luxuries other families had—things we could only dream about.

Our furniture reflected the difficult times we had endured. The couch's springs poked through the thin fabric, causing the middle to sag. The kitchen chairs wobbled, their legs uneven from years of wear. Nothing matched, and everything felt temporary, as if our home was a stopgap rather than a place to settle.

Yet, even amidst the chaos, there were moments of light. We bonded over shared laughter while adjusting the antenna, finding camaraderie in making the best of our situation. Those moments didn't erase the hardships. But, they reminded us that even in the dark times, there was still room for connection and joy in the small things.

## Lesson: Finding Small Joys Amidst Hardship

In retrospect, those nights with the static-filled TV taught me an invaluable lesson. I learned that even in the worst of times, I could find small joys. A cartoon's brief escape or laughter while adjusting the antenna reminded me, for a moment, that I wasn't completely powerless.

It wasn't much, but it gave me the motivation I needed. Those small joys became lifelines, showing me that there was still room for hope amid the chaos. They didn't fix everything. But they gave me the strength to keep searching for the stability and connection I longed for.

Above all, they showed me that joy isn't found in grand gestures or wealth. Sometimes, it's discovered in the simplest things—a fuzzy cartoon, a shared laugh, or the warmth of knowing we're not alone in the struggle.

## The Potato Salad Incident

Growing up, I never liked potato salad or macaroni salad. The sharp tang of mayonnaise mixed with the subtle sulfur of boiled eggs turned my stomach before I even tasted it. That mild distaste became a strong aversion at age four. It was due to a moment far deeper than a childhood food tantrum. It became a raw and unshakable memory that lingered well into adulthood.

It was a warm afternoon, the kind that made the vinyl kitchen chairs stick to bare legs. Sunlight sliced through the window, illuminating the kitchen table where my mom stood. Her shadow loomed over me as I sat, arms wrapped tightly around myself, cocooned in a defensive shield I couldn't escape. The enemy sat before me: a heaping spoonful of potato salad. Its pale-yellow dressing glistened in the sunlight, taunting me. I had refused to eat it, repulsed not only by the sight but by the very idea of it settling, heavy and unwelcome, in my stomach.

She started gently, trying to coax me. But the sharp impatience in her voice betrayed her mounting frustration. "Just eat it," she said, her tone edging into irritation, exhaustion lingering at the edges. My resolve was firm. I shook my head and pushed the plate farther away. Her irritation grew, her movements becoming jerky as she paced back and forth, muttering under her breath.

And then she snapped.

Her hands, unyielding and harsh, seized me before I could react, pinning me to the floor. The cold linoleum pressed against my back as her knees held my arms down, rendering me immobile. The room seemed to shrink, the edges blurring as panic set in. I thrashed, kicking and twisting, desperate for freedom—but it was futile.

I realized then that food had become more than nourishment—it was a tool for dominance, a means for others to assert power over me. Yet, at that moment, all I could feel was the suffocating helplessness of being overpowered.

"Open your mouth," she barked, her voice sharp and commanding, leaving no room for defiance.

I clenched my jaw as tightly as possible, tears streaming down my face in silent protest. But her strength outmatched my resistance. One hand forced my mouth open while the other shoved a spoonful of potato salad inside.

The experience was far worse than I had imagined. The sharp tang of mayonnaise mixed with the dry, overcooked potatoes set off an immediate revolt in my stomach. Each bite was an assault on my senses, the flavors so pungent they felt like an invasion. I gagged. My body rejected the intrusion. But she was relentless, shoving another spoonful into my mouth before I could catch my breath.

When my stomach finally gave in, the taste turned even more vile. The acrid bile, mingling with the already offensive flavor, burned my throat, leaving a bitterness lingering for hours. The humiliation cut just as deeply as the taste. Lying there on the cold linoleum floor, tears and snot streaking my face, I felt impossibly small, powerless, and ashamed.

## The Emotional Weight

The potato salad wasn't the only reason this moment became unforgettable. It was Julie's disregard for my feelings. She forced me to eat something I despised. I stripped away my autonomy and crushed my preferences under her frustration. In that moment, food transformed into something far beyond nourishment. It became a symbol of control, a reminder of how easily power could be wielded against me in ways I couldn't resist.

Afterward, I curled up on the floor, hugging my knees tightly as though I could make myself smaller, less visible. The air felt heavy and thick, still charged with the residue of Julie's anger. I didn't understand why things had escalated so dramatically—why a simple refusal to eat had spiraled into an unrelenting battle. But even at four years old, I knew the sting of shame that came with being utterly powerless.

That feeling didn't leave me when I left the kitchen. It clung to me, growing roots deep in my mind, its presence unshakable. It wasn't just about the food. The incident planted a seed of resentment within me, one that would take years to grow and even longer to understand.

## The Lasting Impact

Now, I can see how those moments shaped me in ways I couldn't fully understand at the time. The incident became something far more significant than a childhood memory. That day left me with more than just a lingering distaste for potato salad—it left me with the weight of feeling insignificant and invisible.

Whenever I saw a bowl of potato salad at a picnic or family gathering, the sight alone would turn my stomach, pulling me back to that kitchen floor. I could feel the cold linoleum against my back, the sting of tears on my cheeks, and the crushing sense of powerlessness. It was never just about the food. It was about what the food symbolized: humiliation, a lack of agency, and the harsh realization that my feelings didn't matter.

## A Lesson in Empathy

Though painful, that memory taught me an invaluable lesson. I learned how quickly negative experiences can take root. A single act of aggression or indifference can create lifelong wounds. It pushed me to listen more deeply, honor boundaries, and approach others with compassion.

When my children reject food, I remember that day in the kitchen. Instead of forcing compliance, I try to understand their feelings, ask questions, and offer compromises. I never want food—or anything else—to feel like a battle for control in their lives.

That memory also taught me how much I had to unlearn. My self-image was shaped by the belief that my feelings weren't valid and my boundaries didn't matter. Untangling that belief from my childhood was a long process. It required time, patience, and a deep commitment to self-reflection. I learned that valuing my own feelings was as important as treating others with empathy and respect.

## The Broader Struggle

The helplessness I felt during the Potato Salad Incident wasn't an isolated event—it defined my childhood. My life was shaped by the decisions of others, often without consideration for my feelings or needs. They decided what I ate, turned a blind eye to the chaos in our home, and left me with a persistent sense of powerlessness that molded my view of the world.

We lived without the basic comforts that other families took for granted, like a stable home or a sense of security. It wasn't just about the food on our plates but about the environment we endured—a place where survival often felt like the only goal.

## Moving Forward

Reflecting on that moment reveals something deeper than just a story about food. It's a story about boundaries, power, and the long-lasting effects of even minor acts of disregard. The sight of potato salad still makes me nauseous. Its taste is not the issue. It reminds me of a time when my voice was silenced and my autonomy ignored.

Yet, that memory has become a guidepost. It reminds me to approach others with compassion and understanding rather than control and force. While the taste of potato salad still turns my stomach, the lesson it taught me has shaped how I live my life. It drives me to choose empathy over dominance. I must honor others' boundaries. I want to create a space where no one feels the helplessness I felt on that kitchen floor.

## Longing for Connection

Through it all, I yearned for a connection with my dad. His absence left a void that nothing could fill. I imagined him as a TV dad. He'd be supportive and encouraging. He'd guide me, celebrate my wins, and value me.

I hoped for a different reality when he returned from the Gulf War. But the man who came back wasn't the same as the one who had left. There was a distance in his eyes, a heaviness in his gait, as though he carried an invisible, crushing burden. Though he was physically present, emotionally, he felt worlds away.

The ache of disconnection grew, and I struggled to bridge the gap between us. I wanted to understand him, to close the distance, but I didn't know how. Instead, I carried that longing with me. It quietly shaped how I sought relationships in the years that followed.

## Searching for Belonging

My complex personality was shaped by my childhood, past hardships, and ongoing struggles. Deep down, I longed to belong, to feel wanted, and to matter to someone. My anger wasn't like hers—it became my armor, a way to bury the emptiness I couldn't confront.

I couldn't tolerate anyone else's anger and had no patience for situations that forced me to face my shortcomings. I hardened myself against the world, a survival tactic that left its scars. Believing I wasn't worth much, I acted like it. I took risks, made mistakes, and didn't care who got hurt in the process.

Beneath the anger and bravado, a quiet, aching need for love and acceptance simmered. I wanted someone to look beyond the trouble I caused—to see the kid inside, desperate to hear that he mattered.

## Enduring and Staying Whole

Her decisions left wounds that my brothers and I have carried throughout our lives. Whether it was enduring her anger or joining her in self-destruction, we became shaped by her struggles. We learned the wrong lessons—lessons that took years to unlearn. Surviving her world wasn't just about enduring the chaos but also navigating the harm it caused.

Her chaotic ways showed me the path I shouldn't take, her anger taught me the actions I needed to avoid, and her neglect forced me to recognize my own worth. Breaking the cycle wasn't easy, but I understood I had the power to rewrite the story she had handed me. Chaos may have been my inheritance, but it didn't have to be my legacy.

# Chapter 2:
# The Cost of Defiance

If the chaos of my early years taught me to live in uncertainty, the years that followed revealed the harsh realities of pain and survival. The chaos wasn't just noise; it was a grim preparation for the storms to come.

Violence was another constant in my childhood, arriving in waves—unpredictable and crashing down without warning. One of my earliest lessons was how quickly anger could escalate—and how painfully it could land. It wasn't just something you heard in raised voices or saw in clenched fists. It was tangible, like the charged air before a thunderstorm—heavy, tense, and foreboding.

I was three years old when my dad made me a promise. He said he'd take me to the sporting goods store to pick out a baseball bat. For days, I couldn't stop talking about it. In my little world, where promises often felt fleeting or broken, this one mattered. I imagined the bat in my hands, gleaming as I practiced swinging it in the backyard. It wasn't just about the bat—it was the assurance that my dad would keep his promise and stand by me.

The day finally came. I remember walking into the store with him, the bright fluorescent lights reflecting off rows of shiny bats, each one lined up like soldiers, holding promises waiting to be fulfilled. I could barely contain my excitement as I tugged on his hand, pointing eagerly to the one I wanted. It was a lightweight aluminum bat with a sleek black handle. He picked it up, turned it over in his hands, and nodded approvingly, agreeing it was a good choice.

But then something shifted. Maybe it was the price tag or something else I couldn't understand, but I noticed the hesitation flicker across his face. His grip on the bat loosened, and after a moment, he carefully placed it back on the rack. "Not today, buddy," he said, his voice carrying a sigh that sounded as if the decision pained him too.

The words landed like a punch to my chest. I stared at him, stunned. "But you promised," I whispered, my voice trembling. He avoided my eyes, muttering something about money. It didn't matter what he said. All I could hear was the hollow echo of a broken promise.

By the time we got back to the car, my disappointment had hardened into frustration, which quickly evolved into defiance. As he stepped out of the car, I reached over and pressed the lock button. The slight click of the doors locking felt like my own tiny act of rebellion. My small hands shook a mix of anger and the adrenaline rush from doing something I knew I wasn't supposed to.

I pressed my tear-streaked face against the window, staring out at him. His expression shifted immediately—confusion giving way to anger. He knocked on the window sharply, motioning for me to unlock the door. I shook my head.

For a fleeting moment, I felt powerful. Though I had little control over my life, in that instant, I had drawn a line he couldn't cross.

But I didn't realize how steep the cost of that defiance would be.

When we got home, the tension that had filled the car followed us inside. The door slammed shut with a force that reverberated through the house, making me flinch. He didn't yell immediately. Instead, the silence that followed was suffocating, thick with unspoken anger—like the air before a thunderstorm, charged and waiting to explode. My heart raced, bracing for the inevitable.

When his frustration finally boiled over, the anger I had seen through the car window erupted, consuming everything in its path.

He grabbed me and dragged me toward the living room. I braced myself for the sharp, painful blows I feared, but then his hand reached for the paddle. The thick, smooth piece of wood had hung on the wall for years, a silent warning. I knew what it was, but I'd never experienced it before.

A loud crack split the air, reverberating through the house as the paddle struck. Pain exploded through my body, radiating from the spot where the paddle landed. My cries filled the room, but they didn't stop him. Each strike felt harder than the last, leaving my small body trembling. The heat of the blows seared my skin, and the marks left by the paddle would deepen into bruises over the next few days.

It wasn't just the physical pain that overwhelmed me—it was the sense of betrayal. This wasn't the dad who had promised me a baseball bat. This wasn't the dad I had believed would protect me. In those moments, I felt abandoned, carrying the full weight of his anger on my own small shoulders.

I don't remember how long it lasted, only that by the end, my body felt foreign to me—like it no longer belonged. I crumpled to the floor, my breath coming in shallow, ragged gasps. Bruises covered my legs and arms, their colors blossoming into angry shades of purple and green. The sting of the paddle still burned, a reminder that would linger far beyond that moment.

My dad said nothing afterward. He didn't apologize, didn't explain. He simply left me there on the floor, his footsteps retreating into another part of the house. Immobilized by pain and fear, I felt trapped, as if time itself had stopped. The silence of the house was suffocating, pressing in on me like a weight I couldn't escape.

A week later, my mom came to pick me up. By then, the bruises had darkened, spreading across my body like ink stains that refused to fade. When she saw me, her face froze. She didn't ask what had happened—she didn't need to. I saw the answer in her eyes: her jaw tightened, and her gaze sharpened. Her anger wasn't loud like my dad's—it was quiet, focused, and deliberate.

She wrapped me in her arms, holding me tighter than ever. For a moment, I felt safe. Then the questions came—questions I couldn't yet voice. How could someone who was supposed to love me behave like that? How could a promise about a baseball bat end with bruises and tears?

## My Mom's Fury and My Dad's Absence

When we got home, my mom placed me on the couch before disappearing into another room. A few moments later, she returned holding a camera. Repeated flashes harshly lit the room as she asked me to remain still. I didn't understand what she was doing at the time, but later, I realized those photos were evidence. She was building a case to protect me and ensure it wouldn't happen again.

A few days later, she walked into court with those photos. I remember little about the hearing, only that I sat on a bench that seemed far too big for my small frame, my legs dangling above the floor. The adults around me spoke in hushed tones, their words a language I couldn't understand. Then, with a sharp crack, the judge's gavel fell. My dad lost all visitation rights. He was gone from my life as quickly as he had left the courtroom.

Soon after, they deployed him to an unfamiliar war zone. My mom explained very little, and by then, I didn't ask. His absence, once sharp and painful, had become more like a dull ache. Unanswered questions had become part of my life's journey.

That day taught me lessons I wouldn't fully understand until years later. I learned promises could break as easily as bones. I discovered that anger was more than just an emotion; it was a force that could ripple out and affect many lives, leaving behind lasting consequences. Loved ones can inflict the deepest pain, and emotional wounds often outlast physical ones.

But survival wasn't just about physical scars. It was about learning to navigate a world defined by chaos and fleeting comfort. My parents' divorce may have laid the groundwork for the instability that followed, but it was the smaller moments—the ones that seemed insignificant at the time—that truly showed me what it meant to live in survival mode. The lessons came not only from the surrounding chaos, but from the scars it left behind.

## The Weight of Responsibility: Caring for Jesse

That need for vigilance and control became a defining theme, especially for my baby brother Jesse. He was born when I was five, the product of a one-night stand that our mom rarely spoke about. Without a stable parental figure, I had to step into a role that no five-year-old should have to, since Jesse's father didn't meet him until he was eight.

While most kids my age were playing with blocks or riding bikes, I focused on learning how to care for a baby. I still remember the first time I heard his cries—sharp, insistent, and piercing through the walls of our tiny trailer. It was early morning, and the sunlight slanted through the windows, casting the living room in soft shades of gold and brown. Our mom's door stayed shut as usual, her rhythmic snores drifting faintly from the other side.

I climbed out of bed, the cool linoleum floor sending a chill through my bare feet and shuffled into Jesse's room. His tiny face was scrunched and red, his cries causing his whole body to shake. The crib bars seemed impossibly high to my small frame, but I managed. Standing on a chair, I hoisted myself onto the edge, my arms trembling as I carefully lowered him into mine. His warmth was a shock against the cool air around us, and I instinctively rocked him, mimicking the movements I had seen adults do.

The diaper was my first real challenge. At five, I was still mastering the art of tying my shoes, yet here I was, trying to figure out tabs, folds, and wipes. The smell was sharp and sour and made my nose wrinkle, but I didn't have the luxury of turning away. My small hands fumbled with the sticky tabs as Jesse kicked his tiny legs, wailing louder as I struggled. Eventually, I got it right—or at least close enough—and fastened the fresh diaper around his wriggling waist.

Next came the bottle. I taught myself to make formula through trial and error, standing on tiptoes to reach the powdered canister on the counter. I measured the scoops, though I didn't fully understand what "measuring" meant. Then, I added water and shook the bottle with all the strength my little arms could muster. The liquid swirled inside, frothy and white, and I tested its warmth on my wrist, just like I'd seen others do. The bottle felt heavy in my hands, a weight that mirrored a burden too large for my small frame.

I'd settle onto the couch, holding Jesse close as blurry cartoons flickered on the screen. The colors and sounds were comforting, even if I wasn't really paying attention. His tiny fingers would curl around mine as he drank, his cries softening into contented gulps. In those quiet moments, there was a peculiar beauty and weight. I loved Jesse fiercely, but even then, I knew what I was doing wasn't normal. I was just a child, yet I had already become someone's caretaker.

Some nights, Jesse's cries felt endless, filling the house with an unbearable noise. I'd rock him back and forth, whispering soothing words I'd heard from adults, words I barely understood. "It's okay," I'd murmur, my voice shaking with exhaustion. "I'm here. I've got you."

The pain I felt went far beyond physical exhaustion. Sitting in the dim light of our living room, I was just a young boy holding a crying infant in my arms with no one else to rely on. Our mom was often passed out in her room, the stale scent of cigarettes and alcohol lingering in the hallway. She wasn't coming to help, and I knew it. I had learned not to knock on her door; it would only make her angry.

The frustration and helplessness swelled inside me during those long nights. I'd clench my jaw to hold back my own tears, rocking Jesse as he sobbed into my chest. His tiny body felt so warm and fragile, constantly reminding me of how much he depended on me. There were moments when I didn't think I could do it, when exhaustion blurred my vision and my arms felt like lead. But I never stopped.

When Jesse finally fell asleep, his face soft and peaceful, I'd sit there longer, afraid to move in case I woke him. The silence that followed his cries felt fragile, like glass that might shatter with the slightest touch. My eyelids would grow heavy, and more than once, I woke hours later still holding him, the two of us tangled together on the couch.

Caring for Jesse was a labor of love and a burden I couldn't fully understand then. I adored him with a fierce, protective love. He wasn't just my little brother—he was my responsibility, my purpose. But that love came at a cost. I learned things no five-year-old should know—that safety isn't guaranteed, that I could bear burdens of care even when too small, and that love and obligation sometimes intertwine.

It forced me to grow up faster than I should have. While other kids played tag or built forts, I was learning how to warm bottles and soothe a colicky baby. I envied their freedom—their ability to laugh and run without a care. I longed to be like them, carefree and unburdened, but my reality didn't allow for that.

Despite the challenges, I found moments of joy in caring for Jesse. His bright, unfiltered laughter was like a balm for my tired heart. I loved how his eyes lit up when I made silly faces or how he'd reach for my hand when I entered the room. Those moments reminded me why I kept going and why I didn't let exhaustion or frustration take over. Jesse deserved love, even in a world that felt chaotic and unkind.

But those early years shaped me in ways I wouldn't fully understand until much later. They taught me to put others first and sacrifice without question. A quiet ache lingered—I longed for a childhood I never had. Jesse became the center of my world, but in caring for him, I often forgot how to care for myself.

Looking back, I see how those experiences built my strength and planted seeds of resentment and confusion. Why wasn't our mom there? Why did this responsibility fall on me? I never resented Jesse despite my questions. I couldn't. He was just as innocent in all of it as I was.

Those years with Jesse taught me what it means to love unconditionally and give everything you have, even when you're running on empty. They taught me the power of resilience—and the cost that comes with it. Above all, they taught me that sometimes, love means carrying more than your share of the weight because there's no one else to do it.

## A Bond Forged in Brokenness

Focusing on Jesse gave me a sense of order in an otherwise chaotic world. When I held him, soothed him, or protected him, I created a small island of stability in the middle of a storm. His dependence on me became my purpose, something solid to hold on to when everything else seemed to slip through my fingers.

Jesse became my anchor, even as the weight of responsibility threatened to pull me under. I poured everything I had into Jesse—the care and love I had craved for myself—desperate to offer him the safety and stability I had never known. I wanted to be his shield, his comfort, his constant—everything I'd wished for when I was young. In that bond, I discovered a healing power, a connection that pushed me to persevere despite the overwhelming brokenness I felt.

But loving Jesse—and my other brother, David—also meant stepping into the role of protector. It was an unspoken vow, a duty I never questioned. David, older than Jesse, had a quieter, gentler nature, a stark contrast to the roughness life had shaped in me. Jesse, though, had a spark of wildness and defiance, yet he was still young, learning the rules of the world. I saw myself in him—how he looked to me for guidance, courage, and strength.

Growing up in our neighborhood wasn't easy. Trivial things—an off-hand remark, a careless glance—could easily spark conflict. Kids formed packs, and if you didn't stand your ground, you became a target. Jesse was scrappy, but he wasn't a fighter. He'd come running to me whenever the neighborhood kids picked on him, his face flushed with anger and fear. "They're messing with me again," he'd say, his voice trembling just enough to reveal how scared he really was.

I always stepped in between Jesse and anyone who thought they could push him around. I'd glare at them, my stance broad, my voice low and steady. "You want to mess with someone? Try me." Most of the time, that was enough. The bullies would slink away, whispering to each other, and Jesse would stay close, his small hand clutching my shirt.

But I knew I couldn't always protect him. Despite my desire to shield him from the world, I realized that wouldn't prepare him for it. He'd have a future without me, and he'd need to be self-reliant. I hoped he wouldn't experience the same paralyzing fear I'd felt during my childhood, the kind that made me feel small and powerless. He needed to learn that he could face his fears—and survive them.

One day, that moment came. Jesse had gotten into it with a group of older, bigger kids. When he came running to me, his eyes wide and pleading, I knelt and placed my hands on his shoulders. "Jesse," I whispered, "you can't keep running to me. You've got to handle this yourself."

His eyes filled with tears, his lip trembling as he shook his head. "But they're going to hurt me," he whispered.

"They might," I said, my voice steady even as my heart ached for him. "But you can't let them scare you forever. Once you face them, you'll see it's not as bad as you think. You're stronger than you know."

Jesse's expression showed my request felt impossible. But after a moment, he nodded. I stepped back, giving him the space to move forward. My stomach churned as I watched him approach the group, his small frame dwarfed by the older boys.

### The Moment of Truth

From a distance, I watched as Jesse squared his shoulders and faced them. His movements were stiff, his fear sharp and evident, his fists clenched at his sides. The boys jeered, their laughter and taunts cutting through the air. My instincts screamed at me to step in, to protect him as I always had, but I held back. This was his moment.

The first punch came fast—a sharp jab into Jesse's arm. He stumbled but didn't fall. His face flushed with fear and anger, and for a split second, I thought he might turn and run. But he didn't. Instead, he swung back—a wild, clumsy punch that missed but was enough to catch them off guard.

The boys closed in, their laughter turning to something darker. Jesse stood his ground, his tiny fists flying in every direction. He wasn't winning, but he wasn't backing down, either. I felt a surge of pride watching him fight, even as my chest tightened with worry.

Eventually, the scuffle ended. The boys backed off when they realized Jesse wasn't an easy target. His breathing was labored, his face flushed, but his eyes burned with a fierceness I hadn't seen before. He had faced his fear. He had taken some hits, but he hadn't turned away.

He came back to me, a swollen lip and a scrape on his cheek marking the battle. I knelt, meeting his gaze. "You did good, Jesse," I said, ruffling his hair. He nodded, his face still tense but with a glimmer of pride in his eyes.

### The Lesson

As I watched Jesse wipe the blood from his lip, his scraped cheek glowing red in the fading sunlight, I felt a confusing mixture of pride and sadness. He had fought back—not perfectly, not cleanly, but with a determination that surprised even me. I wanted to hug him, reassuring him he didn't have to face the world alone. But I also knew he needed to feel this victory for himself, even with its bruises.

That moment stayed with me, not just because of what Jesse accomplished but because of what it revealed about me. It taught me that protecting him didn't always mean stepping in—it sometimes meant stepping back. I had shouldered the responsibility of keeping him safe for years, but that day, I realized he needed to learn to keep himself safe, too.

Love isn't just about shielding someone from pain. It's about giving them the tools to endure, rise above, and grow stronger in the process. Watching Jesse face his fears reflected the battles I had been fighting all along: the struggle to find strength in the face of overwhelming odds and to believe in the possibility of survival, even when the world felt unforgiving.

Jesse didn't just grow stronger that day—so did I. Watching him face his fears forced me to confront my own and realize that sometimes the best way to protect someone is to let them fight their own battles. It's a hard lesson, but it shaped our bond—a bond forged in love, struggle, and the unshakable belief that we could endure whatever life threw at us.

Yet that day wasn't just about Jesse—it was about what we were both learning in a world of survival. His fight reflected everything I had been carrying: the weight of responsibility, fear of failure, and the desperate need to prove I could keep us safe. For years, I had protected Jesse because it gave me purpose, something tangible to hold on to when everything else felt out of control. But in watching him stand on his own, I realized that survival wasn't about control—it was about resilience and finding strength even in the face of fear.

The events of those years shaped me in ways I couldn't fully grasp at the time. I learned survival wasn't just about enduring pain but finding meaning, even when the lessons were hard to uncover. Caring for Jesse taught me the depth of love I was capable of, even as I wrestled with feelings of abandonment and resentment. Protecting him gave me purpose on days when life felt hopeless. But it also revealed the cracks in my foundation—the loneliness, the anger, and the unspoken grief that came from losing the childhood I was never given.

Violence and chaos were constants in my world, but they also taught me something unexpected: the power of choice. I couldn't control the circumstances I was born into but could decide how to respond to them. That realization didn't come all at once, and I stumbled many times along the way, but the seeds of resilience were planted in those moments of struggle.

Looking back, I see those years as a time of hardship and a crucible where my character was forged. The fear, the pain, and the weight of responsibility taught me to endure. More importantly, they showed me the value of compassion—not only for others but eventually for myself. In those small acts of care, whether rocking Jesse to sleep or standing up for him, I discovered the person I wanted to be.

The scars from that time are still with me, but they no longer define me. Instead, they remind me of where I came from and what I've survived. They prove that even in the face of chaos, love and resilience can take root—and sometimes, that's enough to grow something beautiful.

You keep sharpening the skill of survival, one lesson at a time. My bond with Jesse gave me purpose—a reason to stay strong—but life hadn't finished testing me. I wanted to believe I could create a sense of safety for the people I loved, but the next battle forced me to confront fears I wasn't ready to face. This time, it wasn't Jesse who needed me—it was the man who was supposed to protect me.

# Chapter 3:

# The Weight of a Father's Return

When my dad returned from the Gulf War, the man who walked through the door was not the one I remembered. His shoulders, once squared with confidence, now slumped under the invisible weight of something I couldn't yet name. The spark that used to light his eyes had dimmed, replaced by a faraway gaze that seemed to look straight through me. He appeared thinner and quieter, and his movements resembled those of a puppet whose strings were barely holding together.

I didn't have the words to describe what was happening to him. PTSD, paranoid schizophrenia, Gulf War Syndrome—terms I wouldn't understand until much later. But even as a child, I could feel the shift, like the very air around us had changed. He was present, but a part of him seemed to remain overseas, trapped in the deserts of a war I knew nothing about.

At the same time, my mom's marriage to Jason, her new husband, was falling apart. Their arguments had turned to abuse—not toward each other, but toward us. My paternal grandparents stepped in, and their voices were loud enough for Child Protective Services to hear. They reported the neglect, the violence, and the screaming that echoed endlessly in that house. In the aftermath, David and I were placed in my dad's custody. I couldn't ignore the irony: the same man who had lost visitation rights for beating me was now the one responsible for raising us.

## Starting Over with Nothing

When we left our mother's house, we had only clothes on our backs. Jason, her husband, controlled everything, and under his orders, we weren't allowed to take anything with us—not even a single change of clothes. My dad, struggling to regain his footing in a world that no longer made sense to him, couldn't afford to buy us new clothes.

By then, he had frequently entered and exited mental hospitals while doctors dedicated their efforts to balancing his brain's chemical instability. His military career was over, and with it went his income, structure, and much of his dignity. He was broke, waiting for VA benefits and Social Security disability to kick in. Until then, we had to make do with what little he had.

Even then, I felt a small, stubborn determination to find my footing. I didn't know how, but I knew I couldn't stay swallowed by the chaos around me forever. There was something about waking up daily and pushing forward, even when it felt impossible. It wasn't much—a spark—but it was enough to remind me that survival was possible. That flicker of hope became something I clung to, even when the road ahead seemed endlessly bleak.

I remember opening his closet, searching for something to wear to school. The musty smell of old fabric hit me as I pulled apart the hangers, revealing his collection of bedazzled button-up shirts from the 1970s and 1980s. Sequins and gaudy patterns stared back at me—relics of a time long gone. They were all he had; now, they were all I had.

## Lessons in Compassion

Those moments of cruelty taught me more than how to endure. They taught me about compassion and the hidden battles people fight that others can't see. The kids who mocked me did not know about my dad's struggles or the poverty we were drowning in. They didn't know about the frozen pipes in our trailer or the nights I walked home alone in the dark because no one was there to pick me up. They only saw the bedazzled shirt and the boy who didn't fit in.

But it wasn't just my struggles that shaped me—it was also Jesse's. I think back to when he was just three years old, holding a cigarette like it was second nature because Julie thought it was funny to teach him to smoke. Watching her laugh as Jesse inhaled, coughing through watery eyes, planted a more profound seed of helplessness in me. Even at that age, I felt a pull to protect him from the things we couldn't escape. Jesse didn't have a choice in his circumstances, nor did I, but I felt the weight of responsibility for both of us.

Looking at Jesse now, his lifelong battle with that habit feels like more than just addiction—it feels like a consequence of a childhood we never had control over. Those moments remind me that our past doesn't just linger—it imprints itself on who we become. It's easy to judge someone for their choices without understanding the pain that shaped them. Watching Jesse grow up taught me how deeply those early experiences ripple through the years, influencing paths we don't even realize we're on.

## Independence and Loneliness

After school, I joined sports—partly because I loved the competition and partly because it gave me an excuse to stay away from home a little longer. On the field, I wasn't the poor kid wearing sequined shirts or the boy walking alone down back roads. I was fast, focused, and determined. For those brief hours, I felt free, like I belonged to something bigger than my struggles. It wasn't a solution, but it was a reprieve.

But my dad never came to pick me up after practice. He was too busy at his girlfriend's house on the other side of town.

So, I walked—a mile and a half every day, rain or shine. My route took me down a busy two-lane road, where cars sped by without a second glance. I'd cross under a steep overpass, the roar of engines echoing like distant thunder. Then came the railroad tracks, rusty and uneven, the air thick with the smell of oil and gravel. Finally, I'd weave through the woods, where the trees stood tall, their long shadows reaching endlessly into the fading light.

Each day's walk was an endurance test, but it wasn't without its small triumphs. I memorized the path, marking landmarks that became my milestones: the twisted tree just past the tracks, the sound of the creek hidden in the woods, and the faint flicker of our trailer's porch light in the distance. The knowledge of how to get home safely; these small victories were like whispers of resilience. They didn't erase the loneliness, but they reminded me I could keep going, step by step.

The woods terrified me. At night, every rustle of leaves or snap of a twig sounded like a predator lurking out of sight. My imagination ran wild, conjuring images of wolves and shadowy figures. Sometimes, I cried—silent tears slipping down my cheeks as I told myself to toughen up. "Come on," I'd whisper, slapping myself in the face. "You're not a baby."

But those steps through the dark became more than a path home—they proved that I could keep moving forward even in fear. With each step, I was learning something that would echo throughout my life: resilience isn't about the absence of fear; it's about walking through it anyway. I didn't understand it then, but those walks taught me to push forward, even when the shadows around me felt overwhelming.

When I finally emerged from the woods, I'd cross an open field, the tall grass brushing against my legs. In the distance, our trailer stood—its peeling paint and sagging roof a constant reminder of everything we didn't have. If a light was on, my dad might be home, and a microwaved hamburger might be waiting for me. If it was dark, I knew I'd be on my own.

I remember one time a cheerleader's mom gave me a ride home. When we arrived, the trailer was dark, and no one was there. Trying to avoid embarrassment, I lied and told her my dad would be back soon, insisting she didn't need to wait.

Beginning at the age of eight years old, weeks would pass without me seeing my father. I hated my life and blamed God for everything—my shabby clothes, my irresponsible parents, my inadequate school, and the sadness that seemed to shadow me wherever I went. Those feelings of abandonment and anger stayed with me, resurfacing years later as I tried to make sense of my choices and the life I wanted to build.

At school, I endured the worst—the taunts, the rejection—only to return home to an empty house, where silence was my only companion. I would shut my eyes tightly and pray, longing to be someone else. I'd focus on the face of a happy, loved kid at school, wishing desperately that when I opened my eyes, I would be them. I imagined their homes—warm, full of love, where meals were more than just food—they were moments of connection. But every time I opened my eyes, I was still in my body—alone, afraid, in the same rundown trailer.

Those quiet moments of despair were more than just fleeting childhood wishes—they were the seeds of a deeper battle I would fight for years: a struggle to understand my worth and to find a place where I truly belonged.

## The Microwaved Hamburgers

My dad's cooking skills left much to be desired. His specialty was a microwaved hamburger—a raw patty thrown on a plate, dusted with random spices, and nuked until it turned rubbery and gray. Sometimes, he'd forget to season it at all, leaving me with a bland lump of meat that I'd choke down more out of necessity than enjoyment.

Each bite was a stark reminder of the distance between us. He provided for me in the most basic way, but there was no warmth, no intention behind it. It felt more like an obligation than an act of care. I'd sit at the kitchen table, staring at the plate, yearning for something more—not just better food, but a deeper connection, a sense of belonging that always felt just beyond my reach.

But the coldest lessons weren't served on a plate; they came in the form of freezing showers and the harsh realities of survival.

## Cold Showers and Hard Lessons

Winters in our trailer were brutal. The pipes often froze, leaving us without running water. When it came time to bathe, my dad had a simple solution: freezing showers.

The first time he forced me under that icy stream, I screamed. The water hit my skin like shards of glass, and my breath came in short, panicked gasps as I begged him to let me stop. But he didn't. He held me there, his grip unyielding, his voice cold as he told me to "man up."

Even now, I'm unsure if he thought he was teaching me a lesson, preparing me for life's hardships, or simply asserting control over a world where he felt powerless. All I know is how it felt—cold, agonizing, and profoundly lonely.

## Finding Strength in the Pain

Those moments, like the freezing showers and the microwaved hamburgers, shaped me in ways I didn't fully understand then. I can still feel the icy water shocking my skin and hear my dad's cold command to "man up." In those moments, every fiber of my being screamed to give up, but I couldn't. The same feeling hit me as I forced down those rubbery burgers, knowing they weren't just meals—they were a reminder that I couldn't count on care.

That pain taught me resilience. It forced me to endure, even when life felt unbearable. But it also showed me the emptiness that comes when compassion is absent. I longed for the care I never received—a longing that fueled a quiet vow: to break the cycle of pain, to approach others with kindness, and never to let someone feel as alone as I had.

Even now, I carry the loneliness of those years like a scar. When I think back to walking home alone, terrified of the woods, I remember how insignificant I felt. But I also remember the determination to make it through, step by step. That determination guides me today—not just to survive but to choose connection over isolation, compassion over cruelty, and love over indifference.

The pain became more than a memory; it became a strength. Though brutal, those moments gave me a roadmap for navigating the complexities of life, showing me what I wanted to create for myself and others: a world where no one has to endure that kind of emptiness alone.

**Looking back at your own life, what moments shaped you most?** Maybe it's the pain you thought you'd never survive or the strength you didn't realize you had. The cycles we carry can be heavy, but they can also be broken. And sometimes, in the most challenging moments, we uncover who we're meant to become.

## Emotional Scars That Run Deep

Even as a child, I felt the pull of worthlessness, like an undertow dragging me beneath the surface. My mother's anger and neglect sent the message loud and clear: you don't matter. My father's absence, compounded by his explosive temper when he was present, confirmed it. I wasn't safe—not in my home, and not within myself.

This unspoken lesson—that I was unworthy of love, stability, or peace—embedded itself in my psyche. Countless nights, I lay in bed, staring at the ceiling, my chest tight with an ache I couldn't name. My thoughts spiraled: Why do I feel so small? So empty? So... broken?

As a child, I didn't have the words or understanding to untangle those emotions. I didn't know that the shame I felt wasn't mine to carry, that the people who were supposed to protect me had passed it on. Instead, I internalized it. I believed the lies trauma told me: that I was defective, that I wasn't good enough, that I didn't deserve kindness or care.

# FROM **B**ROKEN TO **B**LESSED

## How Trauma Shaped My Coping Mechanisms

The impact of my childhood didn't reveal itself all at once—it was a slow, creeping thing, weaving its way into my life like ivy. It wasn't until much later, as an adult, that I began to understand how deeply those early experiences had shaped me.

In school, I struggled to connect with others. I wanted friends, but I didn't know how to trust them. My instinct was to push people away before they could hurt me, even though I longed for connection. I was like a stray dog—starving for affection but too skittish to let anyone close.

I sought validation wherever I could find it, desperate for anyone to tell me I was enough. This hunger for approval often led me down destructive paths. I said yes when I should've said no. I ignored the red flags in relationships. I compromised my boundaries because I didn't believe I had the right to enforce them.

And then there was the anger. It simmered beneath the surface, a quiet but persistent presence I didn't know how to release. When it boiled over, it erupted in ways that hurt others—and, most of all, myself. I threw punches, yelled at people I loved, and made impulsive decisions that left me with a trail of regret.

## The Long Shadow of Childhood

The scars of my childhood affected every part of my life—not just my relationships. They showed up in my inability to handle stress, my desperate need to avoid conflict, and the self-destructive habits I clung to when everything felt too overwhelming.

By adulthood, trauma ruled my life. Anxiety tightened my chest every time I tried to relax. I overthought everything—every conversation, every decision, every interaction—and lived in constant fear of making a mistake.

Depression crept in, too, a quiet, insidious voice whispering lies in my ear: You'll never be good enough. You're a failure. Why even try? Some days, it was hard to get out of bed. On other days, I moved through the world on autopilot—going through the motions but feeling nothing.

And yet, I didn't recognize any of this as trauma. To me, it was just life. I thought everyone felt this way. I didn't realize that my constant unease wasn't normal—that the chaos of my childhood had rewired my brain, leaving me stuck in survival mode even when there was no immediate threat.

## The Journey Toward Healing

It wasn't until much later—after years of hitting rock bottom and clawing my way back up—that I finally understood the depth of my pain. Therapy became a lifeline, where I could unpack the emotional baggage I had been carrying for so long.

One of the most important lessons I learned in therapy was the concept of self-compassion. For years, I had been my own harshest critic, blaming myself for everything—my parents' failures, my mistakes, for not being stronger, smarter, better. I carried an unbearable amount of shame, convinced that I was inherently flawed.

But self-compassion changed that. It allowed me to look at my past through a kinder lens, to see my younger self not as a failure, but as a survivor. I began to understand that the ways I coped—whether it was isolating myself, lashing out in anger, or seeking validation—weren't signs of weakness. I had developed strategies to survive in a world that had felt hostile and unsafe.

## Reclaiming My Worth

Self-compassion didn't just help me forgive myself—it helped me reclaim my worth. For the first time, I believed that my trauma didn't define me. My past had shaped me, but it no longer had to control me. I could rewrite my story, not with shame, but with empathy.

This shift wasn't easy, and it didn't happen overnight. Healing is a process that requires patience and persistence. There were days when it felt like I was taking two steps forward and three steps back. But slowly, I began to feel a sense of peace where there had once been only turmoil.

I learned to recognize my triggers, name my emotions, and respond to them with care instead of self-criticism. I discovered the power of boundaries—not just with others, but with myself. And I rebuilt what my childhood had stripped away: a sense of safety, stability, and self-worth.

### A Message for Others

Looking back, I see how far I've come. The journey hasn't been easy, but it's been worth it. The scars from my childhood will always be a part of me, but they no longer define me. They remind me of what I've endured and serve as a testament to my resilience.

I share my story with the hope that it might help others who are struggling with the weight of their own trauma. If there's one thing I've learned, it's that healing is possible. It's not about erasing the past; it's about learning to live with it, understand it, and transform it into a source of strength.

Self-compassion was the key that unlocked my healing, and it's a tool I hope others can also find. No matter where you come from or what you've been through, you are worthy of love, peace, and a fulfilling life. Healing is a journey, and it's one we don't have to walk alone.

### Instability and Transience

Growing up in unstable, ever-changing environments taught me resilience. The constant upheaval made me adaptable, but it also left me with a restlessness that lingered into adulthood, shaping my choices in ways I didn't always recognize. At first, that restlessness was destructive, but over time, it became the drive I needed to build a stable life.

Moving between my mom's and dad's homes meant we were always on the go, settling in impoverished neighborhood's—trailer parks, section eight housing, or even the ghetto. By the time I was fourteen, I had counted twenty-eight moves with just my mom, not including all the times we moved with my dad. I attended two different preschools, four elementary schools, two middle schools, and three high schools. While this constant change forced me to adapt, it also deeply impacted my sense of self-worth, making it difficult to feel like I belonged anywhere.

Seeing other families, filled with warmth and stability, gave me a glimpse of what I longed for. Their consistency showed me an environment where people could grow and feel valued. It taught me that a supportive home shapes how we see ourselves and how we envision family and relationships. From those experiences, I learned exactly what I wanted to create: a place where people feel they belong and are genuinely valued.

The impact of these experiences is something I carry with me. My longing for connection and belonging fuels my efforts to provide stability and support for the people I care about. In a way, the ache I felt in my past has become a driving force, urging me to create environments where others feel valued and at home. It's a testament to how deeply our early lives shape who we are and who we strive to be for those around us.

My brother Jesse once got caught smoking a pack of cigarettes at just three years old, which my mom found amusing. Moments like these were just one example of our early exposure to things most kids should never experience. These incidents planted the seeds of habits and choices that would haunt us both in the years ahead.

She made him smoke the entire pack, laughing as he crossed his legs and flicked ashes as if he'd been doing it his whole life. This "joke" of hers marked the beginning of a lifelong habit; Jesse is thirty-four now and has been smoking for thirty-one years.

## Stealing from David

The memory of stealing from David still stings, like an old scar that aches when touched. I was seventeen when I first dipped into his savings account—an act of desperation I convinced myself was temporary, even harmless. Our paternal grandparents had set up the account as a gesture of love and foresight, meant to give David a small financial cushion for his future. I justified my actions at the time with the promise I kept repeating: I'll put it back before anyone notices. But that promise dissolved as quickly as the guilt I buried under layers of excuses.

It started with one withdrawal—just a tiny amount, enough to relieve some of the financial strain I was facing. But that one act led to another, and another until I had withdrawn over $800. I told myself it wasn't theft—not really. David wouldn't miss it, I thought. He was too young to need it yet. But deep down, I knew better. Every time I entered that bank and signed his name on the withdrawal slip, a small voice inside me whispered that this wasn't who I wanted to be.

**The Moment of Reckoning**

I'll never forget the day David found out. He was just a kid—maybe fifteen or sixteen—when he went to the bank to check on his savings. I can still imagine the look on his face when the teller told him that most of his money was gone. Confused and hurt, the thought of him standing there, trying to make sense of it all, twists my stomach.

He didn't confront me directly, not at first. Instead, he went to our grandfather, Don, who pieced together what had happened.

Don didn't yell or lecture me when he found out. That wasn't his way. He had a quiet, steady presence that was both comforting and, at that moment, crushing. Instead of making a scene, he stepped in, as he always did when one of us messed up. He went to the bank and replaced the money himself, restoring David's account without a word of judgment.

But when he looked at me, I could feel the weight of his disappointment. It was heavier than any punishment he could have handed down. His calm demeanor only made me feel worse.

Don was a Freemason, a man of integrity and quiet influence. He had a way of making problems disappear—mine included. He prevented any charges from being pressed with a secret handshake and his signature on the forms. It wasn't the first time he'd bailed out a family member, and it wouldn't be the last. But this time felt different. It wasn't just my guilt that ate at me—it was the realization of what I had stolen beyond the money. I had betrayed the trust of someone who looked up to me and deserved better from his older brother.

### A Lesson in Accountability

Even though I avoided formal consequences, I couldn't escape the guilt that followed me. Every time I saw David after that, I felt the sting of what I'd done. It was a quiet shame, gnawing at me in the still moments of the night. I didn't need a judge or a jury to tell me I was wrong—I knew it with every fiber of my being.

That experience forced me to confront a version of myself I didn't like. I realized how far I had drifted from the values I wanted to live by and the person I wanted to be. It wasn't about the money—it was the trust I had broken, the harm I had caused someone I loved. And while Don's intervention spared me from legal consequences, it didn't erase the internal reckoning I had to face.

In the years that followed, I held on to that lesson: accountability isn't just about repaying what you owe. It's about recognizing the harm you've done and committing to do better. It means facing the parts of yourself you'd rather ignore and choosing to grow from them.

### Protecting Jesse: A Repeat of the Cycle

Five years later, the roles reversed. This time, it was my younger brother Jesse who got into trouble. He had used our mother's credit card without her permission, racking up $800 in charges—almost the exact amount I had taken from David. When our mom found out, she went to the bank, ready to press charges against her son.

I couldn't let that happen. Stepping in, I offered to cover the debt if she returned to the bank and retracted her statement. I scraped together $500 on my own and went to our grandmother, June, asking if she could lend me the remaining $300 until I could repay her. She didn't hesitate, handing me the money without question.

I gave the full amount to our mom, hoping it would be enough to smooth things over. At first, she agreed. But then she saw an opportunity to exploit the situation, planning to take my repayment and the $800 reimbursement from the bank for the fraud. It took a lot of effort to convince her to drop the idea, but eventually, she relented, and Jesse avoided charges.

## The Complexity of Family

Looking back, I wonder if I handled things the right way. By stepping in to protect Jesse, did I rob him of the chance to learn the lesson I had learned the hard way? Sparing him from the full consequences of his actions felt like the right thing to do at the time—it was what family does, after all. But part of me questions whether shielding him from the fallout allowed him to continue down a destructive path.

Jesse didn't have the exact moment of reckoning I did. He didn't feel the weight of his actions the way I did. And in the years that followed, he continued to make similar choices, each one leading him further down a road that would eventually land him in prison.

It's a painful reality to grapple with—that sometimes, the best way to help someone grow is to let them face the full consequences of their actions. Family support is invaluable, but it has its limits. We can't shield our loved ones from their mistakes forever, nor should we. Growth comes from struggle, from the hard lessons we'd rather avoid but can't escape.

## Breaking the Cycle

For me, stealing from David was a turning point, a wake-up call that forced me to examine my choices and the person I was becoming. It was one of many mistakes, but also one of the most important. It taught me about accountability, the value of trust, and the man I wanted to be.

Growing up, I felt a deep sense of disconnection and loneliness, which showed in my choices. I carried resentment and fell into patterns of self-sabotage. But even those damaging choices held the seeds of growth. Facing my mistakes helped me uncover the deeper wounds behind them—feelings of inadequacy, a need for acceptance, and a desperate desire to matter.

Looking back now, I see those moments not as failures but as lessons. They were painful, yes, but they were also necessary. They taught me that growth isn't about being perfect—it's about being honest with yourself, facing your flaws, and choosing to do better.

## Finding Redemption

The road to redemption isn't a straight line. It's messy, filled with setbacks and detours, but it's also where the most profound growth happens. Acknowledging my mistakes and committing to making amends—both to others and myself—became the turning point. It wasn't about erasing the past but learning from it, facing my flaws, and choosing to improve.

These experiences taught me we're all capable of change, no matter how far we've strayed. They revealed the power of accountability, self-reflection, and the courage it takes to break free from destructive cycles. While I can't undo the harm I've caused, I honor the lessons it taught me by striving each day to be better—not perfect, but better.

Looking back, my father's return from war marked the beginning of a battle neither of us could have foreseen. His trauma became the backdrop of my childhood, shaping how I saw myself and others. But it also gave me a gift: the determination to create the life I had once only imagined. The scars of those years run deep, but they no longer define me. Instead, they serve as a testament to what I've survived and the strength to choose compassion—for others and, most importantly, myself.

Breaking cycles isn't easy, but it's possible. As you reflect on your journey, consider the moments that have shaped you—the pain that tested you and the growth it inspired. Redemption begins with a choice: to rewrite your story, heal, and create something meaningful from the struggle. That choice, as hard as it is, changes everything.

# Chapter 4:

# Through Chaos and Compassion:

# Family Bonds Forged in Fire

We were a mix of chaos—humor, recklessness, and heartbreak intertwining to define our relationships. We laughed, we cried, and we endured. At the heart of it all, I learned one crucial lesson: family can both shape and test you. This chapter is about the people who left lasting impressions on my life—Mike, Karl, Kelly, Beverly, and my mom, Julie. Each of them, in their own way, taught me invaluable lessons about resilience, love, and the destructive forces of addiction. Even if you feel your parents didn't get it right, there's still plenty to learn—sometimes, it's about figuring out what not to do.

My mom, Julie, was the oldest among her siblings. She had two younger brothers: Karl, the middle child, and Mike, the youngest. Uncle Mike's life was forever marked by a traumatic accident that changed him in ways. When he was thirteen, he was pouring gasoline into a burn barrel when a gust of wind sent the fuel back onto him, setting him ablaze. He spent the next six months in the hospital, enduring excruciating treatments, including debridement and skin graft surgeries, after suffering third-degree burns over 60% of his body. That traumatic experience altered him profoundly, shaping the unpredictable, troubled man he would become.

In adulthood, Uncle Mike spent more years behind bars than he did as a free man, though it didn't seem to bother him much. One of my earliest memories of him was when he rushed into our house, his face frantic as he whispered to my mom, asking for an alibi. Sirens wailed outside, and the police were closing in. Mike was a wild man, always on the edge, but he was family—and despite his unpredictability, he could be quite entertaining. I remember when I was young, he fired up a chainsaw and chased me around the yard. I can laugh about it now, but back then, I was terrified.

That chaotic humor was Mike's signature, a way of masking the deeper pains he carried. It became his defense mechanism, a way to cope with the struggles that gnawed at him. Yet it also brought us closer, bonding us in moments of laughter, even when we knew it was a cover-up for something far more profound. As I grew older, I began to see past the wild antics and desperation, realizing that beneath it all, there was something more—something darker—that shaped Mike's life.

### A Reflection of Recklessness

I remember working on my beloved 1992 Camaro Rally Sport Coupe, which needed an engine replacement after its oil pan had been damaged. With Grandpa's cherry picker, I managed to pull the engine and set it outside on a tire at my apartment, planning to swap it out for a small block V8. During a visit to Grandpa's, Uncle Mike overheard my situation and casually mentioned, "Well, I've got a 3.1-liter engine in the bed of my truck I can sell you, just to tide you over." Curious, I agreed to take a look.

Inspecting the engine, something didn't feel right. "Mike," I said, "This engine has a hole in the oil pan, exactly like mine. This is my engine!"

Mike looked at me, unphased, and shrugged. "Well, can you help me unload it? I need the space in the back of the truck."

That moment encapsulated Mike's resourcefulness, though it came at the expense of trust. His misguided, often humorous antics were part of his coping mechanism—a strange mix of recklessness and creativity that obscured the deeper struggles he faced. It was as if his chaotic approach to life was both a defense and a desperate attempt to maintain control in a world that seemed to slip further from his grasp.

## The Thin Line Between Humor and Tragedy

Mike's wild streak often veered into dangerous territory. One time, he called me with a plan to go bar-hopping uptown. He asked if he could crash at my place afterward, and I agreed. Then, he requested a ride into town, but I told him I was busy and he'd have to find another way. Undeterred, Mike came up with a bizarre plan—he dialed 911, falsely claiming to be having a heart attack, knowing that the paramedics would transport him to the nearest hospital, Marysville Memorial Hospital. Once there, he simply walked out, continuing on to his drinking destination.

Later that night, Mike showed up at my house around 2:45 a.m., declaring he was starving. I told him to help himself to the microwavable frozen meals I had stocked. When I went to bed, I thought nothing more of it. But the next morning, I discovered all eight meals had been opened. Mike had picked through them, leaving the boxes and trays scattered across the kitchen. I woke him up to find mashed potatoes tangled in his mustache and somehow stuck in his hair. As he sat up, lighting a cigarette, he casually asked for a ride home.

These moments were frustrating, yes, but they were also profoundly human. Mike's antics, though maddening, were his way of filling the emptiness within him—using humor and indulgence to escape the deeper pain he couldn't outrun.

Mike's humor was a shield—a way to deflect the agony he carried. But it also taught me an important lesson: humor can mask chaos, but only for so long. Beneath the laughter and mischief, I saw the real cost of reckless choices. I saw the damage that follows when self-control slips away. Mike's life became a painful reminder of the fragility of our decisions—and how easily it can all unravel when we choose to avoid the pain rather than face it. His humor was a survival tool, but it also taught me that unresolved pain, no matter how well-hidden, eventually demands its due.

## Chaos, Accountability, and the Cost of Recklessness

One drunken night, my Uncle Mike took my car without permission, driving off from where I had parked it at my grandfather's house. In a reckless escapade, he ended up throwing the serpentine belt. Without it, the water pump became ineffective, causing the engine to overheat and blow a head gasket. I had no idea any of this had happened at the time. Weeks later, a friend from school expressed interest in buying the car, so I brought him to my grandfather's house for a test drive. That's when everything unraveled.

The car struggled to start, and when it finally roared to life, it spewed a cloud of thick white smoke from the tailpipe. That's when I knew—a blown head gasket. Embarrassment flooded me. I feared my friend might think I was trying to rip him off, though I genuinely hadn't known the car was damaged. It wasn't until after Mike's death that his brother, Karl, came clean, admitting that Mike had taken the car that night. But even then, doubts lingered—who knows if Karl's story was true? For all I know, Karl could have been the one to steal the car and conveniently blamed it on his late brother, who could no longer defend himself.

This chaotic situation reveals deeper truths about trust, responsibility, and the far-reaching consequences of reckless choices. When someone acts without accountability, it doesn't just affect the moment—it sends out ripples, creating problems for others. In this case, Mike's—or maybe Karl's—decision to take my car left me embarrassed, cost me hundreds of dollars and hours of work, and jeopardized the sale, adding unnecessary stress and tension.

The incident also serves as a reminder of the value of transparency. When the damage to the car became apparent during the test drive, I felt a deep sense of shame. But I knew I had to be honest with my friend. Owning up to the situation and facing it head-on was the only way to navigate it with integrity. It reinforced the lesson that, even when things go wrong—especially when they do—honesty and transparency are key to building trust and preserving relationships.

Life often doesn't offer closure in messy situations like this. I may never know who actually took my car that night, and I've come to accept that. Sometimes, the lesson isn't in uncovering the truth but in learning how to respond when uncertainty surrounds you. In this case, I had to move forward, focusing on what I could control rather than dwelling on what I couldn't.

Growing up in an environment where chaos often reigned, I learned that actions have consequences far beyond what we might initially see. Reckless choices—whether taking someone else's car or hiding the truth—don't just affect the person making them; they ripple outward, touching relationships, opportunities, and trust. At the same time, these experiences taught me the importance of gracefully navigating such situations. I couldn't control the choices Mike—or Karl—made, but I could control how I responded to the fallout.

This story, small as it may seem, illustrates a larger truth about overcoming the influences and chaos of a troubled upbringing. It's not just about what happens to us; it's about how we choose to handle those moments and the lessons we take from them. Through it all, I've learned that transparency, integrity, and resilience truly matter—especially in the face of uncertainty and challenges beyond our control.

## When Humor Fails

Even Mike's humor couldn't mask the toll his choices took. Grandpa Karl, a dedicated over-the-road truck driver, cherished his brand-new GMC truck, constantly washing and shining it. One infamous day, while Grandpa was out working, Karl and

Mike—both fueled by drinks and other substances—called and ordered pizza. They took Grandpa's new truck to pick it up. Mike went inside to retrieve the pizza, only to find out that it hadn't been ordered yet. Furious, he floored the accelerator, angry that the pizza wasn't ready.

By the time they left town, they were speeding at over 100 mph. The reckless driving ended with a catastrophic crash, wrapping the truck around a tree. Both were airlifted to the hospital, miraculously surviving. It was yet another close call—another reminder of the fragility of life and the recklessness that seemed woven into both Karl and Mike's characters.

Mike's recklessness was captivating and heartbreaking—a life teetering between survival and self-destruction. Some moments were so absurd that you couldn't help but laugh at the chaos. But underlying it all was a deep, undeniable pain that, over time, consumed him.

Mike's ability to laugh in the face of chaos was admirable, but it also revealed a painful truth: humor isn't a substitute for healing. His life taught me that even the most vibrant personalities can be consumed by unresolved pain when it's left unaddressed. Sometimes, no matter how much we laugh, the weight of the past is too heavy to carry alone.

### A Final Goodbye

My Uncle Mike battled severe depression and tried to end his life multiple times. I was ashamed of his behavior, compounded by the lies and broken promises. Not being an addict myself, I felt frustrated, helpless, and angry, which only deepened the strain on our relationship. Ultimately, Mike's struggles with depression overtook him. Despite moments of laughter, his demons remained relentless, and in 2003, his life ended from an overdose. He was just 30 years old. Burying him was one of the most difficult days of my life.

In the days following Mike's funeral, the house felt hollow, as though grief had settled into every corner. Conversations became terse, and even laughter—the one thing Mike had always brought to our lives—felt like a betrayal. I remember sitting with my grandfather in the kitchen, the weight of unspoken questions lingering between us: Could we have saved him? We were consumed with guilt, wondering if we could have done more to help him.

In death, Mike left behind a complicated legacy: humor, heartache, and the lessons learned from loving someone who couldn't overcome their struggles. His life taught me that beneath every action lies a story—often one of pain—and that while humor is powerful, it has its limits as a coping mechanism.

Mike's humor was his shield against the chaos of his life, but it also showed me how laughter could coexist with pain—a duality I came to understand deeply.

Mike's death was a stark reminder that addiction and pain can overwhelm even the most vital spirits. In losing him, I learned that love isn't always enough to save someone—but it can still honor their memory. His chaotic life left me with lessons about compassion, loss, and the importance of seeking help when you need it most.

The day of Mike's funeral was heavy with sorrow, but grief's impact was far-reaching. As we laid Mike to rest, it became clear that the weight of his loss was too much for some of us to bear. For my Uncle Karl, that grief turned inward, manifesting in a way that nearly took another life. From the end of the driveway, I heard Barbie, Karl's girlfriend, crying out in desperation. My heart raced as I sprinted toward her, a pit of dread settling in my stomach with each step. As I got closer, I saw Barbie struggling beneath Karl, trying to hold his weight. Just then, my grandfather emerged from the house and entered the garage, his face a mask of panic. In that instant, the horrifying reality struck me: Karl was trying to hang himself.

With frantic urgency, my grandfather rushed over and cut Karl down, the rope falling away to reveal the raw desperation etched on his son's face. When Karl hit the ground, my grandfather knelt beside him, his voice trembling with emotion.

"I lost one son today. What makes you think I want to lose another?" he pleaded, his anguish cutting through the air. That moment underscored the devastating ripple effects of grief and the desperate ways it can manifest. Karl's attempt wasn't just a reflection of his pain; it was a haunting echo of Mike's loss, reverberating through the family.

That day, as my grandfather saved Karl, I witnessed the depth of family bonds—the need to hold each other up, even when the weight of loss threatens to pull us down.

In the aftermath of that day, several important lessons became painfully clear:

1. Mental Health Awareness: Karl's actions underscored the urgent need for mental health awareness, especially during times of trauma. Grief can spiral into despair if left unaddressed, making it essential to recognize the signs of emotional distress in ourselves and those we love.

2. The Ripple Effect of Loss: Losing a loved one doesn't just affect one person; it reverberates throughout the family. My grandfather's heart-wrenching plea illuminated the reality that our actions impact others, emphasizing the need for compassion and support during difficult times.

3. Open Communication: This experience highlighted the importance of discussing feelings, particularly when facing grief. Encouraging open conversations about loss can help individuals process their emotions rather than resorting to destructive behaviors.

4. Family Support: My grandfather's quick intervention to save Karl illustrated the critical role of family support in times of crisis. A strong support system can provide a lifeline, reminding those in distress that they are not alone.

Urgency of Intervention: In moments of suicidal thoughts or actions, timely intervention can be life-saving. My grandfather's decisive response saved Karl's life, reinforcing the importance of being vigilant and ready to help those in need.

That day remains etched in my memory, a powerful reminder of the fragility of life and the depths of human emotion. It teaches me that we must extend compassion and understanding to those who suffer silently, even amid grief. In honoring Uncle Mike's memory, we must commit to looking out for one another, fostering a community where no one feels isolated in their pain.

Mike's humor was his shield against a deeper pain, one that eventually overtook him. That same shadow seemed to follow his brother Karl, whose brilliance often battled against his own self-destructive tendencies.

## Family Ties and the Duality of Karl

Family ties don't automatically guarantee trustworthiness. While it's natural to place faith in family members, setting boundaries and remaining mindful is just as essential when past behavior raises concerns. One of my earliest memories of Uncle Karl was of him stealing money from my mother one night at a bar. From that moment on, I learned to monitor my belongings carefully whenever I visited my grandparents, especially if I knew Karl would be around. By the time I was old enough to drive, I had made a habit of locking my valuables in my car—an act of self-preservation learned far too early.

Karl's life was a constant tug-of-war between chaos and capability, and one story in particular encapsulates the turmoil that defined him. One afternoon, I walked in on him, kneeling naked in a scene that made my stomach churn. He was using a syringe meant for the dogs—the same needle my grandfather used to medicate their pets—to inject heroin. Desperation had driven him to use whatever was available. It was a jarring image, a disturbing intersection of care for the animals and Karl's reckless disregard for his own well-being. That moment revealed the insidious nature of addiction: how it erodes a person's self-worth, distorting their logic and judgment. It was a sobering reminder of the need for compassion and understanding toward those trapped in its destructive cycle.

Yet, addiction was only one facet of Karl's story. Beneath his struggles lay a man of undeniable skill and resourcefulness, especially in mechanics and welding. He had an uncanny ability to transform a rusted, paint-peeling Dodge pickup truck into something that looked surprisingly good with just a quick coat of paint and a few repairs. Watching Karl effortlessly restore broken-down trucks into shining, road-ready vehicles made his addiction all the harder to reconcile. It was as if his skill and creativity were in constant battle with the demons that dragged him down.

Karl's life was a constant balancing act between brilliance and self-destruction. He showed me that talent and addiction can coexist, but one often overshadows the other. His struggles taught me to look for the light in people, even when it's dimmed by darkness, and to cherish the moments when they shine.

Karl's life was a lesson in duality—the brilliance of his talent forever battling the weight of his demons, reminding me that compassion is often the hardest, yet most necessary, response.

## A Tragic End, A Lasting Legacy

Tragically, on July 8, 2024, Karl's life came to an untimely end due to an accidental overdose. At just 58 years old, he became the last of his siblings to pass, marking the end of an era. His death, with heroin and fentanyl found in his system, was a stark and painful reminder of the devastating toll of addiction. But even in loss, Karl's legacy endures. I feel his presence whenever I pick up a tool or tackle a repair. The lessons he taught me—the patience to solve problems, the joy of creation, and the resilience to push through challenges—continue to shape who I am and how I approach life.

Karl's story is one of contrasts: strength and struggle, love and loss, chaos and capability. His life serves as a reminder that, even amidst the darkest moments, there were sparks of light— lessons to carry forward, skills to pass down, and memories to cherish. While his passing marked the end of his struggles, it also solidified the enduring impact he left on those of us who loved him. Karl's legacy lives on in every repair I make and every lesson I share.

Karl's death marked the end of an era, but it didn't erase the lessons he left behind. I feel his presence whenever I pick up a tool or solve a problem. Though his life was cut short, it taught me resilience, creativity, and the bittersweet truth that we are more than the worst parts of ourselves.

## Lessons in Pain and Resilience

These moments taught me profound lessons about the weight of grief and the importance of understanding pain. Mike and Karl's struggles revealed the fragility of life and the enduring bonds of family, even when tested by tragedy. They showed me the need for empathy—to look beyond someone's actions and see the pain beneath.

Reflecting on Mike's humor and Karl's desperation, I'm reminded of how grief can magnify existing struggles, turning humor into a mask and desperation into action. But through it all, I've learned to cherish the humanity in each of us, to honor the lessons of loss, and to find strength in resilience.

Karl's addiction was a reminder that desperation can lead people to take measures they'd never imagine. His life showed me that even those we admire can stumble and that sometimes love means learning how to separate the person from their struggles.

While Karl's struggles were marked by external chaos, my mother's battles unfolded within the walls of our home, revealing a quieter yet equally devastating turmoil.

## Julie's Journey

Like Mike and Karl, my mother also wrestled with challenges. But her struggles didn't start with chaos—they began with resilience, determination, and a desire to create a better life for herself and her family. That determination would eventually be tested in ways that would change us all.

My mother, Julie, attended school through the 12th grade but didn't graduate due to a lack of credits. Instead of returning to school, she chose to earn her GED. She began her career working in factories before becoming a State Tested Nursing Assistant (STNA) and eventually found her passion for home health care. Julie thrived as an independent 1099 contractor; I remember how proud she was when she built lasting relationships with her clients, becoming more than just a caretaker—she became a friend, a confidante, someone people relied on. When I think of her today, I try to hold on to this version of my mother, full of purpose and warmth. Her determination to carve out a meaningful career in healthcare revealed her resilience, proving that even in difficult circumstances, fulfillment and independence are achievable through hard work.

However, Julie's penchant for partying became a darker undercurrent in her life. She started with smoking marijuana, then progressed to snorting pills and cocaine, and toward the end of her life, she even experimented with bath salts. What began as occasional indulgence gradually spiraled into a destructive dependency. Watching her descent into addiction felt like witnessing someone drift out to sea—at first, it was a slow, almost imperceptible loss, but eventually, she was too far gone to reach. Her journey underscored how addiction often begins subtly, only to overtake a person's life, leaving a profound impact on those around them.

My mom's journey was a testament to both the resilience and vulnerability of the human spirit. She showed me how determination can build a life but also how addiction can tear it apart. Her story reminds me to search for strength in others, even when it feels buried beneath layers of pain.

## The Honeymoon That Was Over Before It Began

My mother asked me to house-sit while she and her fourth husband, Keith, left for their honeymoon in Gatlinburg, Tennessee. They departed on a Thursday, planning to return that Sunday. However, to my surprise, she burst through the door on Friday, announcing that she wanted a divorce.

The honeymoon had taken a disastrous turn before it even began. On the drive to Gatlinburg, Keith had consumed an entire fifth of whiskey, leaving my mother to drive the whole way herself. When they arrived, Keith, still intoxicated, decided to try out the heart-shaped jacuzzi in their hotel room. What followed was pure chaos. In his drunken state, Keith ripped the faucet clean off the tub. Water shot up to the ceiling and spilled across the floor, flooding the room.

Naturally, the hotel management was less than thrilled and called the police. When the officers arrived, they immediately noticed a large bag of weed in the room. They asked who it belonged to, but when neither my mother nor Keith claimed ownership, they were both arrested. My mother spent the first night of her honeymoon in jail.

Despite the disastrous start to their marriage, she never divorced Keith. They remained married until her passing. My mom's honeymoon was a stark reminder of life's absurdity and the ways chaos seemed to follow her. In moments like these, I learned to find humor in life's unpredictability—even when everything seemed to go wrong.

### The Fragility of Stability

As Julie's addiction deepened, her ability to manage life's demands slowly unraveled. I vividly remember teaching her how to file her taxes on her PC, a task that revealed the growing gaps in her attention and understanding. One year, she received a letter from the state of Ohio threatening to revoke her job due to unpaid back taxes. She thought she had submitted her taxes online, but it turned out her computer wasn't even connected to the internet.

This was more than just a clerical error—it was a symptom of the increasing challenges she faced, and it highlighted the toll addiction and stress were taking on her. As a self-employed worker, these details were critical, and Julie's oversight left her vulnerable to cascading consequences. Financial stress, when compounded by addiction, can lead to desperate decisions, marking the beginning of her downward spiral.

Julie eventually hired an attorney to fight for her job, but months later, she received another letter, this time giving her just 30 days to pay what she owed. When I insisted we meet her attorney in person, she hesitated, finally revealing that he was out of state. Confused, I asked why she would hire an out-of-state attorney for an Ohio case. She eventually admitted that she had responded to a flyer she'd received in the mail. She had paid this so-called attorney a large sum upfront, along with monthly payments. Tragically, it turned out to be a scam. By the time we realized the truth, she had sent him more money than she owed the state.

This experience was devastating. It marked a critical turning point and was a painful lesson in the importance of verifying professional relationships and handling finances with care, especially during times of stress.

Watching my mom decline through addiction was a stark reminder of how fragile stability can be. Her struggles with even the smallest tasks showed me that addiction doesn't just take away health—it strips away pieces of who you are. Her story taught me the importance of empathy, the dangers of losing oneself, and the urgency of addressing addiction before it destroys everything.

Julie's life showed me the enduring strength of the human spirit, even when weighed down by struggles, and the necessity of holding on to love amidst the wreckage.

## Addiction's Toll

Losing her job sent Julie into a deeper spiral, and her addiction worsened. Bath salts became her escape of choice, but as they grew harder to obtain, she began driving for hours to purchase them, cutting them with pills or cocaine. Her cognitive state deteriorated rapidly. Conversations with her felt hollow—her voice no longer sounded like hers. It was as though she had lost a vital part of herself. Watching this transformation was heart-wrenching. It exposed the profound toll addiction takes, not only on physical health but on identity and relationships. Drugs don't just harm the body; they erode the very essence of a person, leaving those who love them grappling with loss long before they're gone.

As bills piled up and money ran out, Julie began making increasingly desperate decisions. I had been working on my 1992 Camaro RS, removing the engine with plans to install a small block. One day, she called to inform me that the car had been repossessed—even though I owned it outright. Later, while visiting, I noticed my 25th Anniversary RS edition rims on a neighbor's Chevy pickup. Investigating further, I discovered my engine, transmission, intake, and headers in his garage. When I confronted him, he simply said, "Take it up with your mom." It turned out Julie had traded everything for cocaine, security installations, and cash. She had even sent the car to the junkyard for salvage, exploiting a loophole in Ohio's old state laws that allowed her to do so without a title.

Her actions didn't stop there. I had stored furniture and appliances in her garage, including a stove, leather furniture, a refrigerator, and roofing tools. When she asked if I would sell my stove to her friend, I refused, yet she sold it anyway—along with everything else.

I learned of this a week later during a visit. The emptiness hit me like a gut punch when I opened the garage door. The dusty outlines of my furniture stood like ghosts on the floor—reminders of what should have been there. My mom avoided my gaze when I confronted her, her voice tight with forced casualness. "I needed the money," she said, as if that explanation could erase the betrayal. I wanted to yell, but all I could do was stand there, my fists clenching and unclenching as the weight of it settled in.

Losing my belongings to her addiction was a painful wake-up call, a stark reminder of how deeply addiction alters priorities and damages trust. While her actions hurt, they also underscored the desperation that addiction breeds, teaching me the necessity of setting boundaries while maintaining compassion.

### Desperation and Decline

When nothing was left of mine to sell, Julie turned to increasingly drastic measures. She punctured holes in the roof of her car with a screwdriver, covering the damage with branches and limbs, then claimed a large branch had fallen onto her vehicle. Somehow, the insurance adjuster approved her claim, but it was another clear sign of how addiction had clouded her judgment. Damaging her car for a payout illustrated the extreme lengths addiction can push someone to—measures that ultimately cost far more than they gain.

As her circumstances worsened, Julie lost her house and became homeless, sleeping in her car. My grandparents, ever compassionate, bought her a camper to provide stability. But when the water stopped working, she resorted to using buckets for sanitation. Her life had become bleak—a reality I only fully grasped after her passing on October 31, 2017, at just 53 years old. The unanswered questions surrounding her death still linger, a stark reminder of the fragility of life and the toll addiction takes on both individuals and families.

Her actions hurt deeply, but they also revealed the desperation that addiction breeds. Through those betrayals, I learned the importance of setting boundaries while holding onto compassion. Sometimes, love means protecting yourself, too.

## A Complex Legacy

Julie's life was a tapestry of resilience, struggle, triumph, and tragedy. Her determination to succeed in healthcare showed me the power of hard work and the potential for fulfillment, even under challenging circumstances. Yet, her descent into addiction revealed the devastating impact of substance abuse—not just on the individual but on everyone around them.

Julie's life and struggles taught me about resilience, the destructive nature of addiction, and the importance of family bonds. Her complex memory continues to shape my life, teaching me empathy, caution, and compassion—reminding me of the enduring strength found even amidst hardship.

## Don AKA Shadow

My father, Don, was the youngest of three brothers, growing up alongside Kelly, the middle child, and John, the eldest. As a child, he earned the nickname "Shadow" for his constant presence at his brothers' sides, a moniker that hinted at his loyalty and place within the family dynamic.

Despite his smaller stature—standing at just five feet five inches tall and weighing 145 pounds—Don was incredibly athletic and undeniably handsome. He captured the attention of many of the most popular girls at school. As a running back for the Bellefontaine Chieftains, he was a star on the field, known for his grit and determination. His athleticism earned him a scholarship to play football in college, a rare opportunity that reflected both his skill and potential.

However, during his senior year, a devastating hit during a game changed everything. The collision left him with an out-of-body experience, a moment so jarring that it deterred him from pursuing his football dreams any further. Faced with this turning point, he enlisted in the Air Force, serving for four years after high school.

When his contract ended, Don's desire to continue serving led him to join the Army. There, he achieved a prestigious milestone: joining Delta Force, a highly specialized unit known for counterterrorism, hostage rescue, and other high-risk missions. Yet, his time with Delta Force was cut short after my mother accused him of strangling her with his bare hands—a claim that cast a shadow over this chapter of his military career.

## A Tangled Love Story

Between his time in the Air Force and the Army, Don returned home, hoping to reunite with his long-lost love, Vivian. However, fate had other plans. While searching for Vivian, he met my mother, Julie, one of Vivian's friends. Their initial connection was casual—Don moved in with Julie temporarily while continuing his pursuit of Vivian.

But life had other ideas. My mother discovered she was pregnant with me, and this new reality derailed my father's vision of reconciliation with Vivian. Faced with this turn of events, my parents married, sealing a bond that had started almost by chance. A year and a half after my birth, they welcomed my younger brother, David, into the world.

## A Shot Heard Beyond the Darkness: My Father's Moment of Heroism

While attending a mental health group meeting, my father suddenly heard a gunshot ring out from outside. Without hesitation, he sprang into action, rushing outside and scaring off the shooter. His focus quickly shifted to the victim—a woman who had been shot. He began administering first aid, applying a tourniquet to her arm and pressing firmly on her abdomen to slow the bleeding. In that critical moment, his calm composure and willingness to act demonstrated the profound impact one person's courage can have in the face of tragedy.

As the details emerged, the story grew even more heartbreaking. The shooter, a man in his 30s, had been cut off financially by his parents. In a fit of rage, he turned a sawed-off shotgun on his mother. She instinctively raised her hand to shield herself, but the blast tore through her hand and lodged into her abdomen. The depth of the family conflict and its tragic outcome underscored how unresolved tensions can escalate into unthinkable actions when left unchecked.

The police later apprehended the son as he was on his way to kill his father, preventing what could have been an even greater catastrophe. Meanwhile, the mother was rushed to the hospital. Despite the medical team's best efforts and my father's immediate intervention, she succumbed to her injuries days later. The fragility of life became painfully clear, and the devastating consequences of desperation and unresolved anger were hauntingly evident.

Sometime after the incident, my father was invited to what he thought was a routine dinner. Unbeknownst to him, the gathering was actually a ceremony to honor his heroism. During the event, the Mayor of Marysville presented him with a plaque, recognizing his bravery and quick action in the crisis. For my father, who never sought recognition, this acknowledgment served as a powerful reminder of the importance of stepping up when others are in need.

My father's bravery that day taught me that we can make a difference, even in the face of overwhelming tragedy. His courage showed me that small acts of heroism can ripple outward, creating hope even in life's darkest moments.

## A Bond Beyond Time: The Life Lessons of Kelly

Ah, my dear Uncle Kelly. He was a shining beacon of hope during my childhood, a refuge from the chaos that surrounded my life. Just up the street from my father's house in Springfield, Ohio, his home became a sanctuary I treasured. I couldn't have asked for a better uncle, though I often hesitated to visit.

When we first moved to Springfield, Uncle Kelly was married to Katie, a woman who left a lasting impression on me. Aunt Katie was Kelly's second wife and the first proper, well-mannered, and stern lady I had ever encountered. She exuded effortless elegance, her poise and demeanor reflecting a deep understanding of grace and refinement. Her straight posture and quiet confidence commanded respect without ever demanding it.

I was intimidated by her presence, unsure how to behave around her. I was unruly and lacking in manners and respect, qualities she would never tolerate. Yet, through her quiet strength and grace, she taught me the importance of manners, self-control, and the respect one can earn simply through dignity.

Aunt Katie had a rare disorder, Anticardiolipin Syndrome, an autoimmune disease that causes the body to produce antibodies that attack healthy tissues and organs. My Uncle Kelly was her steadfast caregiver, attending to her every need until the very end. One day, while Kelly was at work, my dad noticed that Aunt Katie wasn't doing well and immediately called Kelly, urging him to come home. Kelly rushed back, and as he entered the house, my father stepped outside, knowing what was unfolding.

Two hours later, Kelly emerged, his face heavy with the weight of loss. My dad asked softly, "Has she passed?" Kelly responded in a voice tinged with quiet grief, "Yes, she passed about an hour ago." Aunt Katie had died in his arms, and Kelly held her long after, unwilling to let go. His devotion and strength during her illness showed me the profound resilience of love—the kind of love that doesn't end with death but continues through selfless care in someone's final moments. Kelly's care for Katie was a quiet heroism that often goes unnoticed but leaves an indelible mark on those who witness it. It's a legacy of love that inspires me, reminding me of the profound strength and selflessness it takes to care for someone in their final days.

I have countless cherished memories of Uncle Kelly. He introduced me to the world of firearms, taking me to my first gun range and teaching me the essentials of gun safety. Under his patient guidance, I learned how to load a gun, clean it, and practice proper range etiquette. I'll never forget the time I accidentally pointed a gun at him. Without hesitation, he threw me to the ground and yelled, "You only point a gun at someone you intend to shoot!" That moment, the only time I recall Kelly ever raising his voice, made a lasting impression on me. It wasn't just a lesson in gun safety—it was a lesson in respect, discipline, and the responsibility that comes with handling something dangerous.

Uncle Kelly also took me on a white-water rafting trip, an exhilarating adventure that pulled me away from the chaos of my everyday life. The rush of the water and the thrill of navigating the rapids gave me a sense of freedom and excitement I had never known. He also took my brother and me on a cross-country road trip, traveling through the Badlands in South Dakota and to Yellowstone National Park. Those trips, filled with breathtaking views and moments of awe, opened my eyes to a world beyond the small confines of my childhood struggles.

Through Kelly's adventures, I learned the value of shared experiences, of stepping outside one's comfort zone, and of living life to the fullest. He showed me that life isn't just about surviving the chaos; it's about embracing it with curiosity, joy, and a willingness to discover the beauty in the world around us. Uncle Kelly's influence on my life continues to shape how I view the world, and his legacy of love, strength, and adventure will stay with me always.

Through Kelly, I learned that joy is not just a refuge from chaos but a tool for navigating it and that adventure is an act of resilience in itself.

## The Do-Si-Do of Death

In the Badlands, we ventured into an area that had been roped off—a place we weren't supposed to be. My brother and I followed a narrow path, but at the end, there was nowhere to go but down. I made the leap, dropping ten feet to the level below. However, as I landed on the incline, I lost my footing and fell onto my backside, sliding dangerously close to the edge of a cliff that dropped hundreds of feet below. The rocks in the Badlands are mostly sedimentary—shale, siltstone, or mudstone—soft and crumbly. This makes the terrain unstable, as the rocks break down into loose gravel-like material over time, making footing treacherous in many places.

At that moment, my heart raced as I slid toward the edge. Fortunately, I turned and dug my hands and feet into the fine rock, pulling myself up the incline just in time to avoid what could have been a disastrous fall. I yelled back to David, "Don't come down this way!" Once I regained my footing, I made my way to the other side and called for him to jump down. When he did, I caught him in mid-air and guided him to safety against the rock wall he had just descended from.

We were pressed against the sheer face of the rock, with a steep drop stretching hundreds of feet below us. The sense of vertigo was overwhelming, but I drew on the skills I had learned from my days on roofs—staying calm, focused, and steady. Slowly, I started walking down at an angle, finding solid footholds as I went. When I reached the bottom, I turned and saw David still pressed against the rock wall, his body shaking uncontrollably from fear.

That moment, raw and full of adrenaline, taught me a powerful lesson about the fragility of life and the strength required to overcome fear in the face of danger. It was a stark reminder of how quickly things can go wrong and how the right choices and quick thinking can pull you from the edge of disaster.

I called up to David, instructing him to turn around and take the same angled path I had used to reach safety. For what felt like an eternity, he hesitated, gathering the courage to follow my instructions. But then, disaster struck. As he turned, he slipped, landing on his backside and beginning to slide uncontrollably down the slope.

Without thinking, my instincts kicked in. I sprinted as fast as I ever had, racing toward the spot where my brother was headed. The gap between us was probably a hundred yards, but the thought of him sliding off the cliff sent a surge of adrenaline coursing through my veins. With every ounce of energy, I extended my arm, reaching for him, praying that I could get there in time. In a heartbeat, his hand was within my grasp.

I caught it just as he went over the edge. My body went into overdrive, flinging him back onto the cliff, but my momentum carried me toward the precipice as well. Our hands locked together, and for a split second, terror gripped me—I thought we would both fall. But as my brother was yanked back onto the rock, the force of my swing sent me lurching out over the edge. With our hands still gripping each other tightly, he braced me against the rock and pulled me back onto solid ground, shaken but intact.

That moment—suspended between life and death—taught me invaluable lessons about courage, self-reliance, and the split-second decisions that can change everything. It showed me the power of instinct, resilience, and determination in the face of danger and the undeniable strength we can summon when it matters most. These are the skills I carry with me, constant reminders of our ability to face adversity and survive.

Meanwhile, Uncle Kelly had been standing below, witnessing the entire scene unfold. In his usual laid-back style, he yelled, "I got that on camera!" When we finally reunited with him, he proudly pulled out his camera, eager to show us the footage. But to our disappointment, his camera had a five-second delay, and the footage began with a picture of his foot.

Kelly, ever the storyteller, turned the mishap into a legendary family tale. He framed the picture and dubbed it "The Do-Si-Do of Death," capturing the essence of that wild moment. Only Uncle Kelly could turn something so terrifying into a moment of laughter—a perfect example of his ability to find humor even in life's scariest situations.

That terrifying moment in the Badlands taught me the power of instinct and quick thinking, but it also reminded me of the healing power of humor. Laughter has a way of bringing us back to solid ground, even in the most harrowing moments.

One of my most cherished memories with Uncle Kelly is of a night that perfectly encapsulated his playful spirit. I was staying at his house, and after a few too many drinks, he became a whirlwind of laughter and spontaneity. With a mischievous grin, he tossed me a sword and, in a slurred voice, declared, "Defend yourself!" Before I could even process what was happening, he swung his sword in an exaggerated overhead strike—and, in the process, shattered a low-hanging light fixture in the living room. The sound of glass shattering rang through the house, and for a moment, we both just stood there, stunned. Then, without missing a beat, Uncle Kelly shot me a wry smile and suggested, "Maybe we should take this outside." His eyes sparkled with mischief, and I couldn't help but laugh.

That spontaneous, playful moment was a perfect example of Kelly's ability to bring laughter and light into any situation. It reminded me of the joy and warmth that humor can bring to family life, even in the most unexpected moments.

Through his love, guidance, and adventurous spirit, Uncle Kelly taught me lessons in responsibility, resilience, and the importance of shared laughter. He created a legacy of love, playfulness, and joy, showing me that the best memories are made when we embrace life fully. His influence continues to remind me to face life with courage, nurture humor in our relationships, and create meaningful memories that last a lifetime.

## A Legacy of Love and Laughter: Beverly's Enduring Impact on My Life

That humor was intrinsic to who he was and extended to his relationship with his third wife, Beverly. If Kelly was the adventurous anchor in my life, Beverly was the spark who taught me that laughter could heal even the deepest wounds. She was unlike anyone I'd ever met—she was a hoot. No one could make me laugh as hard as she did. Beverly was sharp, adventurous, and full of life. She had a unique way of turning even mundane moments into cherished memories. Whether it was her relentless teasing or her embrace of spontaneity, she taught me that laughter is a cornerstone of resilience. Beverly and Kelly showed me how humor can bind people together and soften life's most brutal blows.

Beverly's contagious laugh started low in her chest and bubbled until everyone in the room joined in. She had a knack for finding humor in the most unexpected places—like when she spent ten minutes mocking the outdated wallpaper in a diner, her voice dripping with mock sophistication as she called it "a bold statement piece." She could turn even a trip to the grocery store into an adventure, making life feel lighter simply by being in it.

Just weeks after they started dating, Kelly invited Beverly to hike the Grand Canyon. During their hike, he started chafing so severely that he could barely move. Kelly meekly asked to borrow her lip balm, which came in a small container that required you to scoop it out with your fingers. Grateful for the relief, Kelly dipped his fingers in and smeared it where he needed it most.

But before he could reach for more, Beverly pointed at him, eyebrows raised, and said in her sharp, teasing tone, "No double-dipping!"

Kelly froze, caught somewhere between embarrassment and laughter. The absurdity of the situation hit them both, and they laughed so hard that they had to stop hiking for a moment.

Beverly's wit turned what could've been an uncomfortable moment into a family story we've never stopped laughing about.

One of Beverly's favorite stories involved a hilarious moment from my twenties. One evening, after a long night of drinking, a commotion erupted in the office, and Kelly and Beverly walked in to find me sprawled across the computer desk, desperately trying to cover myself with a random assortment of papers while the desk struggled to stay upright. They burst into uncontrollable laughter at the sight, laughing so hard they could barely catch their breath. Kelly still regrets not letting Beverly take a picture of that moment, saying it would've been a perfect addition to their collection of family memories. This moment, like so many with them, taught me the importance of cherishing and creating joyful memories. Beverly's humor and warmth inspire me to cultivate lightheartedness in my family, reminding me that laughter is a legacy worth passing down.

Losing Beverly hit hard. A blood clot following a routine knee surgery took her life far too soon, leaving a void that is still profoundly felt. Her passing was a stark reminder of life's unpredictability and the importance of cherishing every moment with the people we love. In a bittersweet twist, I named my daughter Iona Beverly in her honor. Although they never met, Beverly's legacy lives on in my daughter, a testament to the enduring impact of love and laughter. Thank you, Beverly, for all the beautiful memories. I love you and miss you always.

Through Kelly and Beverly, I learned how to live fully, love deeply, and face challenges with humor and grace. Their stories are woven into the fabric of my life, reminding me to embrace the people around me, take risks, and find joy even in life's chaos. Their legacy of love, adventure, and laughter continues to guide me, a shining example of how the bonds we form can transcend time and loss. Beverly's spirit taught me that humor and love are among the most powerful tools we have to heal, even when life feels unbearably heavy.

## Conclusion

Family is never perfect. It's chaotic and excruciating. But through the chaos, I've found strength—not just within myself, but in the lessons they left behind. From Mike, I learned the power of humor as a survival tool, even if it's not enough on its own. Observing Karl, I realized that talent and addiction can coexist, highlighting the need for compassion, even in the most challenging situations. From Julie, I learned both the dangers of losing yourself and the resilience it takes to keep going. And from Kelly and Beverly, I discovered the joy of embracing life fully, even in the face of loss.

Through Mike's humor, Karl's brilliance, Julie's resilience, and Kelly and Beverly's joy, I've come to understand that family is never simple. It's chaotic, messy, and imperfect—but it's also where we learn to love, endure, and grow. Their lessons—whether in laughter or loss—continue to shape the person I am today, reminding me that amidst the chaos, there's always room for hope, healing, and connection. Ultimately, family is where we face our most significant challenges and find our most profound growth. Through laughter and loss, chaos and compassion, their stories remind me that even amidst imperfection, there is strength, love, and room for healing.

# Chapter 5:
# From Chaos to Redemption

When I slammed David to the ground, the sound of his body hitting the floor echoed through the room—sharp and final, like a thunderclap shattering the silence. In that instant, everything froze. His scream tore through the air, raw and jagged, a sound I knew would haunt me forever.

My hands trembled as I stared at his limp body sprawled on the floor, panic surging through me like an electric current. I dropped to my knees, shaking him, my voice breaking as I called his name over and over. "David, wake up. Please, wake up." The words came out desperately, almost in a whisper, swallowed by the crushing weight of fear.

Time stretched into an agonizing eternity before I saw him stir. His hand moved to clutch his shoulder, his face twisting in pain as he let out a low groan. Relief collided with guilt, leaving me dizzy, my heart hammering so loudly it drowned out everything else. The enormity of my actions settled over me like a suffocating fog, making time seem to stutter—each moment dragging as if caught in quicksand.

Then, I realized that some actions are irreversible. The look on his face, the sound of his scream, the weight of my own hands—they were now etched into me, scars I'd carry long after the moment itself had passed.

Alone in my room that night, the weight of what had happened burdened my chest. Shame and guilt twisted inside me, waging war with my anger. I replayed the moment over and over in my mind, wishing I could take it back but knowing I couldn't.

When the police pulled me out of class the next day and put me in handcuffs, I didn't fight it. I knew I deserved it. This was the price of losing control. The consequence for me was eight months in a juvenile detention center.

I had nothing but time to think inside those sterile, gray walls. The hush of night was immense, punctuated only by distant patrol steps and the slam of a hallway door. I hated who I'd become. That moment with David haunted me like a ghost, but in the quiet moments, I realized something—I didn't want anger to define me. I didn't want this to be the person I grew into.

## A New Chapter: Faith, Family, and Forgiveness

Upon my release, Keith and Theresa Roshon welcomed me into their foster home, offering me a safe place instead of sending me back to my father's. Under their roof, I experienced the structure, warmth, and stability that proper families possess.

The first time I stepped into the Roshon's house, I noticed the faint smell of lavender—clean and comforting, like nothing I'd ever known before. The neatly set dining table gleamed under the soft overhead light, starkly contrasting the cluttered chaos of my childhood home.

As I looked around, a wave of unease settled in my stomach. Could I belong here? I wasn't used to places like this—places where people seemed to care about the details, where everything had a purpose and a place. I was scared to touch anything, afraid of breaking the fragile peace already wrapping around me. But Keith smiled at me, warm and genuine, and Theresa handed me a plate of spaghetti, her eyes kind. At that moment, I experienced a feeling I hadn't felt for years: hope.

At dinner one night, Keith launched into a story about his misadventures fixing the washing machine. His voice carried that familiar mix of pride and self-deprecation, drawing us in with every word. "So there I am," he explained, waving his fork like a tool, "up to my elbows in pipes and detergent, thinking, 'I've got this.' Next thing I know, water's gushing out like Niagara Falls."

The room erupted in laughter, but Keith wasn't done. "Then—because it couldn't just stop there—I step back to grab the wrench, and boom!" He slapped his thigh for emphasis. "I'm flat on my back in a puddle of soapy water, looking up at the ceiling, wondering where my life went wrong."

By the time he finished, we were doubled over, clutching our sides, tears streaming down our faces. Our laughter filled the small dining room, echoing off the walls, weaving us together in an almost sacred way. Dinner smelled like home-cooked love: spaghetti bubbling in its tangy sauce, thick with garlic and oregano; fresh rolls warm from the oven; the sharp, bright snap of salad dressing on crisp greens. The room felt alive, lit not just by the soft glow of the chandelier but by the warmth of voices overlapping, stories being shared, and laughter spilling out like music.

As Keith told his story about flooding the laundry room, I couldn't stop watching how everyone leaned in, captivated by his words. I'd never seen anything like it—this effortless rhythm of family, where everyone had a place at the table, their laughter weaving together like a tapestry. I laughed, too, though part of me wanted to cry. How many dinners had I spent in silence or with tension so thick it choked the air? Only joy existed here; anger and yelling were absent. And it felt so foreign, so fragile, that I was scared it might slip away.

Life with the Roshons was structured and disciplined yet enveloped in love and laughter. Mornings began with making the bed, followed by school, then coming home to complete homework. We had dinner as a family every night, sharing stories of the day and laughing together.

Afterward, we all pitched in to clean up, setting the space for the next day. It was a world I hadn't known, where parents listened with patience.

The home radiated an environment I once only dreamed of: well-mannered children and empathetic parents who listened and didn't shut their kids down. For the first time, I began attending church, where I found comfort and guidance in faith, eventually accepting Jesus as my Lord and Savior. The Roshons helped me see a version of myself I hadn't imagined—capable of change and worthy of love.

Surrounded by Keith's humor and the infectious joy of the people at the table, I experienced a sense of belonging for the first time. It wasn't just about sharing a space or a meal; it was about sharing stories, laughter, and a sense of safety. For a child always braced for the next storm, this felt like basking in sunlight after years of rain.

## A New Wife, a New Life: How My Father's Choices Shaped My Path

At sixteen, I was drawn back into my father's orbit. He was renting an apartment from my foster dad, Keith, and I found myself slipping back into the cycle of his erratic presence. My father's frequent absences and his preference for staying with his girlfriend, Michelle, across town meant weeks would pass without seeing him. I found work with Keith, who maintained the properties he owned in Marysville. Among the tasks, I painted a particular house and suggested to my father that he buy it from Keith, which he did.

One day, seemingly out of nowhere, my father called to announce that he had just gotten married. He had driven Michelle and her two kids to Tennessee, where they had eloped. "Thanks for the invite," I replied, my voice dripping with sarcasm, though beneath it, hurt was clawing at me. Michelle and I had never gotten along, and from the start, she had made it clear that she wanted me and David out of my father's life. I quickly realized she saw us as an obstacle to the new life she was trying to build with him.

## Unwelcome: The Day My Father Closed the Door on Me

After the wedding, he returned home to find me and ten friends passed out in the apartment. He explained that Keith needed the place vacated by 6 PM that day for new tenants, and without warning, I had to leave. My father had rented a U-Haul, and without hesitation, my friends and I loaded up all my belongings, ensuring we met the deadline. The U-Haul's engine rumbled beneath me as I pulled up to the new house, the weight of my father's belongings heavy in the back, just like the pit growing in my stomach.

The house loomed ahead, freshly painted and pristine, a blank canvas of promises. The air was cold and empty as I stepped inside, a stark reminder of the fleeting nature of existence. My boots thudded against the hardwood floor as my father led me through, his voice brisk and mechanical. He listed the rooms quickly: Michelle's kids' room, David's room, and ours, his tone indifferent. The walls seemed to close in as the words sank in. Confused, I hesitated before asking, my voice trembling with a mix of hope and dread, "Where's my room?"

"You don't have a room here, son," he said, his words cold and final.

His declaration hit me like a slap, leaving me breathless. My chest tightened, and for a moment, I thought I might collapse. The silence that followed was deafening, only interrupted by the pounding of my heartbeat in my ears.

I couldn't believe it. I had just moved everything for him, hoping for a place in his new life. But he left me stranded. Hurt, betrayed, and confused, I forced out, "Where should I stay tonight?" He explained that they were staying at Michelle's apartment because the electricity at the new house still needed to be hooked up, but she didn't want me there. What hurt most was that I had moved everything for him without a word, only to be left without a place to go.

I packed what I could fit in my pickup truck, leaving my bed behind because it wouldn't fit. My father promised I could come back for it later. Two weeks later, I returned to find it discarded outside, weathered and ruined.

It was chaos, and I understood. But that moment only added to the strain between my father and me, already worn thin by years of neglect and abuse.

It revealed a truth that took years to fully unravel: love's enduring presence isn't guaranteed, especially from those who are supposed to protect you. It's a bitter lesson, but it taught me the value of showing up for the people who need you and never letting someone you care about feel unwanted. My father's rejection scarred me, but it also showed me the man I refuse to become.

### Shelter in a Storm: The Generosity That Helped Me Rebuild My Life

With nowhere else to turn, I found myself homeless, living out of my truck while finishing high school and working. Occasionally, I stayed with my mother, but her negativity made it difficult to endure, reminding me of the reasons I had left in the first place. When my girlfriend's grandparents discovered my situation, they kindly took me in for a while.

Working alongside her grandfather, Earl, and her Uncle Pat in their home improvement business taught me valuable skills and gave me the support I needed. I threw myself into the work, using it as a way to cope with everything. With every stroke of the paintbrush, a small part of me started to come back together. The rhythmic hum of the sander, the steady slap of paint on bare walls—it gave me a sense of control I hadn't had in years. Watching a house transform under my hands reminded me that change was possible, even for someone like me.

Painting those houses and seeing the transformations I helped create brought a sense of accomplishment and independence. It was therapeutic—an escape from the chaos of my life at home. I am deeply grateful for their kindness and generosity during one of the toughest times in my life.

*Dustin Bryan*

## Left in the Rain: Finding Strength in the Face of Betrayal

One Sunday, not long after my father and Michelle had settled into their new home, I brought my brother, David, back after a visit with our mother. My father wasn't home to let us in, and with no time to wait for him, I helped David enter through an open window. But when my father and Michelle returned, they called the police, accusing David of breaking and entering.

It was difficult to understand why they reacted the way they did, especially calling the police on David simply for entering his own home. The logic and fairness of the situation seemed twisted, leaving me struggling to make sense of it—and, ultimately, to accept it.

The following month brought an unexpected turn. After my father's paycheck was directly deposited into their joint account, Michelle withdrew all the money and kicked him out of the house. She drained the funds and forced him to leave, leaving him scrambling with no resources to fall back on. It was a stark lesson in how much control finances can have over people's lives. My father, without financial independence, was left vulnerable to manipulation. I realized that financial independence wasn't just about money—it was a form of self-protection, particularly in relationships where power dynamics could easily be exploited.

With no plan or resources, my father took David to our Uncle Kelly's house, hoping to figure something out. After discussing their options, they decided David should go to our mother's house since my father couldn't support him. Watching all of this unfold filled me with frustration and disappointment. During their conflict, David was treated as an inconvenience rather than a son who needed a stable home. It was a painful reminder of how adult conflicts—especially financial ones—can spill over into children's lives. I understood then how crucial it is to shield children from these situations. They need stability, not to be shuffled around like pawns in battles they have no part in.

After dropping David off, my father went back to confront Michelle. That was when the real truth hit: Michelle hadn't wanted my father gone; she just wanted David out of the picture. She gained complete control over my father and the house by sending him away. When she saw David wasn't with him, she welcomed my father back. I saw how much was lost in a relationship where boundaries, respect, and communication had been completely eroded. Watching Michelle manipulate the situation to her advantage made me reflect on the importance of mutual respect and understanding in any relationship. Without them, even the strongest bonds can become toxic, breeding pain and resentment.

A few days later, my father messaged me, telling me I had until 9:00 that night to pick up David's belongings or he would throw them out. There was no consideration for the fact that these were David's things, his memories, and his only tangible link to what should have been his home.

The rain fell steadily, drumming against the truck's roof as I approached the house. The porch light flickered, casting a dim, yellow glow over the pile of David's belongings, scattered like debris after a storm. His clothes were soaked through, clinging to the wooden planks in dark, heavy clumps. Books lay open, their pages swollen and curled, the ink bleeding into illegible smudges. The air was cold and sharp, the rain seeping through my jacket as I knelt, my fingers trembling as I gathered each item.

With every piece I picked up, anger and sadness twisted together inside me. How could they treat him like this? Did his belongings, his memories, mean nothing to them? The weight of the soaked clothes mirrored the weight of my frustration, my helplessness. I looked at David, standing silent and still in the rain, his shoulders hunched against the cold. Though he remained silent, his eyes, brimming with lasting hurt, conveyed more pain than words could ever express.

I realized how even small gestures of care—like keeping his things dry or giving me prior notice—would have made a world of difference. The absence of that basic consideration revealed just how important respect and thoughtfulness are in family relationships.

Confusion, anger, sadness, and guilt churned inside me. My father's behavior left me questioning what loyalty and responsibility truly meant in our family. When loyalty becomes selective—dependent on convenience or manipulated by others—it loses all meaning. I had always believed family was meant to protect one another, but that belief felt fragile now, as though it could be stripped away just as easily as David's belongings had been left out in the rain.

As I drove away with David's things piled in the back of my truck, the rain still falling, I made a promise to myself. I wouldn't let him feel alone again. If our family couldn't be the safety net we needed, I would be. That moment taught me the power of showing up for someone when no one else will. It's a lesson I've carried into every relationship since.

Amid this turmoil, I realized that family isn't defined by blood alone but by the love, stability, and trust we choose to build. While my father's actions left me disillusioned, the Roshons introduced me to a different kind of family—one rooted in unconditional care and support.

## Building a Future of Love: Lessons from Pain, Faith, and the Roshons

The Roshons showed me what family could be—what it should be. Their home wasn't perfect, but it was filled with love and stability that I'd never known before. Walking through their front door for the first time, I was struck by how different it felt from any place I had called home. The faint scent of warm lavender greeted me, carrying an unspoken promise of safety. Sunlight poured through the windows, pooling on the polished floor. Everything about their home felt deliberate—not rigid, not untouchable, but in a way that said, You matter enough for this space to be cared for.

In their home, I learned that discipline didn't have to hurt to be effective, that listening could heal wounds I hadn't even realized I carried, and that belonging wasn't something to be earned. It was freely given, as natural as breathing, as steady as the ticking of the kitchen clock. It was the first time I felt loved without needing to prove my worth. In their daily life, unwavering love was abundant.

## FROM **B**ROKEN TO **B**LESSED

The Roshon's dinner table profoundly altered my understanding of family. It was large and solid, its surface worn smooth from years of shared meals, lively conversations, and the occasional misplaced pencil from someone's homework. The food was simple but always lovingly prepared: hearty stews, baked chicken, or pasta dishes, their rich, savory aromas filling the air. Theresa's laugh rang out at the table like a melody, wrapping everyone in its warmth. Across from her, Keith would lean back in his chair, one arm resting casually on the backrest, launching into one of his signature stories—stories that began with humor and ended with lessons so subtle that you didn't realize you'd been taught until long after the plates were cleared.

In those moments, I felt something unfamiliar yet powerful—comfort. It wasn't just the food or the laughter; it was the way the Roshons saw each other, the way they saw me. They asked about my day and waited for my answer as though it truly mattered. They didn't interrupt or dismiss me. They listened. And that simple act of listening became a balm for the parts of me that had grown raw and brittle from years of feeling invisible.

When I think of the Roshons, small details come rushing back—details that made their house more than just a shelter. The scent of fresh cookies mingled with the faint lavender cleaner Theresa used to wipe down the counters. The hum of the washing machine in the background, a gentle rhythm underscoring daily life's chaos. A calendar pinned to the wall, its squares filled with scribbled notes about dentist appointments, school plays, and family birthdays—a testament to the quiet structure that kept their lives running smoothly. Their home wasn't perfect, but it radiated an unspoken promise: Here, you are welcome. Here, you are safe.

### Faith as a Refuge

The lessons I learned in their home extended beyond those walls and into the church they introduced me to—a place that became a sanctuary in every sense of the word. The first time I stepped into that church, my shoes squeaked faintly on the polished floor. The scent of wood polish and candles lingered in the air, and sunlight filtered through the stained-glass windows, casting kaleidoscopic patterns on the pews.

As I sat there, feeling the weight of my past pressing down on me, the pastor spoke of forgiveness—not just the kind we extend to others, but the kind we must offer ourselves. Those words washed over me like cool water, soothing wounds I hadn't dared to acknowledge. I returned to that church week after week, drawn not only by the sermons but by the sense of community that echoed the warmth I'd felt in the Roshon's home. Faith wasn't about perfection or punishment but grace and redemption. It was about believing in the possibility of change, even for someone like me.

The church became a place where I could set down the weight I'd been carrying and look forward with hope. It served as an anchor during turbulent times, a reminder that even the most broken pieces can be gathered and reshaped into something whole. Faith taught me that my past didn't have to dictate my future, and that realization became a turning point in my life.

## The Journey Forward

Looking back, every twist, turn, and moment of despair and hope has shaped me into the person I am today. Life wasn't kind or stable for much of my youth, but those struggles taught me resilience, adaptability, and strength. They revealed the cracks in my family's foundation, but they also illuminated the possibility of building something more substantial.

The time I spent with the Roshons, the generosity of my girlfriend's family, and even the painful lessons from my fractured family all contributed to the person I've become. Those experiences instilled a deep determination to create a different life for my children. I want my kids to grow up knowing they are loved—not just in the fleeting, conditional way I sometimes felt loved as a child, but in the profound, unshakable way I felt loved in the Roshon's home. I want them to feel secure, valued, and seen for who they are. In that promise to them, I finally found peace and purpose.

Reflecting on my time with the Roshon's, I see how their unconditional love and unwavering support shaped the man I am today. Their willingness to open their hearts and homes to a struggling teenager taught me what true compassion looks like and how it can change a life forever. Because of their impact, I deeply respect and admire foster parents who step into children's lives during their most vulnerable moments.

## Foster Care Appreciation

My wife, Rachel, is a Child Protective Services supervisor, overseeing foster care and adoption in our county. Recently, I had the privilege of being a keynote speaker at a foster care appreciation dinner, where I met many foster parents who generously shared their inspiring stories with me. To be a foster parent is to embrace a journey that few are prepared for but many are called to. It's a life marked by endless sacrifices—early mornings, late nights, and countless moments of silent resolve, often made in the face of daunting challenges. These are the unsung heroes who open their hearts and homes to children in need, offering not just shelter but something much more: stability, love, and the chance for a brighter future.

The impact of a foster parent is profound and lifelong. For every child who has experienced upheaval, abandonment, or trauma, a foster parent becomes a beacon of hope and safety. In opening their homes, they extend an invitation to healing—a chance for a child to rebuild trust, rediscover joy, and feel valued and understood. This love goes beyond the surface, leaving a mark on these children that will be felt for years, if not generations, to come.

## Sacrifices That Speak Volumes

The journey of a foster parent is rarely easy. It involves profound sacrifice, often at significant personal and emotional cost. It's waking up early to comfort a child haunted by nightmares, sitting beside them on rough days, and celebrating even the most minor victories. For foster parents, the commitment goes far beyond signing papers or providing shelter. They endure the complexities of healing, often walking a tightrope of patience and resilience as they help children navigate emotional scars that can be overwhelming. The late nights spent soothing fears, the appointments with counselors and teachers, the extra hours spent advocating for educational support or mental health resources—these sacrifices reveal an unwavering love that shines quietly but brilliantly.

These parents must navigate the delicate balance between caring profoundly and allowing children the freedom to learn, grow, and sometimes even stumble. They carry the heartache of knowing their role may be temporary—that they may have to say goodbye to a child they love as their own. Yet, they persevere with selfless determination, ensuring every child feels valued, safe, and worthy of love—even if only for a season. This is no small sacrifice. It is a profound gift, knowing that their time together could end tomorrow.

## The Strength of Unwavering Support

It's impossible to overlook the strength and courage required to be a foster parent. They are often thrown into complex situations, each with unique challenges, where they must adapt quickly and provide stability. Sometimes, they face skepticism or resistance from others involved in the child's life. The patience and empathy required are not easily cultivated, nor are they always reciprocated. Yet, foster parents persist, shouldering the emotional burdens and standing firm as the children entrusted to them work through their traumas and uncertainties.

They are healers, quietly mending wounds they didn't cause. Every moment spent advocating for their foster children—whether through school meetings, therapy sessions, or healthcare appointments—adds to a growing foundation of support that fosters growth and healing. Foster parents are not just providing care; they impart life skills, build confidence, and show these children they are worthy of time, effort, and love. These small yet monumental acts of resilience remind each child that they matter and deserve happiness, security, and love.

## Challenges That Test the Heart and Soul

The foster journey isn't for the faint of heart. There are days when the weight of it all feels overwhelming—when doubts and frustrations emerge, testing every fiber of resolve. Foster parents wrestle with the complexities of helping children who have endured unimaginable hardships, often facing these battles with little guidance or acknowledgment. For many, there are moments of wondering if they're making any difference, especially when confronted with behavioral challenges or emotional resistance. Yet, in those moments, foster parents' commitment truly shines.

The challenges they face—navigating a broken system, fighting for resources, managing sometimes-complicated relationships with biological families—are immense. These struggles test their patience, optimism, and sometimes even their faith. Yet they persevere, driven by the unwavering belief that every child deserves the opportunity to heal and thrive. This resilience defines them: a quiet but powerful determination with an immeasurable impact on these young lives. They understand, perhaps better than anyone, that healing isn't always straightforward or linear. It's a slow process, filled with difficulties and trials, but they walk alongside each child through it all—even on the most challenging days.

## A Legacy of Love

To all foster parents, thank you for your kindness, bravery, and unwavering commitment to making a difference and transforming lives. You give without expectation, love without condition, and stand beside children who may have known only pain and rejection. You are the hidden guardians, the devoted advocates, and the shining beacons who ensure these young people feel seen, safe, and loved.

I think of the Roshons opening their door to me—a confused, angry teenager—and never asking for anything in return. I remember the nights Keith taught me how to repair a leaky faucet or sand down a stubborn wall for painting, always with calm patience, making me feel like I could figure anything out. I think of Theresa's soft laughter echoing through the house as she baked cookies, her presence so warm it seemed to settle over the entire home like a comforting quilt. Foster parents like Keith and Theresa change lives, not in monumental ways, but in the quiet, consistent moments that whisper to a child, "You are safe now."

Your legacy is one of profound love, and we are eternally grateful for it. The lives you touch, the hope you inspire, and the compassion you embody leave an indelible mark on this world. Though you may not always see the fruits of your labor immediately, the seeds you plant in these young hearts will grow and blossom in ways that echo far beyond your lifetime. Thank you for being there for those who need it most, standing firm in the face of challenges, and believing in love's transformative power.

God only knows where I would be had I not found the Roshons when I needed them most. Their love became the lifeline I didn't even realize I was reaching for. They taught me that discipline doesn't have to come from a place of harshness but can be delivered with kindness and understanding. I think back to the nights Keith sat beside me at the dining table, his voice calm but firm as he walked me through homework I thought I'd never understand. Or Theresa, gently guiding me in the kitchen as she showed me how to cook a meal, always encouraging me to believe that I could take care of myself. These weren't just lessons—they were acts of love.

Thank you, Keith and Theresa, for listening patiently and offering guidance and support without judgment. This starkly contrasted my previous experiences, where my feelings often went unheard. In your home, I felt seen and valued for the first time. You nurtured my interests, encouraged me to explore my passions, and celebrated my achievements, no matter how small. Thank you for introducing me to a community within the church that embraced love, compassion, and forgiveness. I remember sitting in those pews, the sunlight streaming through stained-glass windows, and hearing sermons about grace and redemption. Those words resonated deeply because you both lived them every day. Eventually, I accepted Jesus as my Lord and Savior, an experience that profoundly changed my perspective on life.

Keith and Theresa helped me see a version of myself I had never imagined—capable of change and deserving of love. They instilled in me the belief that my past did not define my future and that, with effort and determination, I could forge a new path. Their unwavering support was a beacon of hope during some of my darkest days.

The Roshons also imparted essential life skills that have served me well beyond their home. They taught me how to manage my time effectively, prioritize responsibilities, and approach challenges with a solution-oriented mindset. I remember when Theresa helped me plan a complicated exam study schedule. She sat with me, sketching a plan on a notepad, her voice steady and reassuring. "You've got this," she encouraged, sliding the pen into my hand. "You just need a plan." Whether it was developing a study routine or showing me how to plumb a house, their hands-on approach to teaching equipped me with tools I would carry into adulthood. Each lesson affirmed I was capable of more than I had previously believed.

Another invaluable lesson came through their unwavering support during challenging moments. When I faced setbacks—whether it was struggling with schoolwork or carrying the weight of my past—the Roshons were always there, ready to listen and encourage me to persevere. One night, I returned home feeling defeated after failing a test. Theresa sat beside me at the table, her hand resting lightly on my shoulder. "It's okay to fail," she assured me, her voice gentle but firm. "What matters is that you don't give up. You're stronger than this moment." That belief in me—their belief—became the foundation of my resilience. It changed how I approach life's challenges, helping me see obstacles as opportunities for growth rather than insurmountable barriers.

Their nurturing environment helped me understand the value of empathy and compassion. Their dedication to helping others inspired me to become more socially aware and involved. I saw that my unique experiences were part of the larger human story. This realization motivated me to reach out and support others who were struggling, just as the Roshons had done for me. It fueled my desire to give back, ensuring that no one else would feel as lost or alone as I once did.

I learned from the Roshons that love is freely and abundantly given, not earned. Their love wasn't transactional; it didn't come with strings attached. It was steady, like a lighthouse guiding me through the storms of my past. I modeled my fatherhood on their patience and kindness: I strive to listen, to guide steadily, and to always assure my children of their inherent value—not based on their actions, but on who they are.

Every time I sit down at the dinner table with my family, I feel the echoes of the Roshon's influence. The laughter that fills the room, the gentle questions about everyone's day, and the sense of connection that ties us together all come from what they taught me. I set the table with the same care Theresa showed me—not because the plates are perfect or the napkins match, but because it's a way to say, "You matter." Their love gave me a blueprint for what family could be, and though I'll never be able to repay them entirely, I can carry their lessons forward. I can pass on the light they gave me, hoping it will guide my children through their storms.

The Roshons didn't just give me a home; they gave me the tools to rebuild my life. Because of their unwavering love, I've created a family grounded in faith, hope, and compassion. Their kindness is a light I carry forward, ensuring their legacy of love continues to shine.

# Chapter 6:
# The Silent Witnesses and a Promise Made

When I was 18, my uncle's choices led him to a tragic end that left an indelible mark on my life. He had recently separated from his girlfriend and was trying to numb his heartache in the only way he knew how. I still don't know if this was intentional, but the combination of drinking, pills, and chewing pain patches had devastating consequences. That night, his body was fragile; a thread stretched too tightly, and it finally snapped. He stumbled, unsteady and disoriented, his breath ragged as he tried to regain balance. His foot caught on a rug, and he slipped face-first into a coffee table. The sickening crack of bone against wood echoed through the room, sharp and jarring, freezing the air as though even time itself recoiled.

Blood burst forth as vessels ruptured from the impact. His face swelled almost instantly, turning discolored and grotesque. The blood pooled, seeping onto the table and dripping to the floor below, dark red against the faded carpet. He lay there, motionless, his chest barely rising and falling. The silence that followed was suffocating, broken only by the muffled music playing from a speaker in the corner—a hauntingly upbeat tune that felt painfully out of place in the grim reality of the scene.

Mike's so-called "friends" sat around him, their eyes wide with shock, but not a single person moved. No one called for help. They glanced at each other, their faces pale and uncertain, waiting for someone else to take action. One of them nervously lit a cigarette, the flick of the lighter loud in the oppressive quiet, as though attempting to distract themselves from the horror unfolding just a few feet away. Another stared blankly at the floor, muttering something inaudible as if trying to convince themselves this wasn't happening.

And yet, none of them lifted a hand to help. No one called for an ambulance or even checked if he was still breathing. They sat frozen, paralyzed by fear, apathy, or perhaps the cruel self-interest of not wanting to get involved. The air grew thick with the sharp, acrid smell of alcohol, mingling with the metallic tang of blood. It was suffocating, heavy with the weight of inaction.

Minutes ticked by, each one feeling like an eternity. Mike's body lay crumpled, lifeless, his face pressed against the table's edge, his skin turning a shade of gray that no living person should ever wear. Whether they noticed or not, death was creeping in—silent but undeniable, wrapping its icy grip around him as the room remained steeped in chilling apathy.

The pills and alcohol in his system were already a deadly mix, but the fall accelerated what was bound to happen. His body couldn't take it anymore. This wasn't just an accident—it was a slow, preventable tragedy unfolding in plain sight while everyone stood by and did nothing.

The thought that no one called for help—not one person—has haunted me ever since. He didn't die surrounded by care, concern, dignity, or love. He died on a cold floor in a room full of people too disconnected to recognize the humanity slipping away before them.

They neglected to help him. They failed to call for an ambulance. Instead of staying by his side, they left. They rifled through his pockets as he lay dying, unconscious and alone. They took his money, his pills, his drugs—anything they thought might incriminate them. Later, they would justify it to my grandparents, claiming they wanted to avoid the cops finding the contraband on his person. But no explanation could erase what they did—or, conversely, what they neglected to do.

Even now, I can't shake the image from my memory: the crimson streak on the coffee table, the stillness of Mike's remains, and the way the light overhead flickered as though it, too, was faltering. It was a moment that didn't just mark his end—it imprinted a painful, permanent scar on me.

While Mike's final moments were marked by neglect and cruelty, the aftermath rippled far beyond that room, reaching my grandparents' doorstep the next morning.

### An Ordinary Morning, A Shattering Loss

The scene shifts in my mind to the early hours of the following day. The sun is barely above the horizon, casting a pale, gray light over my grandparents' modest home. Inside, the faint smell of coffee lingers in the air, mingling with the musty scent of old carpets and the creaking of the wood floor beneath my grandfather's heavy boots. It is a home that has seen its fair share of heartbreak, a place where knocks on the door often carry terrible news.

When the sound came—a heavy, deliberate knock against the weathered wood—my grandmother wiped her hands on her apron, her heart sinking with a familiar dread. She exchanged a glance with my grandfather. This wasn't unusual. The county sheriffs had called before, always about one of their children. These visits had become almost routine, like clockwork, in their chaotic lives. But this time, something felt different.

When my grandfather opened the door, the sheriff stood there, his hat in his hands, his face solemn. Behind him, another deputy shifted uneasily, avoiding eye contact. It wasn't just the sight of them that sent a cold ripple of fear through the room—it was the way they hesitated, the way the sheriff's voice wavered when he spoke.

"Mr. and Mrs. Pullins, may we come in?"

That wasn't normal. The officers never came inside. They usually stood on the porch, delivered their message with cold detachment, and left. My grandfather's brows furrowed, his jaw tightening as he stepped aside, letting them enter.

As the officers walked in, the tension in the room became palpable. The air felt heavier and thicker, as though the walls themselves were bracing for the weight of what was coming. The sheriff's boots thudded softly against the floorboards as he approached the small, worn couch where my grandparents sat, their bodies stiff with unease.

"Please, sit down," the sheriff urged, his voice low and calm.

My grandmother clutched the edge of her apron, her knuckles white as she twisted the fabric nervously. My grandfather's hands rested on his knees, his fingers curling slightly. His weathered face remained stoic, but his trembling hands betrayed him.

"I'm sorry," the sheriff began, his voice breaking slightly. He cleared his throat and tried again. "I'm so sorry to have to tell you this. We found your son dead early this morning."

For a moment, time seemed to stop. The words hung in the air, suspended like a blade, waiting to fall. My grandmother's breath hitched with a sharp, involuntary sound that shattered the silence. My grandfather stared at the sheriff, his jaw tightening, his chest rising and falling in shallow, controlled breaths—as though he were holding something in—grief, anger, or both.

"No," my grandmother whispered, her voice trembling. "No, not my son."

Her words cracked in the air, the sound of them shattering the fragile stillness in the room. The sheriff lowered his head, his hands wringing his hat.

"We believe it was an overdose," he said, his voice quiet and heavy. "He was with some... friends. But when we arrived, he was alone. I'm so sorry."

"Friends?" My grandfather's voice was low and sharp, cutting through the room like a knife. "Friends wouldn't leave him to die."

My grandmother sobbed openly now, her body shaking as she buried her face in her hands. The grief spilled out of her in waves, raw and unrestrained, filling the room with its heaviness. My grandfather, ever the stoic one, sat frozen, his eyes fixed on the floor. But the set of his jaw, the way his hands clenched into fists, spoke volumes.

The sheriff's words blurred in my grandparents' ears as he explained the details—the pills, the alcohol, the "friends" who didn't call for help. The officers stood awkwardly, their hats in hand, unable to offer any real solace. They'd done this before. They knew there were no words that could soften the blow, no platitudes that could fill the void left by the news they carried.

When the officers left, the house was quiet again—but it wasn't the same calm. It was a suffocating silence, heavy with grief and regret. My grandmother's sobs still echoed faintly in the background as my grandfather stood and walked to the window, his back to the room, shoulders hunched against the weight of loss.

It was a day that began like so many others—an ordinary day—but it ended with a tragedy that would leave a scar on my grandparents, my family, and me.

## The Cruelest Goodbye

The cruelty of it all is what haunts me most. Mike's death haunts me, not just because he died, but because he was left bleeding and unconscious, surrounded by people who did nothing to help. The way they chose self-preservation over compassion, rifling through his pockets as though his life had already ended. That decision—to take instead of give, to leave instead of stay—added an extra layer of pain to an already unbearable tragedy.

Then there's the image of my grandparents, sitting in that living room, hearing the words they'd feared but hoped they'd never hear. They had weathered many storms, but this one shattered something in them. My grandmother's sobs, my grandfather's silence—they told a story of pain too deep for words. A pain that rippled through our family, reshaping us in ways we're still struggling to understand.

But as I watched my grandparents endure their grief, a thought formed in my mind—one I couldn't yet put into words: I can't let this be my story, too.

## The Promise

That thought stayed with me as I stood at his graveside. I still remember the silence after everyone had gone, leaving just him and me. It was a chilly day; the earth was still freshly turned, its dampness rising in the crisp air. My shoes sank slightly into the soft ground as I stood there, frozen. The only sounds were the distant rustling of leaves and the faint creak of a tree branch swaying above.

I looked down at the unfilled grave, a gaping void that seemed to echo my whirlwind of emotions—grief, anger, regret, and a piercing fear that refused to subside. I was losing not just my uncle but the version of him I once admired. Flashes of memories came unbidden: his laughter booming over the sound of a football game on TV, the way he'd drum his fingers on the steering wheel while blasting Bad Company in the car, the way he always called me "kid" like it was his unique nickname for me.

But now, an uneasy stillness surrounded me. My chest tightened as I stared down at Mike's final resting place, my throat thick with unspoken words. I wanted to blame him for his choices, to scream at him for giving up. But beneath the anger was something more profound—a quiet resolve that took root. I solemnly promised him—and myself—that day: I will not end up like you. My life will be different. I will honor what your life could have been by choosing a better path for myself.

My life will be purposeful. My struggles will not define me but fuel my growth. I will learn to shoulder my responsibilities as a man and, one day, as a husband and father.

That moment became a turning point—one that forever changed how I saw the world. As I stood there, the weight of my family's struggles bore down on me, but it also ignited a fire within me. This wasn't just about avoiding my uncle's fate; it was about breaking free from the cycles of pain and poor choices that had plagued my family for generations. It was about transcending despair and forging a new legacy built on purpose, resilience, and love. This promise became the foundation for how I chose to approach not just my own life but also how I interpreted the struggles and lessons from my past.

## Turning Pain into Determination

From that day forward, I resolved to live with integrity. Refusing to be defined by a complicated past, I vowed not to become just another statistic. I'd witnessed countless instances of people consumed by their pain, and I knew I had a choice: to repeat the cycle of despair or build something new.

It would have been easy to point fingers at my parents or my circumstances and use them as excuses for my failures. Resentment beckoned me like an old friend, whispering, "This isn't your fault. Blame them." But I pushed those thoughts aside. I knew I couldn't let bitterness take root in my heart—it would only chain me to the very past I was trying to escape.

Instead, I made the more challenging choice: taking responsibility for my future.

Growing up, my mother often viewed life through a dark, pessimistic lens, casting a shadow over every day. She would say, "Life is just hard," her voice heavy with resignation, implying that happiness belonged only to others. Her negativity had a way of seeping into everything, coloring the world in shades of gray. It would have been so easy to absorb that mindset and let it become my own. But I longed for a brighter life, one filled with possibility and hope.

So, I made a conscious decision to see the world differently. Where my mom saw barriers, I saw opportunities. Where she focused on what couldn't be done, I focused on what might be possible. I didn't want to live in the shadow of her pessimism. I sought the light of optimism and resilience, even when life tested me in ways I couldn't imagine. Her negativity could have been a weight I carried forward, but instead, it became the catalyst for my determination to rewrite my story. This choice was part of a larger resolve to break the cycles of despair that had defined too much of my family's history.

## Lessons from the Hardest Days

My uncle's death became a harsh yet invaluable lesson. It taught me the devastating consequences of unchecked despair and the absence of healthy coping mechanisms. It was a painful reminder of how important it is to seek connection, to find support, and never to let temporary pain dictate permanent outcomes. His struggles weren't in vain—they motivated me to build a life of purpose and stability.

On my most challenging days, I remind myself of what genuine hardship once looked like. I think back to moments of uncertainty—when I didn't know where my next meal would come from or whether the lights would stay on. Those memories anchor me. They remind me that I've faced worse and come out stronger. My parents shaped my "no-quit" attitude, even if they didn't realize it.

Their struggles, flaws, and mistakes taught me resilience in ways nothing else could. For that, I'm grateful. I don't view those difficult times as a curse but as the forge that tempered me. They gave me a toughness that's hard to rattle and a sense of empathy for others still fighting their battles.

## A Father's Promise: Turning Pain into Purpose

When I became a father, the promise I made at my uncle's graveside took on a whole new meaning. Suddenly, it wasn't just about breaking cycles for myself—it was about creating a new reality for my children.

I am driven by a fire that I stoke every day, ensuring my kids never know the uncertainty of a missed meal or the shame of not having a safe place to call home. I give them the security I longed for as a child, and more importantly, I raise them knowing they are unconditionally loved.

My mission is to build a foundation of stability and belonging for my family. This promise isn't just about meeting their physical needs; it's about providing emotional safety. I want my children to understand that their self-worth is not tied to their circumstances. I want them to grow confident in who they are, supported in their dreams, and resilient in facing challenges.

I lead by example, showing my children that life's hardships can become tools to build something better. I teach them that setbacks aren't the end of the story—they're merely chapters in a larger narrative of growth and redemption.

## Living the Promise Every Day

The promise I made that day at my uncle's graveside is not just a memory; it's a living force that shapes my choices daily. I've learned that it's not enough to make a vow—you must live it. Living it creates a ripple effect that touches everyone around you, especially the ones you love most.

When my daughter feels scared, I kneel down and remind her she is brave. When my son feels defeated, I reassure him that failure is just a necessary milestone on the path to success. Sitting at the dinner table with my family creates the warmth and connection I once longed for. These moments, small as they may seem, are my way of honoring the promise.

That commitment—to live differently, to be better, and to create a legacy of resilience and love—drives every decision I make. I understand now that the promise wasn't just for me; it was for everyone who came after me. It's for my children and their children, a testament to the power of hope and the human capacity for transformation.

My uncle's life, though tragically cut short, continues to teach me lessons about perseverance, responsibility, and redemption. He may not have found peace, but because of him, I have. His struggles gave me a reason to fight harder, to live with purpose, and to ensure that the cycles of pain and despair end with me.

This promise is my guide, my anchor, and my legacy. It reminds me every day that while we can't change the past, we can build a future that honors the lessons it left behind. Through this promise, I am building a life and a legacy rooted in strength, resilience, and love. Though my uncle's friends were silent witnesses to his death, I've resolved to be a vocal advocate for change—transforming the lessons of that night into a legacy of resilience and love. His story reminds me daily of the power of action and our responsibility to show up for those in need.

# Chapter 7:
# The Weight of Her Words: The Power of Mine

The very words we speak often trap us. Words and thoughts hold remarkable power. My mother lived by a cynical personal philosophy: "Life's a bitch, and then you die, so fuck it all, and let's get high." Her approach was a reaction to hardship that became her "philosophy of life," a set of beliefs that shaped her attitudes and actions. Her language was raw, reflecting the bitterness and frustration that shaped her worldview. My mother lived as though life had dealt her a losing hand, often repeating, "I'll always be in debt. I'll never escape this trailer court. I'll never be happy." And guess what? She was right. Words have weight, and continually using negative language about ourselves reinforces a sense of powerlessness.

My mother didn't have the best luck with men. She often spoke of how her first husband, my father Don, physically abused her. Their relationship was toxic and unhealthy, marked by constant screaming and cursing.

My mother seemed to gravitate toward men who reinforced her pessimistic worldview—a pattern I would understand more clearly as I got older. Each relationship repeated the same toxic cycles of control and manipulation.

John initially appeared to be the stability my mother needed, but his true nature soon revealed itself in violence and fear. When my brother Jesse was just 11 months old, John slammed his head against the corner of a coffee table, requiring stitches. Of course, this incident happened behind my mother's back. John lied, claiming Jesse had been running, tripped, and fell onto the table. He instilled fear in us, threatening to kill us and our mother if we ever told anyone what he had done.

One day, my mother forgot her purse on her way to work. It was a small, seemingly insignificant moment that would change everything. She turned the car around and headed back to the trailer, focused only on retrieving her forgotten bag. But as she opened the front door, the familiar creak of the hinges gave way to a scene that stopped her cold.

I crumpled on the floor, clutching my face and sobbing uncontrollably, tears streaming down my cheeks. Julie's breath caught in her throat as she scanned the room and saw John. He stood near the wall, his hands wrapped tightly around David's neck. The cheap wood paneling pressed David's tiny body against it; his feet kicked helplessly in the air, and his face contorted in terror as he gasped for breath.

For a split second, the air seemed to freeze. Then something primal took over my mother—an instinct so raw and unfiltered, it seemed to explode from deep within her. Her face flushed with fury, her hands balled into fists, and her breath came in sharp, ragged bursts, a mix of fear and rage coursing through her veins. Without hesitation, she lunged at him with everything she had.

The trailer erupted in chaos. The confined space amplified every sound—the crash of furniture as her body collided with his, the scrape of boots against the linoleum floor, and the sharp, guttural cry of pain as she swung at him with the full weight of her anger. John staggered back, momentarily surprised, but quickly fought to regain control. His hands flew up to block her blows, but she was relentless, striking him with a ferocity I had never seen before.

The dull thud of her body slamming into him against the railing outside the trailer rang out like a gunshot. The flimsy wooden railing splintered under his weight as he toppled over, landing in the dirt below with a grunt. For a moment, everything went still. The only sounds were my ragged sobs and David's coughing as he clutched his throat, gasping for air.

John staggered to his feet, his face twisted in fury. He stormed back into the trailer, his movements stiff and erratic, like a wounded animal. My mother stood her ground, chest heaving, fists clenched. But instead of attacking again, John ripped the phone cord out of the wall, muttering curses. Then, without a word, he turned and stormed out the door, his boots pounding against the porch steps. He climbed into my mother's car and sped off.

My mother didn't move, her body still trembling with adrenaline. She stood there momentarily, staring at the open door, her fists slowly unclenching. Then, with a sudden shift, she dropped to her knees beside me, cupping my tear-streaked face in her hands as she whispered, "Are you okay? Did he hurt you?"

Her voice cracked, thick with emotion, and in that moment, I saw something in her I hadn't fully understood before—love fierce enough to destroy anything that threatened her children. For the first time, she wasn't just the mother struggling to keep us safe amidst the chaos of her relationships. She was a protector, a warrior willing to put herself in harm's way for us.

David was still coughing, his breaths shallow and shaky. She pulled him close, her hands running over his back, checking for any sign of injury. "It's okay," she murmured, though her voice wavered. "You're okay now. I've got you."

Huddled together on the cold floor of the tiny trailer, the three of us remained there for what felt like an eternity. The air was heavy with the lingering effects of recent events. The room smelled of sweat and fear, and the broken phone cord lay forgotten in the background. The floor beneath us was cold and unforgiving, but it didn't matter in that moment. We were together, and for now, we were safe.

I will never forget the look on her face when she charged at John. It was raw, unfiltered, and terrifying in its intensity. But it was also the first time I truly understood the depth of her love for us. She may have been flawed and broken in countless ways, but in that moment, she was everything we needed: brave, unyielding, and fiercely protective.

## Rebuilding After Betrayal: Finding Strength Through My Mother's Journey

When John vanished from our lives, I thought we might finally find peace. But I quickly learned that chaos has a way of finding its way back in. My mother, still trapped by her insecurities and pain, soon found herself in the arms of another man. Jason, her third husband, would bring a different kind of destruction into our lives—one that left scars just as deep but more complex to see.

Jason was a womanizer and a sexist. He wielded control over my mother in ways I had never seen before. He exploited her low self-esteem to gain power, isolating her from friends and family, cutting off the support she desperately needed, and making her entirely dependent on him.

This became my first lesson about relationships: how the lack of self-worth and confidence can lead to a vulnerability that abusive people are quick to exploit. Jason knew how to pull my mother away from anything that might help her see her value or give her the strength to stand up for herself. Watching this unfold, I began to understand the importance of building one's self-esteem as armor against those who would seek to manipulate and control it. If you don't believe in yourself, someone else will fill that void—not always with good intentions.

But Jason's manipulation didn't stop there; it seeped into every aspect of our lives. He even justified his abusive behavior toward us, defending it as the proper way to discipline "unruly boys." With disturbing ease, he convinced my mother that his cruel discipline was not only necessary but expected. When faced with the choice to leave him or stay, she chose to stay. His manipulation had eroded her sense of self-worth to the point where she genuinely believed she couldn't do better. Under his influence, she began to "discipline" us in the same abusive ways, wielding paddles, belts, and switches.

During this time, social services removed my brother David and me from our mother's home.

This experience taught me an important lesson: how easily an abusive cycle can be passed on when it's seen as normal. Before Jason entered our lives, my mother had always been a gentle parent. But after his arrival, she resorted to painful discipline because she was trapped in his mindset. I realized that breaking the cycle of abuse requires a conscious effort to recognize what is right and what is harmful—even when someone in authority says otherwise.

I believe my mother wanted to escape Jason's control. However, the isolation and emotional dependency he fostered left her feeling as though she had no way out. When abusers sever ties with a person's support system, it becomes harder to see a future outside the abusive relationship. Watching my mother's struggle taught me how vital it is to have a network of supportive friends and family. Relationships are often our most critical lifelines, providing the perspective and strength to make difficult changes.

Then, one day, something broke Jason's control over us, but not in the way anyone expected. Coming home from work to an empty house, a sudden, overwhelming sense of emptiness struck my mother. The walls seemed to echo with a new silence that wasn't just empty but hollow. Her eyes scanned the bare floors and stripped cabinets, her breath quickening as the reality of his betrayal sank in. For a long moment, she stood frozen, her hands trembling at her sides. Then the first sob broke free, raw and guttural, and she crumpled to the floor, clutching the edge of the countertop as if it were the only thing keeping her from falling apart completely.

Jason had taken everything, packed it all into a U-Haul, and left. We later discovered that he'd impregnated a fifteen-year-old girl and ran off with her to Kentucky. While my mom was working, he'd gathered her belongings and disappeared.

The pain of abandonment was deep, but in an unexpected turn, Jason's departure became a blessing. My mother was heartbroken, but without his control, she could finally begin to reclaim her life. Though his absence left a void, it also gave her the freedom to rebuild. From this, I learned the power of resilience and the potential of starting over, even after betrayal and manipulation. I realized that even the most painful losses could lead to a form of freedom.

Witnessing my mother's struggle with Jason made me determined not to repeat the same patterns. I wanted to be different—to value myself and surround myself with people who respected me. I understood that self-worth, awareness of abusive behaviors, and a strong support system were essential safeguards against the control and suffering Jason had inflicted on our family. This experience instilled in me a deep resolve to create a life rooted in respect and love and to build relationships that were nothing like the one I had witnessed between my mother and Jason.

Ultimately, my mother's painful experience with Jason became an invaluable lesson. It taught me how crucial it is to recognize my values, set boundaries, and cultivate relationships that uplift rather than tear down. While I wish she had never had to endure his control, I'm grateful for the lessons it gave me—insights that continue to guide me in building a life free from the cycles of abuse and manipulation.

After Jason's betrayal, my mother had to pick up the pieces of her life once again. But the void he left behind didn't just bring freedom—it also brought vulnerability. It didn't take long for her to be captivated by another man, who introduced yet another type of chaos into our lives.

## The Biker and the Bruises

After her divorce from Jason, my mother became engaged to a man named John Smith. John was quite a character. Standing six foot four and weighing two hundred and fifty pounds, he was the quintessential biker—long hair, biker boots, cut-off shirts, and a wallet attached to his belt loop by a chain. His lifestyle was as reckless as his appearance suggested. John had a penchant for drinking, smoking weed, and snorting cocaine, all of which were paired with a notoriously careless attitude. Unfortunately, he also treated my mother as his personal punching bag.

Before my mother and John got together, he had survived a severe car accident. To preface, this story is John's account, and while it may contain embellishments, it provides insight into his character. Shortly after purchasing a new car, John claimed he was en route to get insurance when another driver ran him off the road. His car veered off an overpass, flipping multiple times before landing upside down on the railroad tracks below. According to John, he awoke to the deafening sound of a train horn. Trapped inside, he said the engine had crumpled through the firewall, pinning him in place. Desperate, he supposedly pushed the engine off himself, crawled out, and landed in a patch of poison ivy just in time to escape the oncoming train.

At the hospital, still covered in poison ivy, doctors informed him that his left leg was broken in ten places and his right in eleven. They handed him crutches, warning that if he wanted to walk again, he would have to avoid relying on a wheelchair. Despite this, John's legs remained permanently stiff; he couldn't bend his knees when he walked. This made for amusing moments as we, as children, would run away laughing whenever he tried to chase us.

But beneath his dramatic stories and stiff-legged gait, John was dangerous. To my mother's shock and devastation, he vanished one day, just as Jason had done before him. About a month later, he reappeared in the most disturbing way imaginable.

That day, John tied my mother to the bed, leaving her naked, gagged, and humiliated. He shaved her pubic area and abandoned her there, exposed and helpless. When I arrived home from school, I heard muffled sounds from her bedroom. Curious and concerned, I investigated, only to find my mother restrained and utterly vulnerable. Horror washed over me as I realized the depths of John's cruelty.

# FROM **B**ROKEN TO **B**LESSED

## A Family Fractured: The Consequences of One Winter Night

When I was 13 years old, my mother came home drunk and loud one school night after a long evening of partying. The chaos woke everyone, and my younger brother Jesse, only ten at the time, bravely confronted her. In her drunken anger, she lashed out, shoving him outside into the winter snow—wearing nothing but his underwear.

Horrified, I quickly went out to bring him back inside. This only fueled her rage. Her anger turned toward me, and she tried to pick a fight. I kept my composure and told her to go to bed, hoping to defuse the situation. She sneered, "When you're old enough to put me to bed, I'll go to bed."

I decided to take her at her word. Without hesitation, I picked her up, carried her to her room, and dropped her onto the bed. For a moment, I thought the confrontation might end there. But within seconds, she burst through the door like a storm, tackling me to the ground.

We struggled as she tried to overpower me, her anger unrelenting. I refused to strike her, but when she began scratching my face and gouging at my eyes, panic took over. I made a decision that still haunts me—I placed my hands around her throat and choked her until she lost consciousness.

The house was silent after that. My brothers, a close friend, and I decided we couldn't stay there any longer. Around 1:00 a.m., we left on foot, walking through the cold night to a nearby hotel. With no money for a room, I called my dad, explaining the situation and asking for help.

By the time the police got involved, the chaos had boiled over. They pressed charges against my mother and removed me from her custody. I was sent to live with my dad, leaving behind the turbulent environment that had shaped so much of my childhood.

Living with my mother often felt like navigating a tightrope without a safety net—one wrong move, and everything could collapse. The lack of structure and stability made us vulnerable to decisions and circumstances that could have unraveled our lives entirely. One of the clearest examples of how close we came to falling through the cracks is Jesse's near-miss with a life-altering crime.

## A Rare "No": The Fragile Line Between Freedom and Consequence

Our life growing up with our mother was anything but structured. There were no rules, no curfews, and no real sense of boundaries. We were left to our own devices, free to roam the streets at night and navigate life's challenges alone. That lack of structure shaped us in ways we didn't fully understand at the time. During his high school years on the East Side of Columbus, Ohio, my brother Jesse found himself drawn to a tough crowd. These weren't just rebellious teens—they were walking a dangerous line that would ultimately lead to devastating consequences.

One fall evening, Jesse's friends came by to pick him up. Normally, he would have gone without hesitation. But that night, in a rare and unexpected moment of intervention, our mother told him he couldn't go out. It was so out of character that even Jesse was taken aback. Her decision might have seemed random at the time, but looking back, it was a moment of profound significance.

That night, Jesse's friends made choices that would shatter their lives. They broke into a home, armed with guns, and terrorized the family inside. They hogtied the homeowners, ransacked the house, and fled with stolen goods. The victims managed to free themselves and call the police, providing a detailed description of the loud, distinctive car the group was driving. It wasn't long before the authorities caught up with them. Inside the car, they found masks, guns, and the stolen items. The arrests were swift, and the consequences severe.

Some of the boys, though minors, were tried as adults and sentenced to prison. Their lives were forever altered by that one reckless night.

It's haunting to think how close Jesse came to being in that car and how easily his life could have taken a similarly irreversible turn. My mother's rare act of setting a boundary—whether it was instinct, luck, or something else entirely—kept him from being swept up in the chaos. It's a stark reminder of how fragile the line can be between freedom and devastating consequences. One small decision, made in a fleeting moment, was all that stood between my brother and a life forever defined by that night.

That night illustrates the profound power of choices—both good and bad. Jesse's friends made a series of decisions that led to devastation, while my mother's simple but rare decision to say "no" gave Jesse a second chance. It also underscores the importance of influence—the people we surround ourselves with and the environments we grow up in. Without structure or consistent guidance, it's too easy to fall into dangerous patterns, where even a poor decision can have lasting consequences.

Looking back, it's clear how one moment, one choice, can change everything. My mother's uncharacteristic intervention delayed what seemed like an inevitable outcome for Jesse. It wasn't a transformative change, just a brief reprieve that kept him out of prison that night but couldn't stop the trajectory of choices that would ultimately lead him there.

Her actions that evening were a stark reminder of the fleeting nature of moral judgment in an otherwise unstable household. That one decision bought Jesse time but couldn't undo the deeper patterns that shaped his life. Genuine change requires more than a single choice—it demands consistent guidance, meaningful support, and sustained effort. These were things our mother, despite that night's intervention, wasn't able to provide.

Though her actions that evening spared Jesse from immediate danger, her pattern of poor decisions resurfaced in other ways. Most heartbreakingly, it became evident when she jeopardized Jesse's recovery after his time in rehab. Her rare moment of intervention was a temporary shield in a storm that required a stronger, steadier hand to weather fully.

*Dustin Bryan*

## A Celebration Gone Wrong: A Sobering Lesson in Toxic Parenting

After my brother completed rehab, my mother decided to celebrate his sobriety with a trip to Put-In-Bay—a destination notorious for its bars and nightlife. The irony of her choice wasn't lost on anyone. Taking someone fresh out of recovery to a place so entwined with alcohol wasn't just a lapse in judgment; it was a glaring example of thoughtlessness and the harmful effects of poor parenting.

Put-In-Bay, known for its vibrant drinking culture, was the last place anyone in recovery should go. This choice wasn't merely inappropriate; it was actively harmful. It demonstrated a lack of understanding and sensitivity to the fragile nature of my brother's sobriety. Instead of creating an environment that supported his recovery, my mother's impulsive actions put him at risk, highlighting a pattern of recklessness that had long plagued her parenting.

When they arrived in Port Clinton, Ohio, they discovered they had missed the last ferry to Put-In-Bay. Not one to let circumstances derail her plans, my mother improvised, deciding they would explore Port Clinton instead. Unfortunately, the evening quickly unraveled. My brothers chose to walk back to the hotel on foot, leaving my mother to navigate the unfamiliar town alone.

The situation took a darker turn when my mother decided to drink and drive. In her confusion and unfamiliarity with the area, she found herself lost. At one point, she stopped in the middle of an intersection during a green light to ask for directions, oblivious to the growing line of angry drivers honking their horns.

This chaotic scene didn't go unnoticed. A nearby police officer and my brothers, who happened to be passing by, saw what was happening. Recognizing her car, my brothers flagged her down and climbed inside, unaware they were being watched. Moments later, flashing lights filled the car as the officer pulled them over.

Her actions that night led to a DUI charge—her third—and jail time. The fallout was swift and heavy, placing an emotional and financial burden squarely on my brothers' shoulders as they scrambled to bail her out. Watching them empty their savings to cover her bail drove home the devastating impact of her choices.

Jesse stood in the jail lobby, gripping the receipt, his jaw clenched in frustration, disappointment radiating from him like heat. My other brother sat silently, avoiding her gaze, staring out the window with a mix of anger and resignation. Their expressions told the whole story: this wasn't just another mistake. It was a betrayal—a stark reminder that even in moments meant for celebration, she couldn't prioritize their needs over her own reckless impulses.

This wasn't an isolated incident. It was part of a larger pattern of selfish decisions that left a trail of emotional and financial wreckage for her children to clean up. Instead of a moment to celebrate Jesse's sobriety and support his recovery, the night became another example of the ripple effects of her toxic parenting. Her actions not only endangered herself and others but also robbed her sons of their ability to focus on their growth and well-being.

This experience carried a deeper message about the critical role parents play in shaping their children's emotional and moral foundation. Parenting requires more than good intentions; it demands accountability, responsibility, and the ability to create environments that encourage growth and positivity. For my brothers and me, this was a painful lesson in how not to parent—a vivid reminder that support means putting others' needs above impulsive desires and breaking harmful cycles with deliberate, thoughtful choices.

Looking back, that night in Port Clinton wasn't just a terrible decision—it was a stark reminder of the ripple effects of poor parenting. But it wasn't the only time my mother's choices left lasting scars. Over the years, her struggles with negativity, toxic relationships, and self-sabotage shaped not only her life but ours as well. Yet, those mighty struggles taught me invaluable lessons, guiding me toward a different path rooted in resilience and self-reflection.

*Dustin Bryan*

## A Reflection on My Mother's Struggles and My Growth

Looking back on the experiences that shaped this chapter of my life, I realize the weight of the lessons I've carried forward. My mother's life—marked by cycles of toxic relationships, impulsive decisions, and a worldview clouded by negativity—became a roadmap of what not to do. Yet, amid the turmoil, there were also glimmers of resilience, moments of fierce love, and growth opportunities that helped me forge a different path.

One of the most valuable lessons was the importance of breaking cycles. My mother's relationships with abusive men, her reliance on negativity as a coping mechanism, and her impulsive parenting decisions all formed repeating patterns that shaped not just her life but ours as well. Watching her struggle taught me that breaking free from these cycles isn't something that happens by chance. It requires awareness, effort, and a conscious choice to rewrite the narrative. I saw firsthand how unresolved pain and self-doubt can trap someone, creating a life where growth feels impossible. This realization drove me to be intentional about my choices—to reject the patterns I grew up with and build a life defined by stability, self-worth, and positivity.

Another lesson I learned is that resilience doesn't come from avoiding pain but from finding the strength to grow beyond it. My mother's rare moments of bravery—whether standing up to John's abuse or giving Jesse a second chance—showed me that even flawed people are capable of extraordinary courage. Though these moments weren't enough to transform her life, they planted seeds in me. They taught me that courage and resilience are choices we must make repeatedly, even when the odds feel stacked against us.

I also learned the immense power of mindset. My mother's negative self-talk—her repeated mantras of "I'll never escape this" and "I'll never be happy"—wasn't just a reflection of her pain; it became the cage that kept her trapped. Her words and beliefs shaped her reality, reinforcing her sense of powerlessness. This showed me how crucial it is to take control of the stories we tell ourselves. While I couldn't change my mother's narrative, I realized I had the power to shape my own. I began using positive affirmations and deliberate actions to reshape my mindset, knowing that our thoughts and behaviors can either limit us or propel us forward.

Most importantly, I came to understand the role of choice. My mother often acted on impulse, prioritizing immediate relief over long-term well-being. Her decision to celebrate sobriety in a setting that undermined it, her repeated return to abusive relationships, and her failure to create a safe environment for us as children all stemmed from choices rooted in pain and insecurity. But I also saw how a single choice—like saying "no" to Jesse that fateful night—could change the trajectory of a life, if only for a moment. This duality—the harm caused by thoughtless decisions and the potential of even small, deliberate ones—taught me to take my choices seriously. Our decisions don't just shape our lives; they ripple outward, affecting the people around us in ways we often can't see.

Through these reflections, I've also come to terms with the idea that my mother's failures don't define her entirely, nor do they define me. It's easy to dwell on the pain and chaos she brought into our lives, but doing so would ignore the ways those experiences strengthened me. Watching her struggle taught me to value self-worth, prioritize healthy relationships, and cultivate resilience through adversity. Her mistakes became my guideposts, and her pain became a powerful motivator for me to live differently.

In the end, my mother's journey—and my journey alongside her—is a testament to the complexities of life and the ways we can transform pain into empowerment. While I couldn't change her choices, I could change how I responded to them. I could take the lessons from her life and use them to create something better for myself. And that's precisely what I've done.

This chapter of my life taught me that even in the most chaotic and broken circumstances, there is an opportunity to grow. The key is recognizing the patterns that harm us, making deliberate choices to break free from them, and cultivating the mindset and relationships that allow us to thrive. It's not a simple process, but it has the power to rewrite even the most painful narratives. In reflecting on my mother's life, I don't just see the mistakes and pain anymore—I see the lessons, the strength, and the foundation they gave me to build a life of my design.

# Chapter 8:
# The Highs, Lows, and Lessons of Poker

Neil was one of my best friends growing up—the kind of friend you could rely on no matter how chaotic life got. In my early twenties, when I was still trying to figure out my place in the world, Neil's mom, Lori Hale (aka Momma Lolo), gave me something I desperately needed: stability. She allowed me to live with their family for a while when I was between jobs and uncertain of what my future held.

Lori wasn't just a roof over my head—she was a source of guidance and love during one of the most uncertain periods of my life. She treated me like family, offering advice and encouragement when I didn't have a clear direction. Her kindness left a lasting impact, showing me that even when life felt aimless, there were people willing to support me—as long as I was willing to put in the effort to find my way. With Lori's support giving me a foundation to stand on, I began to see poker as not just a game but as a way to fight back against the chaos of life.

During those days, Neil and I went to extreme measures to make money. We weren't afraid to take risks, and there was one thing we both knew how to do: play poker. We didn't see it as just a game; for us, it was a skill—a way to take what little we had and turn it into something meaningful. Looking back now, I realize that if it hadn't been for Lori's support during that time, I don't know if I would've had the chance to figure out what I wanted to do with my life. Her influence is another key part of my journey that helped shape me into the man I am today.

I've played poker for years—sometimes with a bankroll I could afford to lose and other times with money I couldn't. For me, poker has never been just a game. It's been a test of strategy, skill, and nerve but also a desperate lifeline. The highs of big wins and the gut-wrenching lows of devastating losses have mirrored my life outside the felt: unpredictable, intense, and always demanding my entire focus.

Over the years, I've studied tournament poker, immersing myself in concepts like the Independent Chip Model (ICM) theory, which teaches you how to make mathematically sound decisions under pressure. ICM forces you to see the chips in front of you as tools to win and as vehicles of survival and leverage—a lesson that extends far beyond the game. With its shifting dynamics and constant tension, the poker table became a classroom for resilience and resourcefulness. While my poker journey has been a rollercoaster of risks and rewards, it has also shaped my mindset, teaching me how to persevere and turn nothing into something.

### The Plasma Donation Buy-In

We didn't make a glamorous decision to donate plasma, but we didn't intend to. It was desperation, pure and simple. Neil and I needed the money, and in our minds, there was no better way to spin $40 into something meaningful than at a poker table. We didn't just see the poker tournament as a gamble—we saw it as an opportunity to claw our way out of being broke, if only we could get a lucky break.

We showed up at the plasma donation center early that morning, the sky still gray with dawn. The building itself was drab, its faded sign barely legible, as if it, too, was barely scraping by. Inside, the air smelled faintly of antiseptic and something metallic, which reminded me too much of blood. Rows of worn-out chairs lined the walls, and the fluorescent lighting overhead buzzed faintly, casting a pale glow over the tired faces of the other donors waiting their turn.

The process was grueling. Eight long hours of paperwork, waiting, and sitting hooked up to a machine that made a faint whooshing sound as it siphoned out my blood, separated the plasma, and pumped the rest back into my veins. The nurse told me to squeeze a stress ball to keep the blood flowing, and I did, repeatedly, until my hand ached and my forearm felt like jelly. I watched the yellowish plasma collect in a bag beside me, each drop feeling like a small sacrifice for the promise of $40.

Neil sat a few chairs away, and we cracked jokes to keep the mood light, though his usual humor seemed strained. "Think about it," he said, grinning through the discomfort. "This plasma could save lives and bankroll our poker dreams. Two birds, one stone." I forced a laugh, but I couldn't shake the hollow feeling in my stomach. This was rock bottom. I was selling parts of myself—literally—to chase a dream that might not even pan out. The thought lingered, gnawing at me as the machine whirred beside me.

When it was finally over, Neil and I shuffled into the parking lot, each clutching a crisp $40 bill. The sun was high now, and the heat made the asphalt shimmer. My body felt drained, like a wrung-out sponge, and my head was swimming from the blood loss. Still, there was a sense of grim determination between us. We had a plan, and this $40 was our ticket.

## The Poker Club: Turning Plasma Into Chips

We made our way to the local poker club, a small, well-lit room connected to the backside of a storefront. The entrance was through an alley at the rear of the historic brick-row building. There was a camera, and you had to ring a buzzer to be let in. The hum of conversation mixed with the clinking of poker chips, creating an oddly comforting rhythm—like the heartbeat of the room. This was where we belonged—or at least, where we hoped to belong after what we'd just put ourselves through.

With our $40, we each bought into a $20 tournament. The cards felt heavier in my hands that day, the weight of what they represented bearing down on me. Every fold, every call, every raise—it all carried a heightened sense of gravity. I wasn't just playing for fun or even for profit. I was playing to prove that the sacrifice had been worth it.

The game was intense, each decision punctuated by the rhythmic shuffle of chips and the occasional murmur of conversation. I played tight, waiting for opportunities, but the cards weren't falling my way. I held on longer than most, grinding through the blinds and antes, but I busted just outside the money. My last hand—a pair of eights that crumbled against a rivered flush—left me staring at the felt, my stomach sinking. All that effort, and I had nothing to show for it. I wanted to punch something but forced myself to sit there, watching Neil play on.

Neil, however, had luck on his side. He was sharp and fearless, pushing his chips in confidently and making people second-guess their decisions. I sat back and watched as he worked his way into the money, finally cashing out for $60. It wasn't life-changing, but it was enough to keep our dream alive.

### The Short Stack Spin-Up

With Neil's $60 in hand, we approached the club manager, who allowed me to "short buy" into a $1/$2 cash game with my last $20. The usual minimum buy-in was $50, but he shrugged and said, "Why not? Good luck." It wasn't much, but it was enough for me to feel like I had a fighting chance.

I sat down at the table, my measly $20 stack looking comically small next to the towers of chips in front of the other players. They eyed me curiously, probably wondering why I'd even bother with such a short stack, but I ignored them. I wasn't here to impress anyone. I was here to survive.

The first hand I played, I picked up pocket jacks—better than I could've hoped. I pushed my entire $20 into the pot before the flop, my heart hammering in my chest as the dealer slid the chips into the middle. Two players called, and I braced myself as the flop came down: Jack of hearts, 7 of spades, 3 of diamonds. I had hit a set.

The rest of the hand played out in a blur, but I had tripled my stack when the dust settled. My $20 had turned into $60, and for the first time that day, I felt like I could breathe. I played cautiously after that, waiting for premium hands and capitalizing on the overconfidence of the larger stacks at the table. By the end of the session, I had turned my $20 into $120—a modest stack in the grand scheme of things, but a monumental victory given where I had started.

### A Small Fortune

The next day, buoyed by the previous night's success, Neil and I entered a $40 buy-in tournament at the local Veterans of Foreign Wars post, better known as the VFW. The room felt brighter this time, the air lighter. Maybe it was the momentum we'd built, or the faint hope that we were finally catching a break.

Neil was on fire again, playing aggressively and making bold moves that paid off. He finished fourth, cashing for $300. I played more conservatively, picking my spots carefully and avoiding unnecessary risks. I ended up finishing third, taking home $400. Between the two of us, we'd turned our plasma donation money into over $800—a small fortune compared to the $40 we'd started with just a day earlier.

### A Celebration Fit for Broke Kings

The win felt surreal. Just 24 hours earlier, we had been sitting in a dingy donation center, squeezing stress balls and hoping to scrape together enough money to play. Now, we had enough cash to cover our expenses and celebrate. And celebrate we did.

We took our friend Jason to Canada for his birthday—a trip we couldn't have afforded before. Crossing the border felt like entering a different world. The city lights of Windsor sparkled in the night, and for the first time in what felt like forever, we allowed ourselves to relax and enjoy the moment.

Each win—and each loss—taught me something new. Every step in my journey from Windsor to the WSOP reflected the same lessons I learned at the plasma donation center: grit, resilience, and hope. No matter how small the starting point, I knew that persistence could lead to something bigger.

### The Plasma Buy-In Legacy

The plasma buy-in wasn't just a story of desperation—it was a story of grit and determination. It was about taking our small amount of money and turning it into something meaningful. It was about finding opportunities where others might see only hopelessness. And while the money we made eventually came and went, the lessons we learned from those two days—about resilience, risk, and reward—stayed with us.

Every time I sit at a poker table, I carry that story with me. It reminds me that even when the odds are stacked against me, a little courage and a lot of heart can go a long way.

### Hot Streaks in Canada

The first night in Canada was electric—a whirlwind of laughter, drinks, and high spirits, blurring into one continuous reel of excitement. Windsor's neon skyline glowed faintly in the night, and the cool breeze off the Detroit River felt like freedom against my skin. We celebrated our recent success and indulged in the thrill of being far from home, away from our worries, with nothing but opportunity. For the first time in months, life didn't feel so heavy.

But by the following day, reality crept back in. I was down to my last $30, the flush of success fading quickly as I counted what little I had left. Sure, the previous night had been fun, but it had come at a cost. The celebration had drained us more than I realized. I could feel the familiar knot of anxiety tightening in my stomach as I stared at the crumpled bills in my hand. How could I let this happen? I wasn't ready to go home broke after everything we'd been through to get here.

The occasional clink of ice in a half-empty whiskey glass on the nightstand punctuated Neil and Jason's snores as they lay unconscious in the hotel room. I couldn't sit still, tortured by the thought of wasting the day nursing regret. Determined to keep the streak alive, I asked Neil for a loan. He groaned something unintelligible before tossing me $20 from his wallet without even opening his eyes.

## Back to the Felt: Chasing Redemption

The walk to the casino was brisk, the morning air carrying a slight chill that made me zip up my hoodie. My legs felt restless, fueled by a mix of adrenaline and desperation. As I entered the casino, the smell of stale cigarette smoke and the faint hum of slot machines greeted me, accompanied by the constant shuffle of chips and the occasional cheer from a lucky player. It felt like stepping into another world, where luck and skill collided in an endless dance of possibility.

The poker room was buzzing with activity. I approached the cashier's cage, clutching my paltry $50—a combination of my last $30 and Neil's $20—and asked to short buy into a $1/$2 cash game. The cashier raised an eyebrow but didn't comment as she handed me my chips, a sad little stack of reds and whites that barely made a dent in my palm. I took a deep breath and made my way to the table, acutely aware of how small my stack looked compared to the mountains of chips in front of the other players.

The first few hands were uneventful—fold, fold, fold. My stack dwindled as I bled out blinds, each chip lost feeling like a tiny punch to the gut. But then, it happened. I picked up pocket aces—bullets, the best hand in poker. My heart raced as I slid my entire stack into the middle before the flop, forcing myself to keep my face neutral. Two players called, their stacks dwarfing mine, but I didn't care. This was my moment.

The dealer burned a card and dealt the flop: Ace of hearts, 9 of clubs, 4 of diamonds. I had hit a set—three aces. The odds were overwhelmingly in my favor, but I couldn't let my excitement show. As the action unfolded, I kept my expression calm, the other players betting into the pot, unaware that I was sitting on a monster. When the turn and river came down blank, I revealed my hand and scooped the pot, more than tripling my stack in one glorious moment. The rush was euphoric. My $50 buy-in had turned into $150, and I was just getting started.

### Running Red-Hot

From that point on, it felt as though the cards couldn't miss. Flushes, straights, full houses—they kept coming, hand after hand, as if the deck was rooting for me. I played smart, capitalizing on my good fortune without taking unnecessary risks. Before I knew it, my stack had grown to $1,000. The chips sat heavy before me, their weight a tangible reminder of how far I'd come in just a few short hours. I felt invincible.

When I finally cashed out, my hands trembled—not from nerves, but from sheer adrenaline. I gripped the bundle of crisp Canadian bills tightly as I left the poker room, the thought of losing even a single dollar too much to bear. Neil and Jason were waiting for me outside, their faces lighting up as soon as they saw the grin on mine.

"How'd you do?" Neil asked, though he already knew the answer.

I held up the stack of bills like a trophy. "One grand," I said, my voice a mix of disbelief and pride.

"Drinks are on you, then!" Jason said, clapping me on the back. And just like that, the celebration began anew.

## Bowling and Day-Drinking: Living Large

We spent the rest of the day living like kings—or at least like broke twenty-somethings pretending to be kings. We found a bowling alley that served cheap pitchers of beer, and the three of us spent hours hurling gutter balls and laughing until our sides ached. The buzz of day drinking on an empty stomach only added to the hilarity, and for a little while, it felt like we didn't have a care in the world.

The celebration spilled into the evening as we returned to the casino. This time, I didn't need to short buy—I slapped $300 on the table and bought in for the maximum. My confidence was sky-high, and the cards didn't disappoint. Once again, I was on a heater, effortlessly turning my $300 into $1,000. The chips seemed to flow toward me like water, and every decision felt razor-sharp. By night's end, I was on top of the world.

## Exit, Stage Left: A Dance Floor Disaster

That night, we hit the town with a vengeance, determined to celebrate our success in style. The details are hazy—a kaleidoscope of neon lights, pounding music, and whiskey shots that burned all the way down. It started with too many drinks in too little time. At first, I managed to power through the dizziness, but the flashing strobe lights and relentless bass soon teamed up against me.

I lurched forward before I could reach the bathroom, and... it happened. Right there on the dance floor.

Jason shouted, "Abort mission!" and quickly tried to shield me from view while Neil scrambled to find a napkin—like that would solve anything. Within seconds, a bouncer loomed over us, arms crossed and face set like stone. He pointed toward the exit and said flatly, "You're done."

Escorted out to a soundtrack of muffled groans and scattered laughter, we stumbled into the night.

The next thing I remember is waking up in the hotel room. My head pounded like a drum, and my mouth was so dry it felt like I'd swallowed a bucket of sand. Sunlight streamed through the flimsy curtains, stabbing at my eyes like needles. I groaned and rolled over, only to spot my wallet lying open on the nightstand.

It was empty. Completely, utterly empty.

## The Hangover: Lessons in Discipline

Panic set in as I scrambled to piece together the night's events. Had I spent it all? Lost it? Given it away? I couldn't remember. All I knew was that the $2,000 I had painstakingly built over the last two days was gone, and all I had to show for it was a splitting headache and a stomach churning with regret.

Determined to salvage what I could, I decided to hit the casino one last time before we headed home. I convinced myself I could grind it back, rebuild the bankroll I'd so carelessly squandered. But as soon as I stepped into the harsh sunlight, the hangover and lingering effects of the night before hit me like a freight train. My stomach turned, and I staggered back toward the hotel, defeated, before even setting foot inside the casino.

The ride back to Ohio from Windsor was brutal. The car was silent for most of the trip, the weight of my mistakes heavy in the air. I stared out the window, trying to process what had happened. The highs and lows of poker had never felt so stark, so extreme. One moment, I was on top of the world; the next, I was scraping the bottom of the barrel.

## A Hard-Learned Lesson

If there's one thing that experience taught me, it's this: poker isn't just about luck or skill—it's about discipline. The highs and lows come fast, and if you're not careful, the euphoria of a hot streak can blind you to the dangers of overconfidence and poor decision-making. Poker is a game of patience and control, and those who fail to respect that are bound to pay the price.

Looking back, I wouldn't trade that trip for anything. It was a crash course in the realities of risk and reward, a vivid reminder that success is fleeting without the discipline to hold onto it. The memory of that $1,000 heater still makes me smile, but it's the lesson I learned in the aftermath that has stuck with me the most. In poker, as in life, the real challenge isn't just winning—it's knowing how to keep what you've won.

## Online Triumphs: From Pennies to Paydays

Before the bright lights of Las Vegas and the cash games in Canada, my poker journey began in the digital realm. Online poker was my proving ground. The stakes were low, but the lessons were invaluable. I didn't have the glitz of a casino or the weight of real chips in my hands—just a laptop, a relentless drive to succeed, and, on more than one occasion, a bankroll that barely deserved the name.

One session stands out as a pivotal moment in my early poker career. I logged into my Full Tilt Poker account one evening, staring at the pitiful balance blinking back at me: 13 cents. That was it. It wasn't even enough for a proper tournament buy-in, but I refused to give up.

I scoured the lobby until I found a micro-stakes tournament—a 10-cent buy-in with 50-cent re-buys. It was a long shot, but it was all I had left. I took one last gamble.

The tournament was a frenzy from the start. Thousands of players crowded virtual tables, all chasing the same improbable dream: turning pocket change into a real payday. The screen was a blur of bright colors and spinning chips as players re-bought aggressively, shoving all in with reckless abandon. My strategy, however, was different. I played tight, waiting patiently for my spots. Every hand felt like a high-wire act, where one misstep could send me tumbling out of the tournament.

As the hours ticked by, my chip stack grew steadily. I found my rhythm, moving from table to table as I outlasted the competition. With every showdown, my heart raced, the tension nearly unbearable as the cards turned one by one. When I finally reached the final table, the adrenaline surged through me. The room around me was silent, but my pulse thundered in my ears.

It came down to three players. The stacks were deep, and every decision felt magnified. Each chip was a lifeline, and every move was a calculated risk.

I didn't win, but I finished in third place out of thousands of players. My payout? Hundreds of dollars.

Sitting there in the glow of my computer screen, I leaned back in my chair and exhaled a long breath of relief and disbelief. I had turned 13 cents into something tangible—a bankroll, a spark of hope, and a powerful reminder that there is always a way forward, no matter how dire things may seem.

### The $5 Miracle

Flushed with confidence, I logged in the next day, ready to ride the momentum. I entered a $5 freeze-out tournament—a single-buy-in event with no re-buys and no second chances. The tournament was grueling, a marathon of focus and discipline. With each passing hand, the pressure mounted, but I stayed composed, making calculated decisions and trusting my instincts. Hours later, when I finally claimed first place, the joy was electric.

But I wasn't done yet. That same day, I entered a $3 re-buy tournament. The competition was fierce, but I felt unstoppable. Every move I made seemed to land perfectly; every read on my opponents was spot on. Hand by hand, I climbed the leaderboard until I once again found myself heads-up for the win. Taking down that final pot felt like more than just a victory—it felt like validation. That day, I turned a few dollars into thousands.

### The PokerStars Streak

Another time, on PokerStars, my account balance had dwindled to just $5. I remember staring at that lonely number, caught between the pang of desperation and the fire of determination. I entered a $4.40 tournament—my last shot—and braced myself for the grind.

The hours melted away as I battled through the field, carefully picking my spots, avoiding unnecessary risks, and steadily building my stack. The competition thinned, and I found myself deep in the money, my confidence growing with every hand. By the time it came down to a heads-up chop of the prize pool, my share was over $1,000.

I could have stopped there, but the thrill of the game spurred me on. The very next day, still riding the high of my win, I decided to push my limits. I opened 15 tournaments simultaneously—a dizzying juggling act that demanded laser focus and nerves of steel. My computer screen became a chaotic mosaic of tables, cards, and chips, each vying for my attention. The tension was palpable as my hands moved with precision, folding, raising, and re-raising across the virtual felt with clockwork efficiency.

Six hours later, I was still in 10 tournaments, my chip stacks steadily climbing. The chaos wasn't enough for me—I decided to add even more pressure by entering a $20 heads-up tournament. This one-on-one duel demanded every ounce of cunning and intuition I had left. The adrenaline was relentless as I bounced between tables, making split-second decisions and somehow managing the mounting chaos.

When I clinched the heads-up victory, it felt like the ultimate triumph. The top prize of $2,500 was mine, and for that moment, I felt truly unstoppable.

### Lessons in Resilience

These online triumphs taught me more than just poker strategy—they instilled resilience, creativity, and the power of perseverance. Turning a few cents or a few dollars into a bankroll wasn't just about skill; it was about refusing to give up, even when the odds were stacked against me.

Online poker sharpened my instincts and honed my ability to adapt under pressure. The digital felt was a battlefield, where every hand was a chance to fight back, claw my way out of the depths, and build something from nothing.

Those moments were more than just wins—they were proof that there's always a way to rise, even in the face of overwhelming adversity. They became the bedrock of my poker journey, preparing me for the bigger challenges and higher stakes that awaited in the live poker world.

## Vegas Adventures: From Desperation to Triumph

It was 2009, and the bright lights of Las Vegas promised adventure, opportunity, and the chance to chase poker glory. When I arrived with my brother Jesse, Neil, and Jason, I felt cautiously optimistic. I had $800 to my name—a modest sum for a week in Sin City but just enough to stoke the hope that I could make something of it.

As the plane descended over the glittering desert oasis, a mix of excitement and quiet uncertainty washed over me. Las Vegas is a city of extremes—one minute, you're soaring; the next, you're free-falling into despair. I'd experienced both before, but as we drove toward The Strip, I silently vowed that this trip would be different.

The first few days in Vegas were a blur of intoxicating energy. Neon lights glowed, slot machines chimed endlessly, and the ever-present allure of a big score loomed large. The Venetian became our home base with its grand canals and faux Italian opulence. We played poker, laughed, drank, and soaked in the surreal ambiance of a city designed to make you forget the outside world.

But the day before we were set to leave, reality came crashing down on me like a ton of bricks.

## The Roulette Gamble

I was nearly broke. My $800 had dwindled to a pitiful $200—a far cry from what I needed to buy into a tournament at The Venetian, let alone survive another day in the city. My friends had left me, and I paced the casino floor alone, feeling increasingly desperate. The clatter of chips and the hum of the crowd seemed almost mocking, as though the city itself were daring me to give up.

Then, I spotted the roulette table.

I'd never been much of a roulette player—it's a game of pure chance with none of the strategy or skill that poker demands. But desperate times called for desperate measures. I approached the table, staring at the spinning wheel, the black and red pockets a blur of motion. My pulse quickened as I weighed my options. I could walk away, accept that my trip was over, and begin the long, shameful drive home. Or, I could take one last shot.

I placed a "complete bet" on a single number—nine separate $10 bets that covered my number and all the numbers touching it on the wheel. It was a long shot, but it would pay 135 to 1 if it hit. The croupier spun the wheel, and I watched the white ball's erratic movements. My heart pounded in my chest as it skipped past my number, only to circle back again. It hovered over the pocket for a brief, agonizing moment as if taunting me. Then, miraculously, it dropped.

The dealer called my number, and for a second, I didn't process what had happened. Congratulations filled the table as the dealer stacked my winnings—$1,350—before me, a welcome reassurance that my luck hadn't deserted me. The relief was overwhelming, almost enough to make me laugh out loud. My desperation had turned into triumph in the blink of an eye, and suddenly, the city didn't seem so cruel anymore.

## The Venetian Tournament: Redemption at the Tables

With my newfound bankroll, I walked to the poker room and bought into a tournament at The Venetian. The plush carpeting, elegant chandeliers, and low hum of focused conversation felt like a sanctuary compared to the chaos of the casino floor. I settled into my seat, my mind sharper and more determined than it had been all week. I wasn't just playing for money; I was playing to prove that I belonged here, to show that I could rise above the setbacks and build something out of nothing.

The tournament was grueling—a marathon of patience and precision. Hours passed as I carefully picked my spots, folding hand after hand while waiting for the right opportunities. The tension at the table was palpable; every bet and raise was a calculated move, chipping away at the competition. My stack fluctuated wildly; each big pot won or lost sent a jolt of adrenaline through my system.

Finally, after what felt like an eternity, I found myself deep in the money. The field had narrowed from hundreds of players to just a handful, and the payouts climbed steadily with each elimination. I felt a mix of emotions when I finally busted in 14th place, earning $2,267. There was disappointment, of course, from coming so close to the final table, where the real glory and big money awaited. But mostly, I felt pride. Just two days earlier, I had been staring at my last $200. Now, I had more than $2,000 in my pocket and a renewed sense of possibility.

## Riding the High: Staying Behind

Flush with confidence and cash, I made a bold decision. I told Jesse, Neil, and Jason I was staying behind while they prepared to head home. "Take this," I said, handing each of them some money for their trip back. "I'll figure things out here."

They looked at me like I was crazy, but I could see the glimmer of understanding in their eyes. This wasn't just about money—it was about the momentum, the sense that I was on the cusp of something big. I wasn't ready to leave the table just yet.

## The H.O.R.S.E. Heater

Over the next four days, my instincts proved right. I entered a H.O.R.S.E. tournament—a mixed game format featuring Texas Hold'em, Omaha, Razz, Stud, and Eight-or-Better. The variety kept me on my toes, forcing me to adapt and think strategically with every hand. The competition was fierce, but I felt like I was in the zone, making reads and plays that seemed almost effortless.

The tension in the room was suffocating when we reached the final table. Every decision felt monumental, a difference between thousands of dollars or walking away empty-handed.

After hours of intense back-and-forth battles, we agreed to a chop, splitting the remaining prize pool among the top players. My share? $3,788.

The high was indescribable. I celebrated with a good meal and a quiet moment of reflection, savoring the sweet taste of success. Just a few days earlier, I had been broke, wondering how I would make it through the week. Now, I was building something real.

Two days later, I entered another H.O.R.S.E. tournament at the same casino. Lightning struck again—I chopped once more, this time for $4,092. My bankroll was growing, my confidence soaring, and I felt unstoppable.

## The World Series Of Poker Dream

With nearly $10,000 in winnings, I took the ultimate shot: entering my first-ever World Series of Poker (WSOP) event, the pinnacle of competitive poker. It felt like the logical next step in my journey, even though the $1,500 buy-in was steep. The tournament drew 770 hopeful players, all chasing the same dream. Excitement buzzed through the air, palpable and intense.

Playing in a WSOP event was unlike anything I had ever experienced. The competition was brutal, and the stakes were higher than ever. But I held my own, navigating the field with both caution and aggression. Every decision felt magnified, every mistake potentially catastrophic. The hours dragged on, and the field grew smaller and smaller until I found myself deep in the money again.

When I finally busted in 15th place, earning $7,903, I couldn't help but feel a sense of pride. Just two weeks earlier, I had been scraping together my last $200 after a desperate roulette bet. Now, my bankroll had swelled to $18,000. Vegas had tried to chew me up and spit me out, but I had fought back—and won.

# FROM **B**ROKEN TO **B**LESSED

## A Rollercoaster of Emotions

The trip to Vegas was a whirlwind of desperation, triumph, and everything in between. The highs were exhilarating, the lows gut-wrenching, but I had proven to myself that I could persevere through it all. Poker is a game of skill, luck, and relentless determination, and this trip tested me in every possible way.

As I boarded the plane back home, my pockets full and my heart lighter, I couldn't help but smile. Vegas had given me a taste of the dream—a glimpse of what was possible when preparation, luck, and courage came together. And while I knew the journey was far from over, I was ready for whatever came next.

## Lessons from the Felt

Looking back on these experiences, it's clear that poker is more than just a game of cards; it's a metaphor for life. The ability to bounce back from adversity, take calculated risks, and stay disciplined in the face of temptation are lessons that extend far beyond the felt.

Every time I was down to my last dollar—or even my last few cents—I clawed my way back. Whether through skill, luck, or sheer determination, I refused to let my circumstances define me. I believe my upbringing instilled that mindset. Growing up in a challenging environment taught me to fight until the end and never give up, no matter how bad things seemed.

I recently entered a poker tournament with a $600 buy-in and a guaranteed prize pool of $500,000 at a local poker club in Columbus, Ohio. The tournament attracted an impressive 1,118 participants, making the competition fierce and the stakes high.

After two grueling days of intense play, I found myself heads-up, competing for the top prize of $72,500. The poker scene in Columbus is notoriously tough, with multiple WSOP bracelet winners and World Poker Tour (WPT) Champions among the field, including the man I faced heads-up.

Although I didn't take first place, the experience was invaluable. I learned important lessons about strategy, endurance, and decision-making under pressure. Ultimately, I walked away with $42,000—a reminder that persistence, focus, and a refusal to back down can yield success, even against tough competition.

## Poker: A Journey of Highs, Lows, and Lessons

Poker has taken me on an incredible journey, one I never anticipated when I first started. From the humbling days of donating plasma to scrape together a buy-in to the exhilarating moments of competing in World Series of Poker (WSOP) events and walking away with thousands of dollars in winnings, poker has been more than just a game for me. It's been a teacher, a test, and a reflection of life itself.

What makes poker unique is its ability to test not only your skill but also your character. Every hand you play challenges your patience, resilience, and adaptability. You can prepare, strategize, and analyze the odds, but poker forces you to make decisions under pressure, often with incomplete information. That pressure reveals who you are—it compels you to conquer your fears, regulate your emotions, and adjust to unforeseen circumstances.

The highs and lows of poker mirror the highs and lows of life in a way few other pursuits can. One moment, you're riding high on a big win, feeling unstoppable. The next, a bad beat brings you crashing back to earth. The swings can be brutal, but they teach you humility and perspective. In poker, as in life, you can do everything right and still lose—but you can also bounce back from seemingly insurmountable odds with the right mindset and a little luck.

If there's one thing poker has taught me, it's this: no matter how bad things get, there's always a chance for a comeback. The key is to stay in the game. You can't win if you fold or let frustration cloud your judgment. Instead, you must keep playing your hand, trust your instincts, and believe in your ability to turn things around.

Poker has always been more than just about winning money or building a bankroll—it's been a journey of personal growth. It has taught me how to manage risk, balance patience with action, and focus on the long game rather than getting caught up in short-term outcomes. These lessons have permeated every area of my life, from business to relationships.

Poker has also shown me the value of self-awareness. To succeed, you must know your strengths, weaknesses, and tendencies. Be honest with yourself about when to push forward and when to step back. The game has taught me the power of discipline—not only in managing my chips but also in controlling my emotions, time, and focus.

Reflecting on my poker journey, I can't help but think back to that day in the plasma donation center. Sitting there with a needle in my arm, squeezing a stress ball until my hand ached, I didn't feel like someone capable of success. I felt like someone clinging to a desperate hope, just trying to survive. And yet, that moment—selling a part of myself to buy into a poker tournament—became the foundation of everything that followed.

That $40 didn't just buy me a seat at the table; it bought me a lesson in resilience. It taught me that even when the odds seem insurmountable, there's always a way forward if you're willing to take a chance. That same grit carried me through countless tournaments, online marathons, and high-stakes games in Vegas. It reminded me that success isn't about avoiding risk or failure—it's about trusting your instincts and staying in the game, no matter how dire things look.

In many ways, poker mirrors life: a series of calculated risks, unexpected setbacks, and hard-won victories. But the real lesson is this: It's not the size of your bankroll or the strength of your cards that determines your fate—it's your ability to adapt, persevere, and believe in your potential.

Just as I turned those drops of plasma into something bigger, I've learned to transform challenges into opportunities, losses into lessons, and small wins into stepping stones for greater success. So, whether you're at a poker table or navigating life's uncertainties, remember: even when you feel drained, empty, and at your lowest, you still have something to give. And sometimes, that's all you need to turn everything around.

# Chapter 9:

# Forged in the Cold: Lessons in Resilience and Confidence

Long before ice baths became a tool for my growth, resilience was being forged in a far less intentional—and far more chaotic—environment: our frigid showers. When I was younger, winter wasn't just a season; it was a challenge. The pipes in our home would sometimes freeze, leaving us without hot water and no alternatives. My dad, never one to coddle, refused to let something as trivial as bone-chilling water stand in the way of a shower. His solution? Forced compliance.

I still vividly remember the first time it happened. I was nine or ten, standing in the cramped bathroom as he turned on the shower. The old, lime-streaked faucet sputtered before releasing a blast of cold water that seemed to cut through the air like a blade. Steam didn't rise; there was no cozy mist softening the room's edges—just the sharp, metallic smell of ice-cold water pouring into the old, worn fiberglass tub.

My dad's voice was gruff but matter-of-fact. "Get in," he said, as if stepping into arctic conditions was as simple as flipping a switch. When I hesitated, he grabbed me by the arm. Before I could say anything, the icy water hit my feet, then my legs, and quickly engulfed my entire body as he held me under the freezing stream.

The shock was immediate and overwhelming. The water hit me like shards of glass, each drop stabbing into my skin. My lungs locked up, refusing to expand, and for a moment, I thought I might pass out. I gasped, sputtered, and tried to twist away, but his grip was ironclad.

"It's just water," he barked over the sound of the spray. "You'll survive."

The freezing water poured over my head, soaking my hair and cascading in icy rivulets down my back. My teeth chattered violently, and I felt my entire body convulsing to generate warmth. My muscles screamed for relief; my mind begged for it to stop, but there was no room for negotiation. No amount of twisting, crying, or pleading would loosen his grip. He would make sure I stayed under that water until, in his mind, the job was done.

The seconds dragged on like hours, each one testing the limits of what I thought I could endure. I fought the urge to scream, instead focusing on my breath—or what little of it I could manage. Shallow, rapid inhales burned in my chest as I tried to center myself to survive the unrelenting cold. I wanted to give in, to collapse, to do anything but stay upright. But I had no choice—I had to stand there and endure.

When it was finally over, my dad released me, and I stumbled out of the tub, my legs shaking so badly I could barely stand. My skin was a deep, blotchy red, my fingers numb, and my body trembled uncontrollably. I wrapped myself in the nearest towel, my teeth still chattering as I stood in a puddle of icy water. There was no comforting pat on the back, no words of reassurance—just a grunt from my dad as he left the room, as if to say, *See? You're fine.*

But I didn't feel fine. I felt powerless, humiliated, and frozen to my core. I wasn't sure if I was angry or defeated—only that I never wanted to experience anything like that again.

I didn't realize then that those frigid showers were planting a seed—one I wouldn't recognize until years later. They weren't lessons my dad intended to teach me, but they revealed a crucial truth: pain and discomfort, while unbearable in the moment, don't last forever. And sometimes, surviving is all you need to do to grow stronger.

## The Turning Point: Ice Baths and the Resilience They Built

Years later, as a teenager playing football and basketball, I willingly entered a similar cold. Ice baths had become a staple in my recovery routine, a dreaded but necessary ritual to soothe aching muscles after grueling practices. Unlike the forced showers of my childhood, I chose ice baths. That choice made all the difference.

The first time I stared down at an ice bath, it seemed like a challenge I wasn't sure I could face. The steel tub shimmered under the harsh fluorescent lights of the locker room, filled with water so cold that chunks of ice floated lazily on the surface. My teammates had already begun climbing in, some grimacing, others gritting their teeth, their breath hissing through clenched jaws as the water consumed their legs.

I hovered near the edge, every instinct screaming to turn back. My hands trembled as I rolled up my shorts, my heart pounding in anticipation of the cold. The room smelled faintly of liniment and sweat, a reminder of the battle my body had just fought on the court. I told myself I could do it. I had to do it. My body needed the recovery, but my mind needed something even more: proof that I could push through.

The moment my foot touched the water, I almost pulled it back. The cold stabbed through my skin, racing up my leg like a jolt of electricity. When I finally forced myself to sink in, it was like being swallowed by the freezing showers of my childhood, only magnified. I felt the icy water relentlessly rise, biting into my thighs and wrapping around my waist until it fully submerged me. The air left my lungs in a ragged gasp, and my body shook violently as it tried to adjust.

"Breathe," I told myself, echoing the words my dad had once said to me: deep inhale, shaky exhale. Each breath resembled a battle, but slowly, the panic subsided. I gripped the tub's edge, my knuckles white, and focused on the sound of the water sloshing gently against the sides. The cold was still there, gnawing at every nerve ending, but I realized something: it would not break me.

Minute by minute, the sharp sting of the cold dulled into a steady ache, and I settled into the discomfort. The pain was temporary, I reminded myself. I'd made it through before, and I could do it again. When I stepped out, my legs were red and numb, my body shivering uncontrollably, but inside, I felt a quiet pride. I'd done it. I'd chosen to face the pain, and I'd come out stronger on the other side.

## How Ice Baths Translated Into Everyday Confidence

Those ice baths became more than just a tool for physical recovery. They were a proving ground where I learned to sit with discomfort and trust my ability to endure. The lessons I took from those moments seeped into every corner of my life, reshaping how I approached challenges.

When I faced difficult situations—whether performing a tough shot on the basketball court, speaking up in class, or stepping out of my comfort zone to approach a stranger—I reminded myself of the cold. I thought about how the ice water had numbed my legs, how my mind had screamed at me to quit, and how I'd found the strength to stay. If I could handle that, I could handle this—one steady breath at a time.

Even now, when doubt creeps in, or fear threatens to take hold, I carry the memory of those ice baths with me. They remind me that discomfort is temporary and that I build confidence not by avoiding challenges but by choosing to face them, even when every fiber of my being begs me to retreat.

## Take Care of Your Physical Well-Being

I sensed I was out of my element when I stepped back into the gym. The heavy metal plates clanged, and upbeat music thumped, filling the air with vibrant energy. The faint scent of rubber mats and sweat lingered. A group of regulars stood near the free weights, chatting confidently as if this were their second home. I tightened my grip on my water bottle, glancing around and mapping out the equipment. The dumbbells gleamed under the overhead lights, perfectly lined up and slightly intimidating. I felt like a rookie stepping onto a court full of seasoned pros.

Instinctively, I gravitated toward the weight section. Growing up playing sports, lifting weights had always been second nature—a place where I could challenge myself and experience strength. But after being away for so long, the sight of the gym felt almost overwhelming, like stepping back onto a field after years on the sidelines. The racks of dumbbells gleamed under the harsh fluorescent lights, the clanging of metal plates echoed through the air, and the sheer energy of the place left me both eager and out of place. It wasn't just about picking up where I left off—it was about rebuilding something I wasn't even sure I still had.

There was something satisfying about gripping the cold metal of a barbell, feeling its weight press against my palms, and pushing myself to see how much I could lift. I started with small, manageable goals—40-pound dumbbells for shoulder presses and squats with an empty barbell to improve form. My form was shaky at first, and my muscles trembled under the strain, but each rep felt like a tiny victory.

One day, I spotted the basketball court tucked behind the gym's cardio section. The rhythmic sound of a ball bouncing on the polished hardwood floor called to me, stirring memories of late-night games at Eljer Park and the adrenaline rush of close matches. I added basketball to my routine, not as an afterthought, but as cardio, because it didn't feel like work. I'd dribble the ball across the court, practicing my layups and free throws until sweat soaked through my shirt.

On the days I craved a break from basketball, I stuck to the elliptical machine. The steady rhythm of my feet gliding over the pedals provided a way to clear my head. In those moments, the gym transformed into more than just a physical space—it became my sanctuary. It was where I worked out my frustrations, found clarity, and rebuilt my confidence.

What surprised me most wasn't just the physical changes—though I noticed my muscles becoming more defined and my endurance improving—but the way my mindset shifted. Lifting weights taught me discipline, and basketball brought me joy, but the undeniable reward was the deep sense of pride that followed every session. Each drop of sweat that rolled down my face proved I was showing up for myself.

Over time, I carried myself differently. My shoulders were no longer slumped under the weight of insecurity. I walked with purpose, my chin lifted, my posture steady. Even the way I shot hoops changed—no hesitation, no second-guessing. I trusted my instincts, both on and off the court.

### Develop Your Personal Style

For much of my early life, clothes were just a necessity—a way to cover my body and avoid drawing attention to myself. My wardrobe was a mix of hand-me-downs and cheap T-shirts, chosen more for their practicality than any sense of self-expression. My reflection in the mirror often appeared like a stranger staring back at me—someone disconnected from my aspirations. But all that changed when I bought my first tailored dress shirt for a new sales job.

I still remember the moment I tried it on. The crisp fabric slid over my shoulders and fit perfectly, the collar sitting snugly against my neck. As I buttoned it up and glanced in the mirror, something shifted. The person staring back wasn't the unsure, self-conscious version of me I'd grown used to seeing. This version stood taller, looked sharper, and carried himself with a quiet confidence I hadn't felt before. That shirt wasn't just an article of clothing; it symbolized the person I wanted to become.

From that day forward, I started paying attention to how I dressed—not for others but for myself. I experimented with authentic styles, choosing clothes that aligned with how I wanted to feel: put-together, capable, and confident. It wasn't about chasing trends or spending a fortune. It was about making intentional choices that reflected who I was becoming.

That shift in how I dressed rippled into every area of my life. I noticed a change in how people treated me when I walked into a room wearing clothes that fit well and made me feel good. Conversations flowed more naturally, opportunities opened up, and I felt more at ease in my own skin. It wasn't just about how I looked but about sending a message: You're worth the effort.

## Understand Yourself and Set Goals

Self-awareness is a powerful thing, but it's not always comfortable. When I first took an honest look at myself, I saw all the cracks and imperfections I'd been avoiding. I saw the doubts that held me back, the fear of failure that kept me from trying, and the moments when I let opportunities slip through my fingers. But I also saw something else: potential. Confidence, I realized, wasn't about ignoring those cracks. It was about using them as the foundation to build something more substantial.

I started small, setting goals that felt achievable but meaningful. At the gym, my first goal wasn't to lift the heaviest weight or master every machine. It was to show up three times a week with no excuses. When I hit that goal, I set another: add five more pounds to my bench press, run a little faster on the elliptical, or practice my jump shot until it felt automatic. Each goal I reached became a reminder that I could trust myself to follow through.

There were days when progress felt invisible, like leaving the court after missing shot after shot or finishing a workout without hitting the numbers I'd hoped for. But then there were the breakthroughs—those moments when I'd sink five free throws in a row or add another plate to the barbell and feel it lift effortlessly. Those wins, no matter how small, proved that I was capable of more than I'd believed.

## Confidence is a Journey, Not a Destination

Confidence, I've learned, isn't about being perfect or fearless. It's about showing up, even when you're scared or unsure, and proving to yourself that you can handle whatever comes your way. The people I once admired for their unshakable confidence weren't born that way—they'd faced their own cold water, their own moments of doubt and discomfort, and they'd chosen to keep going anyway.

Effort, persistence, and resilience build confidence—like sinking a game-winning free throw or braving an ice bath. It's earned in the moments when quitting feels more effortless, but you choose to keep going. Confidence isn't a gift—it's a reward, waiting on the other side of the hard things you dare to face.

I never thanked my dad for those freezing showers. But now, every time I face something that feels unbearable, I remind myself: It's just water. I'll survive. And when I do, I'll be stronger for it. As much as I hated them, those moments in the cold taught me that I could endure discomfort and push through fear. They laid the foundation for every challenge I've faced since—on the court, in the gym, and in life.

No matter how tough it gets, I carry that lesson with me: survival is the first step to resilience, and resilience is the key to growth.

# Chapter 10:
# Beyond Fear: The Courage to Grow

Recruiting, aside from sales, was an essential part of my younger job. My task wasn't just to persuade others to buy a product—it was to convince them to buy into me, to see me as someone worth following. The mere thought of approaching strangers felt like standing on the edge of a cliff, staring down into an abyss of judgment. My stomach churned whenever I imagined walking up to someone cold, my mouth dry as sand, fumbling to find the right words. What if they laughed? What if they dismissed me without a second thought? What if I froze, paralyzed by my insecurities? Each "what if" felt heavier than the last, pressing down on me like the thick, stifling air before a summer storm.

I remember one particular day—a crisp fall morning, the air smelling faintly of damp leaves and distant smoke. My manager had said, "Today, we're hitting the shopping plaza." The shopping plaza! The phrase alone tightened the knot in my chest. It was crawling with people, all going about their day—business suits striding with purpose, moms juggling toddlers and shopping bags. None of them were expecting me. None of them wanted to be interrupted. I knew this because I had been in their shoes before, dodging eager salespeople with hurried excuses or a practiced, polite smile. Soon, I would join their ranks—the people everyone avoided.

As we neared the plaza, the air buzzed with chatter, footsteps, and the distant hum of car horns. My manager, flashing an amused grin, turned to me and said, "Remember, every no is just paving the way to a yes. Don't take it personally." Easy for him to say. He walked with the confidence of someone who'd been told yes a hundred times before. For me, every no still stung like a sharp jab, whispering, See? You're not good enough.

The first person I approached was a tall man in a dark overcoat, his face concealed behind reflective sunglasses. My heart pounded as I stepped into his path, my pulse so loud in my ears that it almost drowned out my voice. "Excuse me, sir," I began, my tone trembling. He didn't even break stride. He merely shook his head and kept walking, leaving me standing there with flushed cheeks as if I had been caught doing something shameful.

Stopping was beyond me. I couldn't give in. I knew that if I walked away, I'd be surrendering to that gnawing voice inside me—the one that thrived on fear and self-doubt. So, I turned to the next person. And the next. Each interaction felt like stepping into a lion's den. Fear pricked my skin, and adrenaline coursed through my veins. Rejections piled up like fallen leaves, one after another, each one pressing on me, heavy and relentless. Yet, somewhere within that sea of no's, something unexpected began to shift.

The discomfort didn't exactly fade—it still sat in my chest like a heavy stone—but I noticed a shift. Each rejection stung a little less. Each interaction felt slightly less daunting than the one before. I wasn't confident yet, but I wasn't crumbling either. I realized the world didn't end when someone said no. The fear didn't swallow me whole. Unexpectedly, I discovered a spark of resilience in that simple realization.

By the end of the day, I was far from perfect, but I felt proud. Not because I had recruited anyone—if I'm honest, I didn't. But despite the overwhelming urge to retreat, I faced my greatest fear and kept going. That day, I learned something I would carry with me for the rest of my life: fear only holds power if you let it. And growth never happens inside your comfort zone.

## The Paralyzing Power of Fear

Everything is always scary in the beginning. Fear grips you, curling around your thoughts like a fog that distorts your sense of reality. In their infinite creativity, our minds build barriers out of shadows—looming, insurmountable things meant to protect us from the unknown. Often, these barriers act as cages, confining us to what is safe and familiar. We convince ourselves that the cage keeps us safe, but all it really does is keep us small. We pace the same restricted path, peering out at the open world beyond, afraid to rattle the bars we've built ourselves.

At first, fear kept me frozen. It wasn't the kind of fear that made you scream or run; it was quieter but just as paralyzing. Endless questions circled in my mind like vultures over a carcass, whispered by doubt. What if you fail? What if people laugh at you? What if you're not good enough? These words sank deep, feeding the gnawing pit of anxiety in my stomach. My self-doubt caused me to second-guess every decision, hesitate at the starting line, and convince myself I couldn't meet the challenges ahead. Fear, I realized, was a master of disguise. It slipped into my thoughts as caution, prudence, or even practicality, and before I knew it, I was standing still, making excuses.

Life, however, doesn't allow perpetual stagnation. At some point, you must decide: remain paralyzed or take the first shaky step forward. That moment came when I realized that the thing I feared most wasn't failure or rejection—it was stagnation. I didn't want to look back years later and see that I had let fear dictate the course of my life. So, I started small. I took a deep breath and did the one thing fear never wanted me to do: I acted.

That first step was terrifying. It felt like jumping into an icy river—my breath caught, my muscles stiffened, and every fiber of my being screamed to retreat. My initial attempts were painfully awkward. I remember approaching someone at a sales event. My hands were clammy, and my heart was pounding like a drumline in my chest. My voice quivered, my words stumbled, and I could feel the heat of embarrassment rising to my face. The person politely declined, and the rejection stung, like a slap across the face. I walked away, struggling to hide the lump forming in my throat.

I repeated it again and again. Each interaction was another plunge into that icy river. Every time, the shock of rejection hit me square in the chest, urging me to retreat to the warmth of my comfort zone. But each time, I resisted. Somewhere between the discomfort and the humiliation, I noticed something. The cold no longer felt as unbearable. Fear still lingered, but I was no longer its captive. The embarrassment that used to linger for hours now faded faster, replaced by an unexpected sensation: pride. Not pride in the outcome, but in the effort—the act of facing what terrified me and stepping into the unknown.

The process of overcoming fear, I realized, was exactly like an ice bath. At first, it was unbearable. Every nerve in my body screamed for me to escape. My breathing was shallow and frantic, and my thoughts scattered. But as time passed, something shifted. The water didn't feel as cold anymore. What had once been pure torture became almost manageable. And then—unexpectedly—it became empowering.

By embracing discomfort, I was rewiring the way I viewed fear. It wasn't an enemy to defeat but a companion to acknowledge. I came to understand that fear wasn't there to stop me; it was there to challenge me, to test my resolve, and to remind me that growth is never easy. Over time, what had once terrified me became second nature. Approaching people, asking for what I needed, putting myself out there—these weren't insurmountable barriers anymore; they were opportunities to practice courage.

The biggest lesson I learned was this: fear will never entirely go away. It will always linger at the edges, waiting for a moment of hesitation to creep back in. But it needn't paralyze you. Fear loses its power if you can endure the initial shock and sit with the discomfort long enough to find your footing. And what you're left with is something far more significant: a sense of freedom, possibility, and strength you never knew you had.

Overcoming fear in sales didn't just transform my career—it reshaped how I approached challenges in every area of my life. Years later, I found myself drawing on those same lessons when fear appeared in new forms.

Fear may have taken on different shapes—speaking to an audience, sharing my story—but at its core, it was the same familiar challenge: a call to action, cleverly disguised as hesitation.

## Transforming Fear into Growth

I had committed to breaking through my fear of talking to strangers back then. I focused on building skills and developing resilience. Soon, I became adept at selling to strangers, recruiting new team members, and even standing in front of large groups to conduct training sessions. What once felt impossible became second nature through persistence.

Eventually, my efforts paid off. I earned the title of national marketing director and achieved success that seemed unattainable in those early days. Along the way, I discovered something profound: fear diminishes when we face it repeatedly. Each time we confront what scares us, we expand our comfort zone. The unknown becomes familiar, and what once seemed impossible becomes a stepping stone to even greater things.

Despite my success in sales, I left the industry in my mid-20s. Over the years, the stage—the spotlight—became a distant memory. The skills I had honed in my sales career, the confidence to command a room, and the ability to connect with an audience lay dormant, like a box of forgotten tools gathering dust in a dim corner of my mind. Life moved on, and I shifted my focus to other pursuits. For a long time, I didn't have the opportunity—or the need—to stand in front of a crowd or pitch an idea.

It wasn't until recently that I felt the pull back into the spotlight, though the context was entirely different this time. It began with a simple request at church. "Would you give a communion meditation?" they asked. At first, I hesitated. The thought of standing in front of people again, of sharing something personal and vulnerable, sent a ripple of unease through me. I hadn't spoken publicly in years. Could I still do it?

A communion meditation is brief—five minutes, maybe less. Yet, those minutes should carry deep meaning. The speaker's role is to guide the congregation into reflection and help them deepen their understanding of Jesus' sacrifice, along with the significance of bread and wine as symbols of His body and blood. The weight of this task settled over me as I sat down to write. This wasn't a pitch or a presentation. It was something deeply personal.

The day of the service arrived. The church sanctuary buzzed with the low hum of whispered conversations and the occasional shuffle of footsteps across the worn carpet. I stood at the front, my hands gripping the edges of the podium. My palms were damp, and I could feel the tremor in my knees, hidden beneath the fabric of my jeans.

"Good morning," I began, my voice tight and a little too high. I cleared my throat, took a steadying breath, and spoke. I shared a glimpse into my past—the abuse, the neglect, the homelessness, how I had grappled with challenges, wrestled with doubt and ultimately found solace in faith. As I spoke, I could feel the room shift. The nervous energy in my chest unraveled, replaced by something steadier. I saw nods, small smiles, and a few furrowed brows of deep thought. When I finished, I returned to my seat, my heart still pounding but lighter. After the service, people approached me, and their words were full of warmth and encouragement. One older woman squeezed my hand and said, "Your words touched my heart."

That moment reminded me of something I had understood during my early sales days: fear, no matter how overwhelming, isn't unique to me. It's a universal experience, but so is the ability to rise above it.

That experience ignited something in me—a flicker of realization that my story mattered. My journey, struggles, and resilience had the potential to speak to others in ways I had never imagined.

Not long after, another opportunity came—this time, one that felt far more daunting. I was invited to be the guest speaker at a foster care appreciation dinner. This wasn't just five minutes in front of my church family. This was a room full of people who lived and breathed the foster care system: foster parents, child protective service workers, prosecutors, judges, magistrates, and the most important guest of all, my foster mother, Theresa, who had flown in from Florida just to be there. These people shaped lives, made decisions, and witnessed both the darkest corners and the rare triumphs of the system.

The stakes felt immeasurably higher. I knew my story had to reach the rawest parts of me, forcing me to confront what I had always kept locked away. In the quiet of my home, days leading up to the event, I drafted and redrafted my speech. The night would deepen, and I'd sit hunched over my laptop, the glowing screen illuminating the darkness, the words blurring together as I struggled to capture the complexity of my experiences and the profound gratitude I carried. The hum of my desk lamp seemed louder in the stillness, and I felt the weight of the responsibility pressing on my chest. How could I find the right words to express the respect and gratitude these people, their efforts, and sacrifices deserved?

### The Weight of a Hundred Stares

When it was finally time to speak at the dinner, I stepped before the room, feeling the weight of a hundred stares. The scent of roasted chicken, buttery rolls, and freshly brewed coffee hung in the air, mingling with the faint floral notes from the centerpieces on each table. The room buzzed with muted conversations and occasional bursts of laughter, that polite hum that precedes an event with an air of formality. Plates clinked softly against silverware as people finished their meals, the sound almost like an undercurrent of anticipation. I smoothed my hands over my shirt, feeling the tremor in my fingers, and glanced around, anchoring myself in the familiar faces scattered among the sea of strangers.

Near the front, my foster mother, Theresa, sat with her hands folded neatly in her lap, her posture perfectly straight. Her gaze met mine—a steady, warm anchor that softened the knot of nerves twisting in my chest. Gratitude swelled inside me as I took in her expectant expression, the quiet pride shimmering in her eyes. She had seen me at my most broken, yet here I stood, hoping to make her proud. At the table beside her sat Sara, my wife's friend and coworker, her amiable smile offering a flicker of comfort amid the weight of the moment.

I spoke, my voice trembling slightly as I waded into the story of my childhood—the chaos, the uncertainty, and the moments of grace that had carried me through. My throat tightened when I spoke about the Roshons, the family who had taken me in when I needed it most, and the profound impact they'd had on my life. When I mentioned Theresa, my voice caught on her name, and I glanced at her. Her eyes glistened, her lips pressed together with equal pride and tenderness.

As I continued, the room seemed to shrink, the distant hum of clinking plates fading as the audience leaned in. Faces came into sharper focus, each reflecting emotion—tearful eyes, softened gazes, furrowed brows deep in thought. Toward the back, a middle-aged woman pressed her hand to her mouth, holding back a sob, her shoulders trembling slightly. Near the front, a man nodded in silent agreement, his jaw tight, his expression a mix of sorrow and resolve. The occasional rustle of napkins punctuated the stillness, accompanied by soft sniffles. The collective energy in the room became palpable, an unspoken connection that bound us all together. Every word I spoke felt heavy with gratitude and a shared understanding of struggle and resilience.

When I finished, there was a beat of silence. The silence stretched, heavy and uncertain, long enough to make me doubt myself. I heard a faint rustle of fabric as someone shifted in their chair. My pulse pounded in my ears, drowning out everything but the whisper of doubt: Had I said enough? Had I connected? The air felt thick, unmoving as if the entire room was holding its breath with me.

Then, like the first crack of thunder after a long stillness, a single pair of hands clapped. And then, like a wave, the room rose to its feet. The applause filled the air, a sound so loud and overwhelming it seemed to wrap around me, drowning out the doubts I'd carried with me.

Sara was the first to stand, clapping enthusiastically, followed closely by Theresa. She rose slowly, her face wet with tears, her hands clasped as if holding the weight of the moment in her palms. She beamed at me with a pride so profound it was almost overwhelming.

As the applause swelled, I let the moment wash over me. I had walked into that room carrying the weight of my story, unsure if I could do it justice, uncertain if I could meet the expectations of those who had lived and breathed the foster care system. But as I stood there, amid the swelling applause, an internal shift occurred. This wasn't just my story—it was our story. A story of struggle, resilience, and the power of connection. At that moment, I understood that sharing it wasn't just an act of courage—it was an act of gratitude.

## The Power of Facing Fear

As I stood there, listening to the applause, a realization washed over me: fear hadn't disappeared—it never does. But when I faced it, I found strength. That night and the moments leading up to it taught me a truth I carry with me to this day: fear only holds power over us until we confront it. Every experience, from my early days in sales to that first communion meditation to the foster care dinner, was a lesson in resilience. Each of those moments came with its own flavor of fear. The cold calls in sales carried the sharp sting of immediate rejection—like a slap you brace for but still feel deeply. The communion meditation felt more like standing on a narrow ledge, vulnerable to judgment or misunderstanding. And the foster care dinner? That fear was heavier—like a stone pressing down on my chest, layered with the weight of responsibility and the faces of those who had lived the foster care experience themselves.

I've come to realize that fear—whether it's fear of public speaking, vulnerability, or rejection—is universal. It speaks to each of us in different voices, some loud, others insidious, whispering doubts that swirl like smoke in the back of our minds. Its goal, however, is always the same: to keep us from growing. It's the chill of hesitation when your hand hovers over the phone before making a call. It's the tightening in your throat when you prepare to speak your truth. It's how your pulse quickens and your thoughts scatter just before stepping into the unknown.

The key to overcoming fear isn't running from it—it's stepping into it. Fear thrives when we turn away, feeding on our avoidance. I used to think fear was something to conquer, something to crush beneath my feet like an enemy on the battlefield. I imagined myself wrestling it to the ground, victorious. But it's nothing like that. When you turn your back on it, fear becomes a large, dark, ominous shadow. But when confronted, the shadow loses its substance. You realize it's not as powerful as it appears.

When I look back on those early days in sales, I can't help but smile at the irony. The first cold call, the first awkward conversation—they terrified me in ways that felt disproportionate at the time but were undeniably real. I can still feel the sticky dampness of my palms as I gripped the phone, my heart pounding like a relentless drum. My voice would waver, betraying the nerves I tried so hard to conceal. A simple "no, thank you" or a curt dismissal—every refusal felt like a whip crack, damaging the fragile self-assurance I was trying to build. Each rejection reinforced the self-doubt whispering in my ear: *See? You're not good enough.*

Despite their discomfort, those moments ultimately strengthened me. I now see them as the early strikes of a sculptor's chisel—awkward, imprecise, and sometimes painful but essential. Each rejection chipped away at the fear that had once encased me. The slow grind of pain revealed a hidden strength—something sharper, more resilient. I didn't realize it then, but I was shaping resilience, one "no" at a time.

Now, I see every challenge as an invitation. The sweaty palms, the trembling voice, the quickened pulse—they're no longer warnings to retreat. They're signals that I'm standing on the edge of growth. Reminders that I'm about to step into something meaningful.

Each challenge offers an opportunity to grow, to share, to connect. To face fear and emerge transformed on the other side. This book invites you, the reader, to confront your fears and unlock your inner resilience.

When I think back to those cold calls, the communion meditation, and the foster care dinner, I realize that the common thread isn't the absence of fear. It's the decision to move forward anyway. Fear never truly disappears—it lingers, waiting for the next opportunity to raise its voice. But no longer am I controlled by that voice. Instead, it reminds me that I'm stepping into something that matters.

Therefore, embrace the discomfort. Take that first trembling step, even when your palms are sweaty, and your heart is pounding. The fear may feel overwhelming, but I promise you, it will lose its power when you face it. In its place, you'll discover extraordinary courage, growth, and strength—born from overcoming fear.

## Fear as a Gatekeeper

This principle applies to every area of life. Fear often acts as a gatekeeper, silently standing at the threshold of our dreams and goals, daring us to approach. Its presence is unmistakable—an unsettling knot in your stomach, the tightening of your chest, or the restless swirl of doubts that keep you awake at night. It doesn't shout or force itself upon you; it whispers. Soft but persistent, fear speaks directly into the places where you feel most vulnerable: You're not ready yet. You're not good enough. What makes you think you can do this?

These whispers may feel as real as the ground beneath your feet, convincing you to turn back, to stay in the safety of what you know. But fear is a master of illusion. It wants you to believe it's an insurmountable obstacle, an immovable wall blocking your path. Yet, as I've learned through my journey, fear isn't a wall—

it's a challenge. It's the gatekeeper of growth, standing between you and what's possible. Only in deciding to turn back lies the true test of strength.

The thing about fear is that it thrives on avoidance. The more we retreat, the larger it seems to loom, its shadow stretching further into our lives. However, confronting fear directly diminishes its power. What once seemed like an immovable wall reveals itself as a doorway. The whispers that once paralyzed you become background noise, growing fainter with each step you take.

When we face our fears, we take control of our lives instead of letting fear dictate our choices. It's difficult—your palms might sweat, your knees may tremble, and your heart could pound like a drum in your chest. However, at that moment, you realize that fear was never the true obstacle. As you step forward despite the discomfort, the real challenge was believing you could walk through the door all along.

## The Ripple Effect of Courage

Facing my fears didn't just change my life—it created a ripple effect. Courage, I've learned, isn't a solitary act. It's like throwing a stone into a still pond: the initial splash may seem small, but the ripples stretch far beyond what we can see. Every act of courage has the potential to touch others, inspiring them to take their own steps into the unknown.

After my communion meditation at church, something remarkable happened. People approached me during coffee hour in the days and weeks that followed. The air was thick with the earthy aroma of freshly brewed coffee, mingling with the warmth of donuts and cookies set out on the countertops. But it wasn't the treats that made the biggest impression—it was their words. Their voices were quiet yet brimming with sincerity as if my vulnerability had created a safe space for them to share something of their own.

One man, older with a weathered face that seemed to carry the weight of many untold stories, shook my hand firmly. His grip was steady, but his voice trembled as he said, "Your story made me think. I've been carrying some things I must let go of, and hearing you talk about your struggles gave me hope."

Another woman, someone I'd only exchanged polite smiles with in the past, pulled me aside near the coat rack. Her voice faltered, emotion thickening her words as she shared fragments of her own story. "I never thought of my pain as something that could help someone else," she admitted, tears rolling down her cheeks. "But maybe... maybe it can."

Their words stayed with me long after the conversations ended. I realized that my willingness to step into fear—to open up and share my story—had opened a door for others. My moment of vulnerability had become a catalyst for healing and connection, leaving me profoundly humbled.

Then, there was the foster care appreciation dinner, where the ripple effect of courage became undeniable. As I stood before everyone, the weight of my words seemed to settle over the room like a heavy, comforting blanket. The air felt thick with emotion, charged with the silent understanding shared by people who had lived and breathed the foster care experience.

The room was still, save for the occasional clink of a fork against a plate. I could see the impact of my story in their faces—the tearful eyes of a foster mother near the back, her expression a blend of exhaustion and fierce pride. A child protective services worker leaned forward slightly, nodding in silent agreement, her face softening as I spoke of the moments of grace that had carried me through my darkest times.

As the applause faded and people rose from their seats, they approached me individually. Their voices were quiet, but their words carried the weight of their experiences. A foster parent told me, "Hearing your story reminded me why I do what I do, even when it's hard." His voice cracked slightly on the word "hard," and I could see the strain etched into his face.

Another woman, a child protective services worker with kind eyes and a tired smile, admitted, "Sometimes this job feels thankless, but your story reminded me that what we do matters."

My foster mother, Theresa, hugged me tightly, her arms wrapping around me in a way that spoke volumes. I could feel her tears dampening my shoulder, but her pride radiated from her like warmth on a frosty night.

In those moments, I realized something profound: courage isn't just about overcoming your fears. It's about creating space for others to confront theirs. When you step into the unknown, face your fears, and own your story, you give others permission to do the same. It's a cycle of inspiration and growth—a ripple that begins with a single courageous act and spreads outward in ways we can't always predict.

Sharing your fears, struggles, and triumphs doesn't just liberate you; it liberates those around you. It's an invitation to others—a quiet but powerful message that says, You can do this too.

Courage, I've learned, is not just a gift you give yourself—it's a gift you give to others. Its ever-expanding influence is what makes courage beautiful. It carries on, reaching further than we ever imagined, touching lives we may never see, and reminding us that every step into fear has the potential to create something extraordinary.

## Writing This Book: A New Frontier

Standing before a crowd taught me to embrace discomfort, but writing this book presented a new challenge. Unlike a speech, where audience reactions are immediate, writing feels like sending my fears into the world without knowing how they'll be received. Yet, just like with cold calls or public speaking, I learned that action—no matter how imperfect—is the antidote to fear.

In the early days of this process, I often found myself sitting at my desk, fingers hovering above the keyboard. The cursor blinked like a steady, unrelenting heartbeat, as if asking, Are you ready? I wasn't. Not at first. Doubt crept in like a shadow, whispering, What if your story isn't good enough? What if people judge you? Are you a good enough writer? What if they don't understand? How will your family feel? How will this affect your life and theirs?

Taking a deep breath, I dove in—just as I had with public speaking and those first shaky cold calls years ago. Writing this book wasn't just an exercise in storytelling; it was a confrontation with myself. The same fears that had haunted me during cold calls and public speeches returned in full force, echoing every doubt and insecurity. But, just as I had learned to answer fear with action, I now had to do the same, one imperfect sentence at a time. The first words were messy, awkward, and filled with uncertainty. But they were a start. With each sentence, with each page, my confidence grew.

There were moments, late at night, when the house was quiet and the weight of the stories I was telling pressed heavily on my chest. Reliving some of my darkest moments, peeling back layers of pain and fear to uncover the lessons buried within—it was exhausting. But it was liberating, too. With every chapter, I felt lighter, as if shedding the final remnants of fear and doubt that had clung to me for years.

I reminded myself why I was writing this book: not just for me, but for you—the reader. I wrote this for those who might see pieces of their own story in mine and feel a little less alone. For the one standing on the edge of their fear, unsure if they have the strength to take that first step.

Fear is universal. Whether it's the fear of public speaking, sharing a painful truth, or facing rejection, we all encounter it. But we don't have to let fear control us. The only way to overcome it is to confront it—to wade through the discomfort and doubt until you find solid ground on the other side.

Writing this book has been an act of courage—a new frontier in facing my fears. It has taught me, yet again, that growth never happens in the comfort zone. Much like public speaking, sales, or any other challenge, the process has been messy, uncomfortable, and deeply complex. But it has also been profoundly worthwhile.

Like every chapter in this book, this one stands as a testament to the power of perseverance. It's a reminder that fear is an inevitable part of life—but it doesn't have to define us. We have the strength to confront it, the capacity to learn from it, and the resilience to emerge stronger than we ever imagined.

I'm sharing my story not as someone who has conquered fear but as someone learning to coexist with it. My hope is that by stepping into my fears, I can inspire you to step into yours. Because on the other side of fear, you'll find growth. You'll find purpose. And you'll discover a bolder, stronger, and more capable version of yourself than you ever dreamed possible.

## Expanding the Boundaries of Comfort

Each time I stepped into the unknown—whether it was making cold calls, standing at the front of the church, or baring my soul at the foster care dinner—I stretched the boundaries of my comfort zone a little further. Each step left an indelible mark, reshaping the edges of who I thought I was and what I believed I was capable of.

Looking back now, I see how every fear I faced left behind a more courageous, more resilient version of myself—a version I couldn't have met without taking that first trembling step.

When I reflect on those moments—each time fear threatened to paralyze me, each time I acted despite the shaking in my hands and the pounding in my chest—I realize something profound. Facing fear isn't about reaching a destination or checking off a goal. It's about growth.

Real growth. The kind that stretches you, reshapes you, and leaves you marveling at how much larger your world has become. The kind of growth that makes you wonder why you ever believed the walls of your comfort zone were immovable in the first place.

Fear, I've realized, is like standing at the edge of a dark forest. Towering trees rise like sentinels, their long shadows stretching endlessly into the unknown. The undergrowth whispers with unseen movement, and your mind races with thoughts of what might lurk within. It's so tempting—so incredibly tempting—to turn back, to retreat to the familiar clearing where everything feels safe and predictable.

But the clearing remains unchanged. It stays small, confined, and unremarkable. The magic, the growth, the transformation—those lie within the forest. Only when you gather your courage, take that first hesitant step into the shadows, and venture into the unknown do you begin to discover paths leading to something new.

Each time we step out of our comfort zone, we expand its boundaries, creating room for possibilities we never imagined. What once felt terrifying eventually becomes second nature. Conversations that used to make your palms sweat and your voice waver become moments of genuine connection. The speeches that once made your knees buckle transform into opportunities to inspire. Challenges that once seemed insurmountable shrink into stepping stones beneath your feet.

The more we face our fears, the smaller they become. We begin to see that they were never as powerful as they seemed.

I've learned that fear isn't the enemy—it's a compass. It points us toward the places we've been avoiding, the places where our greatest potential lies waiting to be uncovered. Fear whispers, Here is the path you've been too scared to take. Here is the version of yourself you've yet to meet.

Fear doesn't exist to stop us—it exists to guide us, to show us where we need to go.

When I think about how fear has shaped my journey, I no longer see it as a wall—I see it as a doorway. And on the other side of that doorway lies a version of myself I've yet to meet—a stronger, braver, more resilient me. Fear doesn't vanish. Even now, it lingers in the moments before I try something new. Its familiar voice rises: What if you fail? What if you're not good enough?

But now, I respond differently. Instead of shrinking back, I lean in and ask, What if I grow?

Stepping into fear isn't easy—it never has been and never will be. My hands shook as I stood on stage, my voice faltering as I shared my story with strangers. I stared at blank pages, the cursor blinking accusingly, daring me to type something that might be judged, misunderstood, or ignored. Fear, in those moments, was loud—almost deafening. Yet, even with trembling steps, hesitant words, and imperfect sentences, I found that action quiets the noise.

Action diminishes fear. It doesn't erase it, but it steals its power. Each time I've chosen action over retreat, I've discovered strengths I didn't know I had.

Courage, I've learned, isn't the absence of fear—it's the decision to act despite it. It's the trust that discomfort is temporary and that growth is waiting on the other side. It's moving forward with shaking knees and a pounding heart, knowing that each step brings you closer to the person you're meant to become.

When I think back to the person standing in the shopping plaza that day, paralyzed by the fear of a simple conversation, it feels like a lifetime ago. That same fear—the one that whispered You're not good enough—is the same one I've confronted time and again, each time in a different form. And each time, I've learned to lean into the discomfort, trusting that growth is always on the other side.

This chapter isn't just a reflection on my journey—it's a call to action for both of us. To you, the reader, who feels fear tightening its grip, who wonders if you have the strength to face what scares you, let me remind you: you do. You always have. That knot in your stomach and that trembling voice in your head aren't signs of weakness—they're evidence that you're standing at the threshold of something meaningful. Something worth pursuing.

It's time to stop viewing fear as an adversary and start seeing it as an invitation to grow. Discomfort isn't something to avoid—it's something to embrace. Step boldly into the unknown, even when the ground feels unsteady and the shadows obscure the path ahead because growth waits on the other side of fear.

And beyond that growth lies a life shaped by passion, filled with deep contentment, and brimming with the freedom to dream without limits.

Imagine the doors that could open if you stopped letting fear dictate your next move. Picture the dreams that could take shape, the lives you could impact, and the person you could become—not despite your fears, but because you had the courage to face them.

Fear will always find its way into our lives, arriving in new forms and challenges at every stage of our journey. But it doesn't have to control us. We hold the power to decide how we respond. We can choose to let it confine us, or we can let it guide us toward something greater.

What if you stopped letting fear hold you back? What if you saw it as a compass pointing you toward your greatest potential instead? Take the first step—just one. Let your voice tremble, let your heart race, but step forward anyway. Because beyond fear lies the life you're meant to live—the version of yourself you've been waiting to meet.

Then take another.

Soon, you'll look back and marvel at how far you've come. You'll see the boundaries of your comfort zone stretched and redefined in ways you never thought possible. You'll realize how each step transformed fear into fuel, discomfort into resilience, and possibilities into reality.

This is how we grow, evolve, and create lives filled with meaning.

Imagine a life where fear no longer holds you back—not because it has disappeared, but because you've learned to walk alongside it. Picture yourself stepping into the unknown again and again until the unknown becomes familiar—your destination all along.

Beyond fear lies the life you were always meant to create.

Looking back, I see that each step I took—whether nervously approaching a stranger in the shopping plaza, speaking from my heart during a communion meditation, or standing before a room of foster care advocates—wasn't just about conquering individual fears. Each moment was a piece of a more significant transformation, one that slowly reshaped my relationship with fear. What began as small, shaky steps grew into a pattern of stepping forward, even when the path wasn't clear. Facing fear taught me it isn't a wall blocking the life we want—it's a doorway. And every time I moved through it, I wasn't just overcoming fear; I was building a life where fear no longer dictated my choices. That's the real ripple effect of courage: when you face fear, you don't just change yourself—you inspire others to do the same, creating a wave of growth that stretches far beyond what you can see.

# CHAPTER 11:

# GRACE OVER ANGER: CHOOSING KINDNESS IN A CHAOTIC WORLD

Life moves quickly, and often, we're just trying to make it through the day. We juggle work, family responsibilities, personal challenges, and the constant pull of technology. Amid all this, it's easy to lose sight of one essential thing: compassion.

Compassion is about noticing when someone is struggling and responding with kindness. It means understanding their pain and offering a helping hand. In today's world, where competition and success are often prioritized, compassion is frequently overlooked. This is especially true during stressful moments when our patience is wearing thin. Ironically, these are the very times when compassion is most needed.

Modern life is exhausting. Research shows that burnout, anxiety, and stress are more prevalent than ever. Constant notifications, a relentless stream of news, and the pressure to achieve leave many feeling drained and disconnected. This disconnection often manifests in subtle ways—snapping at a coworker, ignoring a friend's message, or losing our temper in traffic.

## Compassion: A Remedy for Stress and Disconnection

Compassion has the power to counterbalance the chaos. When life feels overwhelming, it can help alleviate stress and restore a sense of connection. Compassion invites us to pause and remember our shared humanity. This small but profound shift in perspective can bring peace not only to the person receiving kindness but also to the one extending it.

Consider how often stress prompts negative reactions. A driver cuts us off, and we feel a surge of anger. A coworker makes a mistake, and we respond with irritation. These reactions may feel instinctive, but they only add to the emotional burden we carry. Compassion disrupts this cycle. It encourages us to ask, "What might this person be going through?" That single question transforms judgment into understanding and frustration into kindness.

Science reveals that acts of kindness benefit both the giver and the receiver. Compassion reduces stress, boosts happiness, and even strengthens the immune system. It creates a ripple effect of positivity, spreading goodwill that benefits everyone.

But what happens when compassion is absent? When stress and disconnection take over, we become blind to the struggles of others, leading to deeper issues in our relationships and society as a whole.

## The Cost of a Compassionless World

Without compassion, we risk becoming emotionally blind. We become so focused on our own struggles that we fail to recognize the pain of others. This fosters isolation and leads to problems like strained relationships and conflict.

Stress often amplifies minor conflicts. A tense conversation at work, a misunderstanding with a friend, or a disagreement with a stranger can easily escalate without compassion. This damages relationships and cultivates a culture of anger and mistrust.

On a broader scale, a lack of compassion contributes to issues like inequality and discrimination. When we fail to recognize the struggles of others, we miss the opportunity to effect meaningful change. Compassion, on the other hand, helps us connect and inspires action. It reminds us that we are all part of the same human experience, bound by shared hopes, fears, and dreams.

The impacts of compassion—or its absence—are seen not only on a societal level but also in our day-to-day interactions. While large-scale challenges may feel daunting, compassion often reveals its transformative power in small, personal moments.

Understanding the cost of a world without compassion highlights why choosing compassion is so crucial. While it's not always easy, it is always worth the effort.

## Compassion as a Choice

Compassion is a choice. It's the decision to respond with kindness, even when it's difficult. Choosing compassion doesn't mean neglecting your own needs or tolerating destructive behavior. It means approaching situations with empathy and striving to understand others.

This choice begins with small, everyday moments. Imagine you're in line at a grocery store, and a frustrated person ahead of you takes their anger out on the cashier. It's easy to feel irritated or pass judgment, but what if you paused and considered what they might be going through? Perhaps they've had a rough day or are dealing with struggles you can't see. A kind word or a simple smile from you could change the entire moment.

Compassion isn't always easy, especially when we're stressed or upset. But it's always worth it. When we choose compassion, we not only help others, but we also create peace within ourselves.

These small choices accumulate. They improve our lives and make a real difference in the lives of others. The more we practice compassion, the more it becomes a natural habit.

## The Transformative Power of Compassion

Compassion has the power to transform people, relationships, and communities. It fosters connection, helping to combat feelings of isolation and loneliness. It reminds us that, despite our differences, we are all human.

Compassion becomes truly powerful when it becomes part of who we are. This doesn't happen overnight—it takes practice and intentional effort. We must confront our own biases and assumptions. But over time, compassion can feel like second nature.

The process starts with small acts of kindness. And as these acts ripple outward, they can create profound change.

## Building Compassionate Habits

Compassion grows through simple habits. Here are a few ways to practice it every day:

Listen carefully: Give your full attention when someone speaks. Don't interrupt or rush to offer advice—just listen.

Give compliments: A kind word about someone's effort or actions can brighten their day.

Pause before reacting: When you're upset, take a deep breath. Think about how you can respond with kindness instead of anger.

Perform small acts of kindness: Pay for someone's coffee, hold the door open or offer a helping hand.

See shared humanity: Remember, everyone deals with struggles you may not see.

Even minor acts of compassion can create a ripple effect. Compassion isn't just an abstract concept—it's built through small, everyday actions that remind us of our shared humanity.

## Everyday Acts of Compassion: Small Gestures, Big Impact

Compassion isn't about grand, dramatic gestures. It's about small, everyday actions. Holding the door for someone, offering encouragement, or listening without judgment can make a huge difference.

I've seen this firsthand as a truck driver. One busy day, I stopped for coffee at a gas station. The cashier looked overwhelmed by the rush. When I told her, "You're doing a great job," her face lit up. She smiled and said, "You just made my day."

It took little effort, but that small moment had a significant impact. It reminded me how easy it is to brighten someone's day. People often feel invisible or unappreciated; a kind word can remind them they matter.

Small gestures go further than we think. Studies show that people often underestimate the power of their actions. A compliment, a smile, or a simple act of generosity can stay in someone's mind long after the moment. Kindness inspires more kindness, creating a chain reaction that connects people in unseen ways.

The next time you meet someone who seems distant or irritable, pause and think about what they might be going through. Everyone has struggles. A little compassion can soften your judgments and help you respond with kindness.

## Lessons from the Road: A Microcosm of Society

As a truck driver, I've spent countless hours observing people. The highway feels like a microcosm of society. Drivers move fast, slow, cautiously, or recklessly, each revealing their own worries and priorities. Every moment on the road offers a choice: react with frustration or respond with understanding.

One stressful day, I found myself stuck behind a slow-moving car on a narrow highway. Frustration built as I counted the minutes slipping away. When I finally passed the car, I glanced at the driver. An older woman gripped the wheel tightly, her face a picture of focus and worry.

In an instant, my frustration disappeared. She wasn't trying to slow me down—she was simply doing her best in a situation that felt overwhelming to her. What seemed like an inconvenience to me was an act of courage for her. That shift in perspective changed everything.

Driving often reveals the hidden struggles people carry. Angry or reckless drivers aren't necessarily careless—they might be grappling with stress, grief, or anger. Recognizing this helps me respond with patience and kindness instead of irritation.

The road has taught me an invaluable lesson: Everyone is fighting battles we can't see. By choosing empathy and understanding, we ease others' burdens and make the world a kinder, more compassionate place.

### The Ripple Effect of Kindness

Kindness has a remarkable ability to spread far beyond the initial act. When we show kindness, it often inspires others to do the same. This ripple effect isn't just a feel-good idea—it's supported by science. Studies reveal that emotions and behaviors are contagious. A single act of kindness can influence the person who receives it and extend to everyone they interact with afterward.

I've witnessed this ripple effect firsthand while volunteering at a food pantry. One busy day, a stressed family came in seeking help. They had recently lost their job and were struggling to make ends meet. While assisting them with packing groceries, I shared a few kind words to remind them that the community was there to support them.

A month later, that same family returned—not to ask for help, but to volunteer. They had gone from receiving kindness to spreading it. That moment was a powerful reminder of how even small acts can create a cycle of positivity that uplifts everyone involved.

Kindness also has profound benefits for mental health. When we show compassion, our brain releases feel-good chemicals like oxytocin and serotonin. This creates a positive feedback loop—kindness boosts our mood, and that uplifted mood motivates us to extend more kindness.

By choosing kindness, we don't just brighten someone else's day; we contribute to a chain reaction that can transform individuals, communities, and ourselves.

## Self-Compassion: The Foundation of Grace

Kindness isn't just something we extend to others—it's also something we owe to ourselves. In a world that celebrates perfection and relentless productivity, we often become our own harshest critics. But self-kindness is just as vital as kindness to others.

Self-compassion means treating yourself with patience and understanding, especially when you stumble or make mistakes. It's about recognizing that imperfection is a part of being human. Instead of harshly criticizing ourselves, we can choose to offer support and encouragement, building the emotional strength to navigate life's challenges.

I learned this lesson during a particularly tough period in my life. I had made mistakes in both personal and professional relationships, and my immediate reaction was anger and self-criticism. But then it struck me—why not show myself the same compassion I would offer a friend in the same situation?

I started by changing how I spoke to myself. Instead of fixating on my failures, I began acknowledging the effort I was making to grow and improve. This small shift transformed how I felt. It brought a sense of calm and confidence, allowing me to move forward with clarity. It also made it easier to extend compassion to others.

When we practice self-kindness, we create a strong foundation within ourselves. This foundation not only helps us weather life's storms but also enables us to extend grace and kindness to the world around us.

When we learn to extend compassion to ourselves, it becomes easier to offer it to others. Self-kindness strengthens our ability to empathize, creating a foundation for more meaningful connections. By recognizing our struggles and treating ourselves with patience, we gain the emotional resilience needed to see and respond to the pain in others.

## Letting Go of Anger: Emotional Freedom and Mental Clarity

Anger can become toxic when we hold on to it. It clouds our judgment, skews our perspective, and breeds negativity. Carrying anger is like lugging around a heavy weight—it drags us down and keeps us from moving forward. However, letting go of anger can lead to peace and mental clarity.

I'll never forget a memory from truck driving school that illustrated this truth. We watched a video of a tragic crash caused by anger. In the video, a truck driver grew furious after being cut off by a car. Consumed by his frustration, he chased the car down a steep mountain road, driving recklessly in an attempt to retaliate.

As the truck barreled down the incline, it gained too much speed. On a sharp turn, the driver lost control, and the truck crashed. Tragically, the driver lost his life.

Our instructor summed it up with a quiet but powerful remark: "This happens when you let anger take the wheel." The room fell silent. None of us ever forgot that lesson.

Years later, I still think about that video as I navigate the highways. I've witnessed countless situations where drivers make dangerous choices fueled by frustration or impatience. Each time, I find myself asking, Was it worth it? The answer is almost always no.

Choosing grace over anger means letting go of resentment and frustration. Forgiveness isn't just about freeing others—it's about freeing ourselves. When we release anger, we gain the mental clarity to make better decisions, solve problems, and find emotional balance.

## Grace Over Anger: How to Stay Calm in Conflict

I teach my wife and kids one simple rule: Don't honk your horn or yell at people while driving. Instead, take a deep breath and let it go.

Why? Because you never know what someone else is going through. The person who cut you off might have just received terrible news. Maybe they're reeling from a betrayal or rushing to the hospital. They might not be thinking clearly.

Reacting with anger—whether by honking, yelling, or making rude gestures—might seem harmless at the moment, but it can escalate the situation. That person could respond recklessly, using their car as a weapon or making an impulsive, dangerous move.

Staying calm isn't just about avoiding conflict. It's about protecting yourself and everyone around you. No fleeting moment of frustration is worth risking someone's safety.

This approach is rooted in empathy. Instead of viewing others as obstacles, we can see them as people navigating their own challenges. They might be overwhelmed, grieving, or distracted by stress. When we choose not to respond with anger, we give them—and ourselves—the space to move through the moment without adding more tension.

Before reacting, I always ask myself: Is it worth it? Could this conflict be avoided by simply letting it go? Teaching my family this mindset helps them understand that staying calm doesn't mean weakness—it means wisdom.

Every time we take a deep breath and choose not to react, we set an example for our loved ones. We show them how to handle frustration with patience and dignity. In doing so, we create a safer, calmer, and more compassionate world, one choice at a time.

## The Neuroscience of Compassion: Why It Matters

Compassion isn't just a moral choice—it's part of our biology. When we show kindness, our brains release oxytocin, often called the "love hormone." This powerful chemical helps us feel connected to others, reduces stress, and strengthens our emotional resilience.

Research has shown that acts of compassion activate the brain's reward system, creating feelings of happiness and fulfillment. This explains why being kind often leaves us with a sense of warmth and connection.

Interestingly, even observing acts of kindness can affect us. For instance, seeing someone help a stranger might inspire us or fill us with hope. This reaction isn't just emotional; it's deeply rooted in our brain's design, encouraging empathy and social connection.

Understanding this reminds us that kindness isn't just beneficial for those we help—it's also profoundly good for us.

## Compassion in Leadership: Building Stronger Communities

Compassion isn't just a personal virtue—it's also a powerful leadership tool. Leaders who practice compassion foster trust, teamwork, and a sense of belonging in schools, workplaces, and communities.

Compassionate leaders actively listen, value others' contributions, and provide support, creating an environment where people feel seen and appreciated. This approach encourages collaboration and inspires everyone to perform their best.

I witnessed this while volunteering at a local charity. The leader wasn't solely focused on achieving results. She made time to listen to the volunteers, celebrated their efforts, and ensured everyone felt valued. Her compassion brought the team closer together, motivating us to work harder and with more enthusiasm.

That experience showed me that compassion in leadership isn't a weakness—it's a remarkable strength. It builds unity, trust, and inspiration. Compassionate leaders lead by example, encouraging others to act with kindness and empathy in their own lives.

## On the Curb: Finding Connection in Unexpected Places

One sweltering evening in California, I parked my truck at a hotel and noticed a homeless man sitting by a stop sign. The sun was unrelenting, and he had no shade. His weary expression lingered in my mind as I walked past him into Wendy's.

While ordering, I couldn't shake the thought of him sitting out there, seemingly invisible to the world. Compassion nudged me into action. I bought him a meal and added a Frosty to help cool him down.

When I handed him the food, his face lit up. "Hey," I said, "I thought you might be hungry." His quiet smile and heartfelt thanks spoke volumes. Instead of leaving right away, I decided to sit down beside him on the curb.

We ate together and talked. He told me his name and shared how a series of unfortunate events—losing his job, then his home—had left him where he was. Sitting there on that curb, I realized he wasn't just a "homeless man." He was a person with dreams, struggles, and a story like anyone else.

That moment opened my eyes to how often we walk past people without truly seeing them. We assume we know their story or avoid them out of discomfort. But when we pause to listen, we realize their stories aren't so different from our own.

When we finished eating, he looked at me and said, "Most people don't even look at me." His words lingered in my mind, a stark reminder of how often we turn away—not because we don't care, but because we don't know how to help.

As I walked away, I thought about how many people like him feel unseen daily. I realized how small gestures—just a meal, a conversation, a moment of attention—can remind someone of their humanity. That moment wasn't just about helping him; it was about seeing him and, in doing so, connecting to something greater within myself.

Walking back to the hotel, I realized that compassion isn't about grand gestures. It's about being present, listening, and showing up—even if it's as simple as sitting on a curb with someone who feels unseen.

That evening reminded me that we're all connected. Simple acts of kindness have the power to reveal the best parts of humanity. Sometimes, it's not about solving someone's problems—it's about letting them know they matter.

## The Long-Term Benefits of Compassion

Compassion is transformative. It benefits our mental, emotional, and even physical well-being. Acts of kindness can reduce depression and anxiety, strengthen relationships, and lead to a more fulfilling life. But the impact of compassion doesn't stop at the individual—it extends to society as a whole.

When we practice compassion, we build trust and foster cooperation in our communities. It brings people together, creating a sense of connection and belonging. Compassion lays the foundation for stronger neighborhoods, more supportive workplaces, and healthier cultures.

In a world often marked by division and chaos, compassion becomes a powerful tool for healing. It bridges gaps, resolves conflicts, and inspires positive change. Choosing compassion, however, requires effort. It means pausing in moments of frustration or indifference and consciously deciding to care.

Compassion challenges us to see others as fully human—complex, vulnerable, and deserving of kindness. By making this choice, we don't just transform our own lives; we also create ripples of positivity that touch everyone around us. In doing so, we help build a world that's kinder, more united, and more resilient.

Compassion isn't about solving every problem or eliminating all pain—it's about showing up, being present, and reminding others they matter. In choosing compassion, we don't just brighten someone's day; we lay the foundation for a kinder, stronger world, built one small act at a time. Every small act of kindness ripples outward, touching lives in ways we may never see. In choosing compassion, we create a world where everyone feels a little less alone—and that's a world worth striving for.

# Chapter 12:

# From Dreams to Despair: A Promise to Myself

When I was younger, I promised myself that if I could make $100,000 a year, I would do whatever it took to achieve it. That number wasn't just a financial benchmark—it was proof—proof that I could rise above the struggles of my upbringing, where abundance was a distant concept and "enough" was a dream we could barely afford. That $100,000 wasn't about extravagance; it was about freedom, stability, and breaking the cycle of hardship.

I grew up in a world where abundance was something you glimpsed through the shiny storefront windows of a mall you could never afford to enter. I still remember the sharp sting of wanting something as simple as new shoes, only to know the answer would always be "no." Money wasn't just tight—it was nonexistent like air slowly running out in a sealed room. I didn't grow up dreaming of luxury; I dreamed of enough. Enough to keep the lights on without fearing the next bill. Enough to fill a grocery cart without counting every item twice. Enough to breathe. But I wanted more than just "enough."

I wanted freedom, security, and the ability to build a future so different from my past that even I would hardly recognize it. That $100,000 goal became a symbol of hope. It wasn't about extravagance; it was about breaking the cycle—proving to myself—and maybe to the world—that I could be someone who didn't just survive but thrived. It was a quiet rebellion against everything life had told me I couldn't be.

By the grace of God and through relentless effort, I've been fortunate to reach that milestone. But what I didn't understand back then, standing on the edge of that dream, was the cost. The road to success was a difficult path—a labyrinth full of dead ends, sharp turns, and pitfalls that threatened to swallow me whole. For every step forward, there were days when I felt pushed two steps back. The weight of failure pressed down so heavily it felt suffocating, like trying to breathe through a straw while the world collapsed around me.

I quickly learned that success is never given; you earn it, inch by inch, through sheer determination and by facing discomfort head-on. I still remember the late nights when exhaustion clung to me like a second skin, my eyes burning as I stared out the windshield of my cargo van, which blurred from lack of sleep. My body ached from the hours, my mind from the constant hum of worry: Was I doing enough? Could I make this work? The coffee that once tasted like motivation now felt like survival fuel, its bitter warmth barely cutting through the fog of fatigue.

There were moments when it felt easier to give up than to keep going—days when the sacrifices seemed too steep: the hours missed with family, the hobbies I abandoned, the sleep I surrendered. But deep down, I knew that if I stopped, I'd be letting down not just myself but the younger version of me—the boy who had dared to dream of more in a world that offered so little.

Of course, I made mistakes—plenty of them. Some were small, like chasing the wrong lead or mismanaging a task. Others felt catastrophic, like watching a deal I'd poured months of work into fall apart in the last hour. Those moments felt like gut punches, leaving me breathless and doubting my abilities. The shame of failure stung the most, a cruel whisper in my mind:

Maybe you don't have what it takes. But I learned to get back up, even when the weight of doubt felt unbearable. Each failure, painful as it was, taught me lessons I couldn't have learned any other way. Over time, those lessons became the bricks in the foundation of my resilience.

When I started my career, I didn't have a roadmap, connections, or a family name that opened doors. I didn't have a mentor who could tell me which path to take or warn me about the pitfalls. All I had was raw determination and an unshakable belief that if others could succeed, so could I.

I realized that success wasn't about being the most intelligent person in the room or the most talented—it was about showing up, day after day, even when everything inside you begged to quit. It was about persistence, about taking what little you had and building on it, brick by brick, step by step. Some days, the progress was so small it was almost invisible, but I kept moving forward.

I remember the first time I saw my bank statement reflect that six-figure milestone. It should have felt like a victory. After all, I'd finally done it—I'd reached the goal that had fueled me for so long. But instead of triumph, I felt an unexpected mix of emotions: pride, yes, but also exhaustion, relief, and a quiet realization that this wasn't the end of the journey. If anything, it was just the beginning.

Because here's the thing about success: it's not a final destination. That $100,000 wasn't a finish line but a mile marker. The lessons I learned on the way to that milestone truly mattered. I knew that success is more than money; it's about who you become in the process. It's about the strength you build from surviving failure, the wisdom you gain from your mistakes, and the character you develop when you keep going despite the odds.

Looking back now, I understand that every long night, painful setback, and moment of doubt shaped me. They taught me that resilience isn't just about enduring hard times but finding meaning in them. It's about learning to see the struggle as part of the story, not something to be avoided but to be embraced.

I'm grateful for the lessons, even the hard ones. They've shown me that genuine success goes far beyond numbers. It's about breaking barriers, creating a purpose-filled life, and proving that you can achieve far more than you ever imagined. And while I've been fortunate to achieve the goal I once dreamed of, I now understand that the greatest reward isn't the money or the title. The greatest reward is the journey itself.

So, to the younger version of me who dared to dream in the face of despair: thank you for holding on. You taught me that dreams, even the ones that feel impossibly far away, are worth chasing. And to anyone reading this, wondering if they have what it takes to reach their goals, I want to tell you: you do. The road will be hard and will test you in ways you can't yet imagine. But if you keep going and lean into the struggle, you'll find that the person you become is worth every step.

### Early Sacrifices for Success

When Rachel and I first got together, life felt full of promise, but it also demanded tough choices. I had been living on the road, chasing work from one state to another, my life scattered across miles of highway. When I left the road behind to take a local delivery job driving a cargo van, it felt like a turning point. It was a practical decision, one made with the future in mind. But practicality came at a cost, and the challenges it brought were as heavy as the boxes I loaded into that van each day.

My new schedule was grueling—a test of endurance I hadn't expected. The alarm would scream at 2:30 a.m., jerking me awake from sleep that felt like it had barely begun. The house was silent, wrapped in darkness, making me feel like the only person awake in the world. I'd fumble for my clothes in the dim light, trying not to wake Rachel as she slept soundly beside me. The smell of stale coffee from the day before lingered in the kitchen, a reminder of the routine I was already falling into. By 3:00 a.m., I was out the door, the air sharp and cold against my face as the world around me lay still and lifeless.

The workday stretched endlessly, often feeling like a marathon with no finish line. The cargo van rattled as I drove over uneven roads, the engine's hum and the thud of shifting boxes my only company. My hands, calloused and dry, gripped the wheel tightly as I fought off fatigue. The days blurred together in a relentless loop—loading, driving, delivering, and unloading. All the while, the clock seemed to move slower than it should. When I finally pulled into the driveway at 9:00 p.m., the house would be dark again, Rachel waiting patiently inside. I'd shuffle through the door, my body aching and my mind too numb to process anything beyond the need for food and sleep. I was a ghost of myself, barely able to engage in conversation, let alone enjoy the life I was working so hard to build.

But no matter how exhausted I felt, I clung to the promise I made to my Uncle Mike: to live a life of purpose, to work hard, and to rise above the circumstances I came from. Uncle Mike wasn't the man you'd call a role model—not in the traditional sense. He carried the weight of depression and the silent struggles that had worn down his spirit over the years. He was a broken man, often lost in the haze of his pain. But his story wasn't just one of struggle—it was a cautionary tale. Watching him wrestle with his demons, I saw the cost of neglecting pain and allowing hardship to take root and flourish.

Uncle Mike may not have been a shining example of resilience, but he became my motivation. His life, marked by unspoken battles and unrealized potential, was a stark reminder of what I didn't want for myself. While he may not have had the strength to rise above his circumstances, I was determined to honor him by doing exactly that. I made a silent vow that I would not let life break me the way it had broken him. Every time I woke up in the middle of the night, bone-tired and tempted to stay in bed, I thought of Uncle Mike. His struggles became a fire inside me, pushing me to keep going even when the grind felt unbearable.

The fire within me wasn't just fueled by ambition—pain ignited it. Memories of my mother's harsh words echoed in my mind like distant thunder, her negativity a constant refrain from my childhood. "You'll never amount to anything," she'd say, her voice sharp and unyielding. My father's absence loomed like a shadow over every stage of my life, leaving a void of guidance and love. These wounds could have held me down, chaining me to the same cycles of pain and doubt I had grown up in. But instead, they became fuel. Every moment of neglect, cutting remark, and time I felt abandoned—they all burned inside me, driving me to prove that I was capable of more.

As the alarm blared and darkness surrounded me each morning, I reminded myself of how far I had come. I thought of the life I was trying to build for Rachel, Gabriel, and myself. I wasn't just working to pay bills or put food on the table. I was working to break the chains of my past, to create a future that wasn't defined by the limits others had placed on me. My mother's criticism had planted a seed of determination—not to prove her wrong, but to prove to myself that I was more than the narrow expectations she had for me. My father's absence, though painful, taught me self-reliance. These early wounds could have become excuses to give up, but instead, they fueled my drive to keep going.

There were moments when the exhaustion felt insurmountable, like a weight pressing down on my chest. Some nights, I'd sit on the edge of the bed, head in my hands, wondering if it was all worth it. The long hours, the sleepless nights, and the toll it took on my body and mind seemed overwhelming. My muscles ached from lifting and moving heavy boxes and chemical pails all day, and my thoughts often felt like a jumbled mess of worry and fatigue. But those moments, as painful as they were, taught me something profound: success isn't about talent or luck. It's about perseverance. It's about showing up, day after day, even when every fiber of your being screams for you to quit.

Looking back now, I see those early sacrifices as the foundation of everything I've built since. The long hours weren't just temporary hardships—they were a crucible that tested my resolve and shaped my character. They proved I could endure, adapt, and grow, even in the face of relentless challenges. Each sleepless night, each bone-weary morning, was a brick in the foundation of the life I was determined to create.

Most importantly, those sacrifices solidified the bond between Rachel and me. She saw everything I was putting into this—every early morning, every late night, every ounce of effort I could muster—and stood by me. Rachel didn't just tolerate the grind; she supported me through it. She understood that the long hours and the exhaustion weren't just for me—they were for us. Her unwavering belief in me gave me the strength to push through, even on the most challenging days. We weathered those early storms together, leaning on each other when the weight felt too heavy to carry alone. In those moments of shared struggle, we built the foundation of our relationship, brick by brick, with resilience and love.

Now, when I think back to those grueling days, I don't just see sacrifice—I see proof. Proof that I could rise above my circumstances. Proof that I could endure and overcome. Every 2:30 a.m. alarm, aching muscle, and moment of doubt was worth it. Those sacrifices weren't just steps on a path; they were the bedrock of the life I promised myself, Rachel, and Uncle Mike I would build. A life of purpose, one that refused to be defined by the pain of the past. It was worth every ounce of the struggle it took to create.

## Entering the World of Piggyback Trucking

After my daughter was born, my perspective on life and work shifted. I was already a parent to Gabriel, my stepson, but having a newborn added an extra layer of urgency and purpose. It wasn't just about providing anymore—it was about being present. I didn't want to become the walking zombie I'd been in my previous job, drained to the point where I could barely engage with my family when I was home. So, I made a change that would allow me to show up differently—physically and emotionally.

Returning to the road as an independent contractor felt like the right move, but this time, it came with a new purpose and direction. The work was demanding, but it had a rhythm that allowed me to spend weeks on the road and then come home for a few days to a week at a time. When I was home, I was truly home—fully present for Rachel, Gabriel, and my daughter. I wasn't just hauling freight anymore; I had stepped into the specialized world of piggyback trucking, a job that required precision, endurance, and a willingness to master something new. It wasn't just a career shift—it was a deliberate decision to balance the demands of work with the life I was building at home.

Fortunately, the Bellinger family became my guide in this specialized industry. The Bellingers were piggyback trucking veterans, their decades of experience woven into the stories they shared over coffee as we prepared for the day at the hoist, surrounded by tools, grease-stained clothes, and the smell of diesel. They were rough around the edges, hardened by years on the road, but their generosity in sharing their knowledge was unmatched.

"You see, kid," Mr. Bellinger would say, squinting through a haze of cigarette smoke, "this business ain't for the careless. Every bolt, every saddle mount, every strap—it's gotta be just right, or you're not just risking a load; you're risking lives." His voice carried the weight of years of trial and error, and I hung on every word, eager to absorb the hard-earned wisdom he offered.

Piggyback trucking isn't for the faint of heart. It's as much a craft as it is a job, requiring meticulous attention to detail and an unwavering respect for the rigs you're hauling. The process involves hitching multiple semi-trucks together, stacking them like a mechanical train using specialized tools and saddle mounts. Each connection has to be flawless—not just tight, but perfect. A mistake could turn a 75,000-pound convoy into a deadly missile on the highway.

I'll always remember my first attempt at stacking trucks. The clang of the tools echoed in my ears as I worked under the scorching sun, sweat dripping down my face and stinging my eyes. My hands trembled as I tightened the bolts on the saddle mount, double-checking and triple-checking every connection. After securing the last truck, I stepped back to admire my work: three rusted semis hitched together, ready to roll.

The first drive was nerve-wracking. As I pulled onto the open road, the weight of the load pressed down on me—not just the physical weight of the trucks, but the responsibility of keeping them—and everyone else—safe. The rigs groaned and creaked with every turn, and each bump in the road sent a jolt of tension up my spine as the trucks whipped this way and that. My hands gripped the wheel tightly, and I scanned every mirror and gauge. But as the miles stretched on, something shifted. I found a rhythm, a calm amid the chaos. The engine's hum and the steady beat of the tires on the asphalt became almost meditative.

What drew me to piggybacking was the potential. Unlike being an owner-operator, piggybacking offered the opportunity to earn well without the crushing financial burden of owning and maintaining the trucks. I let out a low whistle the first time I saw my paycheck. The money was good—better than I'd ever made before. But it wasn't just about the income. It was about the sense of accomplishment. I wasn't just hauling loads—I was mastering a craft.

Over time, I saw my path more clearly. I realized I didn't want to work under someone else's authority forever. I discovered a growing desire to run my own business, and with every successful haul, that ambition grew stronger. After gaining experience and building connections, I finally took the leap and started my own driveaway company.

## The Turning Point: How I Transformed Hard Work into a Thriving Company

Starting the business was both exciting and terrifying. I filed the paperwork to run under my own authority, hired my first drivers, and took on the tremendous responsibility of managing a team. At first, it felt like I was juggling a hundred things at once—driver schedules, meeting regulations, finding contracts, and fixing problems whenever a truck broke down. But over time, what seemed like chaos became a system, and that system led to success.

One of my earliest clients became the foundation of that success. They purchased 1,000 trucks a year and trusted my team to haul every single one. I still remember the day I closed that deal. His office was small, the air thick with the scent of freshly brewed coffee and the faint musk of new carpet. My heart pounded as I laid out my pitch, hands slightly damp with nerves, but my voice steady. When the handshake came—firm and confident—I knew it was a game-changer.

Managing that account was no small feat. We moved each truck with precision and care, meticulously coordinating schedules to meet all deadlines. But we delivered—every time. My team and I proved ourselves through consistency and reliability; the reward wasn't just financial. It was the trust and respect of an industry that doesn't hand either out lightly.

In those early days of running my company, revenue soared—six figures a month. It was more money than I had ever dreamed of earning, but the true fulfillment wasn't in the paycheck. It was in the pride of building something from the ground up—something that was truly mine. For the first time, I felt like I was living the dream and creating generational wealth.

But the dream came with its share of challenges. Managing drivers wasn't just about assigning routes—it was about understanding people, building trust, and solving problems before they became disasters. One broken-down rig in the middle of nowhere could ripple through the entire operation, throwing schedules into chaos and straining client relationships. I learned to think on my feet, adapt to the unexpected, and stay calm under pressure.

Regulations were another constant hurdle. The trucking industry is a maze of rules and requirements, and staying compliant requires meticulous attention to detail. I spent countless nights poring over documents, the glow of my laptop screen the only light in the room, while Rachel slept soundly in the next room. The stakes were high, but so was the payoff.

Looking back, entering the world of piggyback trucking wasn't just a career move—it was a turning point in my life. It was the moment I stopped being just another driver and started building something of my own. The lessons I learned on the road—discipline, attention to detail, resilience—became the foundation of my business.

But more than that, piggybacking taught me the value of taking risks. It's easy to stay where it's comfortable, to stick to what you know. But stepping into the unknown, whether it's hauling your first piggyback load or starting your own company, is where growth happens. The Bellingers taught me the technical skills I needed to succeed, but the road taught me something even more valuable: to trust my abilities, bet on myself, and pursue opportunities aligned with my goals and values.

When I look back on those days, I see not just hard work but transformation. I see the trucks I hauled, the miles I drove, and the business I built as proof that the limits we see are often the ones we place on ourselves. Breaking through them is never easy, but it's always worth it.

## The Crash During COVID: When the Foundation Crumbled

Then COVID-19 hit, and everything I had worked so hard to build came to a screeching halt. One day, my business thrived, humming with the steady rhythm of contracts and deliveries. The next day, I felt the life drained from the company. The pandemic wasn't just a disruption—it was a seismic shift that sent shockwaves rippling through the entire trucking industry. My customers, who primarily dealt with used trucks, stopped buying altogether.

At first, I didn't fully grasp the scale of what was happening. Supply chain disruptions started slowly, like a faint tremor before an earthquake. But soon, part shortages caused massive delays in new truck production, grinding manufacturing lines to a halt. The bottleneck rippled through the industry, leaving transportation companies unable to trade in or sell their old trucks. Without new inventory coming in, the used truck market froze solid.

The effects were immediate and devastating. Prices for used trucks skyrocketed because of the laws of supply and demand, creating a precarious situation for my customers. Holding inventory that was both expensive and unpredictable became a massive risk. I could hear the unease in their voices during phone calls, the uncertainty laced through every word. Most paused purchasing altogether, hoping to ride out the storm. Others weren't as lucky. Some of my long-term clients—the very foundation of my business—succumbed to the financial strain and closed their doors for good.

It felt like the ground beneath me was breaking apart, piece by piece. Hauling trucks was my livelihood, but now my drivers and I were stuck with no trucks to haul. The business I had poured my heart into had come to a complete stop. An overwhelming silence replaced the steady flow of opportunities I once relied on.

Desperation crept in, an insidious companion that clouded my judgment. I couldn't sit back and do nothing—I had people depending on me—my drivers, family, and employees. I felt the weight pressing on my chest like a boulder I couldn't push off. In that pressure cooker environment, I made a decision that felt like the only option. I dipped into my savings and used them to purchase a fleet of trucks and trailers, hoping to create opportunities where none seemed to exist.

I told myself it was a bold move—a calculated risk entrepreneurs take when faced with adversity. I owned seven pieces of equipment outright, and for a moment, that felt like a solid foundation from which to build. But as weeks turned into months and the market remained frozen, I realized it wasn't enough. Revenues dwindled, the cost of maintaining the equipment mounted, and my "bold move" began to feel more like a gamble I couldn't win.

Desperate to stay afloat, I took the next step: I used those assets as collateral to secure loans, funneling the borrowed money into more purchases. Each transaction felt like a temporary lifeline—a chance to buy more time until the market rebounded. I convinced myself it was only a matter of months before things returned to normal. But normal never came.

Instead, I found myself trapped in a vicious cycle. The loans stacked up faster than I could pay them down. The equipment I had believed would provide flexibility and control became a financial burden. Maintenance costs soared, interest rates loomed overhead like dark clouds, and the weight of it all pressed down on me. What had started as a plan to save my business now felt like quicksand—each step forward only pulled me deeper, with no clear way out.

I remember sitting at my kitchen table one night, staring at a stack of overdue bills. The room was silent, save for the faint hum of the refrigerator, and the darkness outside the window mirrored the storm brewing inside me. With unanswered questions racing through my mind, I gripped a long, cold mug of coffee. How had it come to this? How had the dream I had built with so much care become a nightmare I couldn't escape?

I learned some hard truths during that time—truths that cut deep. Desperation distorts your perspective, making options that seem rational at the moment appear incredibly risky in hindsight. I had acted out of fear and a deep need to protect what I had built—and the people who depended on me. But in my attempt to shield my business from the storm, I had walked straight into another one.

The crash during COVID-19 wasn't just a financial disaster; it was a personal reckoning. Watching my business teetering on the edge of collapse felt like a punch to the gut—an ache that followed me everywhere. I had built something I was proud of, something that represented years of sacrifice and hard work. Watching it unravel was like losing a part of myself.

Yet, that period forced me to confront some of the most fundamental aspects of who I was. It challenged my resilience, tested my adaptability, and demanded that I redefine what success truly meant. I had to learn, painfully, that even the best-laid plans can fall apart. That survival sometimes means knowing when to hold on—and when to let go.

The pandemic taught me that success isn't just about growth—it's about sustainability. It's about making decisions that align with long-term goals, even when the short-term feels uncertain. It's about having the humility to admit when a strategy isn't working and the courage to pivot, even if it means starting over.

Looking back now, I realize that the crash wasn't the end of my journey—it was a detour, one I didn't expect but one that taught me lessons I carry with me to this day. Sometimes, the road to success isn't a straight line. Sometimes, it's full of sharp turns, steep climbs, and unexpected setbacks. But if there's one thing I've learned, it's this: resilience isn't about avoiding failure—it's about rising after the fall.

## A Crooked Insurance Agent: Betrayal and the Lessons It Taught Me

Just when I thought the struggles couldn't get any worse, the next blow came from an angle I never expected—betrayal. After the financial strain of the COVID-19 crash, I thought I was steadying the ship. But I was about to learn a hard business lesson: trust must be earned; it's not simply given.

It all started with my driveaway insurance policy renewal, which I handled with little thought. Like most business owners, I trusted my insurance agent to guide me. He had previously managed my coverage, and I assumed he had my best interests at heart.

When my policy was up for renewal, the agent pitched me a new idea: merge my driveaway policy with my freight policy. He presented it as a streamlined solution that would simplify my coverage while saving me money. On paper, it made perfect sense. He walked me through the process, sending over detailed documents that appeared legitimate. His tone was smooth, his explanations confident, and I trusted his expertise without hesitation. When he instructed me to wire $5,000 to complete the coverage, I didn't think twice. I signed the paperwork and sent the money, confident that my business was still protected.

For months, everything seemed fine. The trucks were moving, the drivers were working, and the insurance policy sat in the back of my mind, as it always had. But then, disaster struck.

My father-in-law, one of my deck drivers, had been involved in an accident. He was transporting a set of four piggybacked trucks when he sideswiped a tractor-trailer parked on the shoulder of the road. Thankfully, no one was injured, but the damage to my customers' vehicles was significant. My heart sank as I listened to the details, but I reassured myself that accidents happen—and that's what insurance is for.

The following day, I submitted a claim, expecting the process to unfold as it always had. But instead of a swift resolution, I was blindsided by a denial. The insurance company informed me that my policy didn't cover driveaway operations. The words barely made sense at first—of course, I had driveaway coverage. I'd paid for it. I'd signed for it. But as the conversation unfolded, the horrifying truth came to light: the agent had never added the driveaway coverage to my policy.

I felt my stomach drop, a sickening wave of dread washing over me. I searched through my files, retrieving the documents he had sent, only to discover they were forged. The carefully crafted paperwork I had trusted turned out to be nothing but a facade. That $5,000 wire transfer I had sent to complete the policy had gone straight into his pocket.

The realization hit like a punch to the gut. I had been conned. And the consequences were catastrophic.

The fallout was swift and brutal. Not only did the insurance company deny my claim, but they also dropped me entirely. In the trucking industry, losing your insurance isn't just a setback—it's a death sentence. Operating without coverage is illegal, and I couldn't haul a load without insurance. My business came to a grinding halt.

I remember sitting in my truck that night, staring at the empty parking lot, my hands trembling with anger and despair. How could this have happened? How had I trusted someone who would betray me so completely? I replayed every interaction with the agent, searching for warning signs I might have missed. But hindsight, as they say, is 20/20.

The financial strain was crushing. I now had to find a new insurance provider, a process made infinitely more difficult by the black mark of being dropped from my previous policy. On top of that, I was still dealing with the fallout from the accident—repair costs, lost contracts, and the mounting pressure of keeping my business alive. Every day felt like a battle, and the weight of it all was almost too much to bear.

But the financial toll wasn't the only damage done. The betrayal cut deeper than money. It was personal. I had placed my faith in someone who had lied to me and jeopardized everything I had worked so hard to build. My drivers, my family, my livelihood—all hung in the balance because of one man's greed.

The emotional toll rippled through every part of my life. Nights became sleepless marathons of worry, my mind racing with worst-case scenarios. My wife, Rachel, tried to comfort me, but the strain was palpable. I felt like I had let everyone down as if I had failed to protect those who relied on me.

Looking back, I realize that as painful as this chapter was, it taught me some of the most valuable lessons of my career. First, trust isn't something you give freely in business—it has to be earned and verified. I had mistakenly assumed someone's past behavior guaranteed their future actions. I had let myself believe that expertise equaled integrity. Now, I know better.

I also learned the importance of due diligence. It's not enough to take someone's word at face value, no matter how convincing they seem. You must dig deeper, ask the hard questions, and double-check every detail. It's uncomfortable but far less uncomfortable than the fallout from blind trust.

That experience was a turning point for me. It forced me to adopt a more cautious, measured approach to every business decision. I began vetting partners and contractors with a fine-tooth comb, leaving no room for doubt or ambiguity. The sting of that betrayal sharpened my instincts and strengthened my resolve to protect what I had built.

Ultimately, that crooked insurance agent didn't just teach me a lesson about business—he taught me resilience. He forced me to confront the cracks in my system and rebuild them stronger than before. While I wouldn't wish that experience on anyone, I can say this: it didn't break me. It made me more vigilant, determined, and committed to ensuring my business would not only survive but thrive.

Reflecting on that chapter, I see it as a hard-earned lesson in trust, vigilance, and perseverance. Though the scars from that betrayal still linger, they are a testament to how far I've come—and how much stronger I've become because of it.

## A Perfect Storm of Challenges

The trucking industry is unforgiving even in the best of times, but during this chapter of my life, it felt like the universe was conspiring against me. Each challenge piled on like bricks on my chest, threatening to suffocate the business I had built from the ground up.

## Soaring Diesel Prices

The next major blow came with the relentless surge in diesel prices. When fuel costs skyrocketed to $5.50 a gallon during the Biden administration, it felt like someone had tightened a noose around my finances. Every mile traveled burned away fuel and the little profit I had left.

I'd stand at the gas pump, watching the numbers climb higher with each gallon, my stomach sinking with every click of the meter. Jobs that had once provided a decent return no longer broke even. It was brutal. Every load became a financial balancing act, and the margin for error disappeared entirely.

I started obsessively tracking every expense, desperate to cut back wherever I could. But no matter how meticulous I became, there was no escaping the reality of those inflated diesel prices. The trucks had to run, the drivers had to be paid, and I had to keep the business moving, no matter how razor-thin the margins became.

## The Damage Claim That Tipped the Scales

As if the fuel crisis wasn't challenging enough, another blow came from a damage claim tied to a high-value equipment shipment. One of my owner-operators had delivered the load, and everything seemed fine—until the broker came calling.

## FROM **BROKEN** TO **BLESSED**

I was furious when I learned of the claim. The broker immediately blamed me for the damage, even though the receiver dragged the equipment out of the trailer with a forklift, slammed it to the ground, and continued scraping it across the pavement. None of that mattered to the broker. To them, I was ultimately responsible.

Their verdict set off a devastating chain reaction. First, they withheld payment for the load. Because I had already factored that invoice to get an advance, I was now on the hook for the amount owed to the factoring company. To make matters worse, I had already paid my owner-operator for completing the job. The money was gone, leaving me scrambling to cover the shortfall.

But the fallout didn't end there. The broker also barred me from hauling additional freight for them until the consignee resolved the claim. Losing a major broker is devastating in the trucking industry. They were a consistent and lucrative source of work. Without them, it felt like a dagger to the heart of my business.

I remember those phone calls vividly—hours spent trying to reason with the broker, explaining that I couldn't afford to wait months for a resolution. My voice was steady, but my hands trembled as I gripped the phone, stress coursing through me like an electric current. No matter how clearly I laid out the urgency of the situation, their response was always the same: "Policy is policy." They insisted their hands were tied until the claim worked its way through the system.

Frustrated but determined, I shifted my focus to the consignee, repeatedly urging them to cooperate with my insurance company to expedite the process. But my appeals fell on deaf ears. They refused to take action, stalling for months. Nine agonizing months passed with no progress—until they abandoned the matter entirely.

Looking back, their motives became clear. By dragging out the process, they avoided paying the transportation bill altogether. What felt at the time like incompetence was, in reality, a calculated tactic to sidestep their responsibilities.

## Insurance Woes and Mounting Pressure

As all this unfolded, another devastating blow loomed on the horizon: my insurance company announced they were dropping my policy. Without insurance, my business couldn't legally operate. The timing couldn't have been worse. My finances were already in disarray, and now I was scrambling to find a new insurer willing to take me on during a crisis.

The desperation was suffocating. I spent countless nights staring at my laptop, scouring the internet for coverage, poring over dense policy documents, and sending out frantic inquiries. The glow of the screen was the only light in the room, casting long shadows on the walls as I worked deep into the night. Rachel would often peek in, her eyes heavy with worry, her presence a silent reminder of the stakes we were up against. But I had no answers. The pressure felt insurmountable, like racing against a clock I couldn't see.

## Signing Onto Other Companies

With no other options, I made the decision I had fought hard to avoid: I signed my trucks onto other companies to operate under their authority. It felt like a last resort, a reluctant surrender of the independence I had spent years building.

Initially, I hoped this arrangement would buy me some time to get back on my feet. But the reality was far worse than I had imagined. The margins under these agreements were razor-thin, barely enough to cover costs. Worse yet, the logistics were a constant headache. By handing over control of my trucks, I had tied my success to companies whose priorities didn't always align with mine.

Delays plagued the jobs, miscommunication was rampant, and every day seemed to bring fresh frustrations. What I had envisioned as a temporary lifeline quickly devolved into a nightmare that tested my patience, resolve, and belief in the business I had worked so hard to build.

# FROM **B**ROKEN TO **B**LESSED

It was humbling, to say the least. I had gone from running a thriving business to working under someone else's authority while desperately trying to hold together the crumbling pieces of what I had built.

## A Risky Pivot to the Oil Fields

In a last-ditch effort to save my business, I pivoted again—this time to the oil fields. Hauling sand to frac sites in New Mexico seemed like a promising opportunity, with the allure of high payouts and steady work. Fracking operations required constant sand deliveries, and I convinced myself this could be the break I needed, the chance to turn everything around.

But the oil fields were as harsh and unforgiving as they were unpredictable, especially during the dead of winter. No matter how high the truck heaters were turned up, the relentless cold seeped into the cabs, chilling my drivers to the bone. Crossing a creek required chaining tires, and the bitter wind howled endlessly, cutting through every layer of clothing. The freezing nights were brutal, and the cold wreaked havoc on equipment, causing breakdowns at the worst possible moments.

For an entire month, I kept two trucks on standby 24/7, ready to haul sand at a moment's notice. However, the frozen ground refused to cooperate with the drilling attempts, delaying the work. My drivers and I waited on edge, the hours dragging as we hoped for calls that never came. The few loads we managed to haul didn't even begin to cover the costs of keeping the operation running.

Then, as if to twist the knife, the company I was working with sent me an invoice—for $4,000. The reason? I hadn't hauled enough loads to pay for the trailer rentals and insurance costs. That bill felt like a slap in the face, a cruel punchline to an already devastating chapter.

## The Weight of It All

By this point, the stress had become unbearable. Every problem felt like an insurmountable mountain, and I no longer had the strength to climb. The soaring diesel prices, the mounting damage claims, the endless insurance battles, and the oil field debacle had left me battered and beaten. It felt like I was locked in a losing battle—throwing everything I had into the ring, only to watch it slip through my fingers.

Yet, even in my darkest moments, a tiny spark refused to extinguish—a stubborn belief that I could navigate this storm. I had faced challenges before, and while this was unlike anything I had ever encountered, I clung to the hope that, somehow, some way, I would survive.

This chapter of my life was a perfect storm of trials—a relentless test of my resilience and determination. Looking back now, I can see how every setback shaped me, forcing me to adapt, learn, and grow in ways I never imagined. But in the thick of it, all I could do was hold on and pray for the storm to pass.

## The Breaking Point

When I reached my breaking point, it felt like I was trying to keep a sinking ship afloat with a bucket that had no bottom. Money was pouring out faster than I could patch the holes, and no matter how frantically I scrambled to stay ahead, the tide kept rising.

I remember the suffocating anxiety that gripped me as I sat at my desk late into the night, staring at numbers that refused to add up no matter how many times I recalculated. The glow of my laptop screen illuminated the grim reality—stacks of unpaid invoices and overdue notices piled high, each one a glaring reminder of how far things had spiraled out of control. My hands trembled as I typed emails to creditors, making promises I wasn't sure I could keep, hoping against hope that they'd give me just a little more time.

# FROM **B**ROKEN TO **B**LESSED

## Borrowing to Stay Afloat

Payroll deadlines were the sharpest knife. My drivers were my responsibility, and the thought of them not getting paid was unbearable. I borrowed against everything I could—business loans, personal loans, lines of credit—just to ensure they received their checks on time. Each loan felt like signing away another piece of myself, another fragment of my future.

But the debts began piling up faster than I could manage. Every time I borrowed, the repayment terms grew harsher. Interest rates soared, deadlines tightened, and the patience of lenders wore thin. I signed personal guarantees on several loans—a decision I would come to regret more deeply than I could have ever imagined. At the time, it felt like the only option, a desperate attempt to keep the business alive just a little longer.

## Losing It All

When the defaults hit, the repercussions were swift and brutal. The banks wasted no time coming after me. One by one, they reclaimed everything I had poured my heart into—the trucks, the trailers, the very things that once rumbled with promise and carried the weight of my dreams. In their place was only emptiness, where my hard-earned success used to stand. Watching those rigs being hauled away was gut-wrenching. Years of sweat, sacrifice, and dreams vanished into the distance.

One cold morning, I stood there, watching a tow truck hitch up one of my rigs. The driver wouldn't meet my eyes. I wanted to scream, to argue, to somehow reverse what was happening—but I was speechless. The bank owned it now. My chest felt hollow as I stood there, arms crossed tightly against the chill, fighting back tears that burned at the edges of my vision.

## The Personal Fallout

What happened next was even worse. The personal guarantees I had signed on those loans made me a target. Courts issued judgments against me, and creditors drained my accounts one-by-one. It started with the business accounts. One morning, I logged into my bank to find a balance of zero. They seized every dollar. The notification from the bank was cold and impersonal, but the reality of it hit like a gut punch.

Then they came for my personal finances. They froze my PayPal, Venmo, and Cash App accounts—accounts I had relied on for day-to-day transactions—and wiped out their balances. I tried to stay composed, to think logically about what to do next, but each notification chipped away at my resolve.

## Losing It All

The final blow came a few months later when they drained the last of my personal checking account. I sat in stunned silence, staring at the transaction history on my screen. The words "legal hold" appeared next to the withdrawal, a tidy euphemism for taking everything I had left. It wasn't just about the money—it was the sheer helplessness of it all. Everything I had worked so hard to build had crumbled in a matter of months.

## From Stability to Chaos

Just two years earlier, I had been in a position of strength. My credit score was above 750, my savings account was healthy, and my business account held multiple six-figure balances. We were generating six figures a month in revenue, and I had no credit card debt weighing me down. Back then, I felt invincible, like I had cracked the code to success.

Now, I was unrecognizable to myself. Suits were being filed against me, judgments were stacking up, and I felt like I was drowning in a sea of obligations I could never hope to fulfill. Every time my phone buzzed with a new notification, my stomach would twist, dreading yet another creditor demanding money I didn't have.

## The Emotional Toll

The stress was all-consuming. Sleep became a distant memory as I lay awake at night, staring at the ceiling, my mind racing with calculations, contingency plans, and worst-case scenarios. I tried to act like everything was fine when Rachel or the kids were around, but the cracks in my façade were starting to show. There were days when the weight felt unbearable—I couldn't summon the energy to pretend anymore.

I'd sit in the kitchen during the early hours of the morning, the coffee growing cold in my hands, feeling utterly defeated. The silence was deafening, broken only by the occasional hum of the refrigerator. It wasn't supposed to go like this. I had worked so hard and sacrificed so much, yet here I was—stripped of everything I had built, left with nothing but a mountain of debt and a trail of broken dreams.

## The Hard Lessons

Looking back, I can now see the warning signs I missed, the mistakes I made, and how desperation clouded my judgment. Signing those personal guarantees had felt like a necessary evil at the time, but they became a noose around my neck when the business faltered.

This period taught me some of the hardest lessons I've ever faced. I learned that success can vanish as quickly as it arrives and that even the most carefully laid plans can unravel when unexpected challenges arise. I learned that resilience isn't just about pushing through tough times—it's about facing the painful reality of your situation and figuring out how to rebuild from the ground up.

The breaking point was devastating, but it also marked the beginning of a new chapter. It forced me to reevaluate my business, my decisions, and my priorities. And while it felt like the end of the road, it was, in fact, just the beginning of a new journey.

## Starting Over

Filing for bankruptcy wasn't just a financial decision—it was a profoundly personal reckoning. As I sat at the table, staring down at the papers, the pen in my hand felt impossibly heavy. It wasn't just ink and paper—it was every hope and dream I'd poured into my business over the years, all crumbling in real-time. My chest tightened as I scribbled my name on the lines, the sound of the pen scratching against the paper somehow deafening. My pulse pounded in my ears, and I could feel the heat rising in my face as shame washed over me.

The attorney across from me cleared her throat softly, breaking the silence. "You're doing what you have to do," she said, her voice low and even, but it sounded hollow. I nodded without looking up. What could I say to that? It didn't feel like I was doing what I had to do—it felt like I was surrendering.

I couldn't stop the thought from clawing into my mind: I've failed. I've let everyone down—my family, my employees, myself. I thought of Rachel, who had believed in me every step of the way, of Gabriel, and my daughter, whom I had promised to provide for. My signature on that line felt like admitting I couldn't keep those promises. My hands shook as I put the pen down.

Later that night, when I got home, Rachel was waiting for me in the kitchen. The light above the sink cast a soft glow over the room, but everything felt heavy, like the air had thickened. I dropped my keys on the counter and stood there momentarily, unable to speak. She stepped closer, searching my face.

"What's wrong?" she asked gently, though I knew she already had an idea.

"It's done," I said, my voice rough and quiet. I avoided her gaze. "The bankruptcy... it's done."

Her expression softened, and she reached for my hand. "You did what you had to do," she said, echoing the attorney's words from earlier. But this time, they didn't sound hollow. There was no judgment in her voice—only understanding.

I pulled my hand away and sank into the chair at the table, burying my face in my hands. My voice broke as I admitted, "I don't know how this happened. I worked so hard. I gave everything I had to make this work. And now it's all gone—the business, the savings, the trucks—everything. I've failed."

"You haven't failed," she whispered, kneeling beside me. "You're still here. We're still here. This is just a test. Not the end."

I wanted to believe her, but the weight of the day pressed harder. Filing for bankruptcy wasn't just about numbers or debts—it was a public declaration of defeat. It's one thing to fail in private, to struggle quietly behind closed doors. But this was different. This was official. Permanent. Undeniable.

I'd spent years building something I was proud of—a thriving business, a steady income, financial freedom. And now, all of that was gone. I wasn't just starting over from zero; I was starting from less than zero, burdened by debts I couldn't pay, obligations I couldn't meet, and the crushing weight of disappointment.

That night, after Rachel had gone to bed, I sat alone at the kitchen table, staring into the darkness. The hum of the refrigerator was the only sound, louder than usual, almost mocking the silence that enveloped me. I clasped my hands together, resting my forehead against them, and let the tears come.

"I worked so hard for this," I whispered to no one. "Why wasn't it enough?"

The question hung in the air, unanswered. Late nights, endless miles, and years of sacrifices flooded my mind. I thought of my employees and drivers, their faith in me. I thought of Uncle Mike and my promise to honor his memory by living purposefully. And I thought of the younger version of myself—the boy who had dared to dream of breaking free from the cycle of struggle he was born into. I felt like I'd let them all down.

As the hours passed, a quiet realization took root. Fragile, small, but steady—I was still here. The business had crumbled; the savings were gone, but I was still standing. And as long as I had air in my lungs and a heart beating in my chest, I wouldn't give up. I would fight.

Sitting there in the stillness, I made myself a promise: this would not be the final chapter of my story. I didn't know how I was going to rebuild, but I knew I had to try. Not just for me but for Rachel, the kids, and that boy who had once dreamed of more.

I would fight—for the future of my family, for the promise I made to my dead uncle, and for that scarred, neglected, hungry little boy who still lingers in the corners of my memories.

I leaned back in my chair, closed my eyes, and prayed. "God," I whispered into the silence, tears streaming down my face. "I don't know what to do. I don't know where to go from here. But I'm still here. Please show me the way. God, give me strength to persevere and help me find peace in the chaos."

It wasn't a prayer that brought instant clarity or struck like a bolt of lightning. But in the stillness that followed, a sense of quiet resolve stirred within me. I thought of Rachel's words: This is just a test. Not the end.

"Rachel's right," I murmured, my voice barely audible over the hum of the refrigerator. "This isn't the end."

And then I thought of my children. Gabriel and my daughter didn't care about bankruptcy filings or repossessions. I wasn't a failed business owner to them—I was their dad. My presence, my love, and my ability to provide security mattered more to them than anything else. They didn't need six-figure revenues or a fleet of trucks. They needed me.

"Starting over isn't the same as giving up," I said aloud as if saying it would make it real. And as I sat there, the weight on my chest lifted just a little. My faith gave me the strength to stand, and my family gave me the purpose to keep going. Maybe Rachel was right. Perhaps this was just a reset. Maybe I hadn't failed after all.

# FROM **B**ROKEN TO **B**LESSED

## The Stigma of Failure

What they don't tell you about bankruptcy is how isolating it can feel. The shame is suffocating, like a heavy fog that settles into every corner of your mind. I replayed every decision and every risk, dissecting where I had gone wrong. I thought about the loans I shouldn't have taken, the trust I shouldn't have placed in others, and the warning signs I had ignored. It was like reliving the collapse in slow motion, but I couldn't do anything to stop it this time.

For someone who had built a thriving business from scratch and tasted the satisfaction of success, losing everything felt like losing a part of my identity. Who was I without the company I had poured my heart into? Without the six-figure monthly revenue, the confidence that came with knowing I was providing for my family, and the pride of creating something that was mine? Those questions haunted me, gnawing at the edges of my resolve.

## A Lifetime of Resilience

But if there's one thing I've learned, it's how to survive. My childhood was a masterclass in resilience. I grew up in a home filled with instability, my mother's constant negativity acting as a steady drumbeat in the background, and my father's absence leaving a void I had to fill on my own. I learned early on how to adapt, find strength in the chaos, and keep moving forward—even when the odds seemed impossibly stacked against me.

Those experiences became the foundation I leaned on during this time. Filing for bankruptcy was humbling, but it wasn't the end. I refused to let it be. The pain of starting over wasn't unfamiliar to me—it was just another mountain to climb, another challenge to overcome. And even though the path ahead seemed impossibly steep, I knew I had to put one foot in front of the other.

## Rebuilding from the Ground Up

Starting over meant stripping everything down to the basics. The first few steps felt small, almost insignificant, but they were all I could manage. I took stock of what I could control and focused on rebuilding from there. Each small victory—a bill paid, a new opportunity explored—felt like a step forward, a glimmer of hope in the darkness.

The hardest part wasn't the work itself; it was rebuilding my confidence. Bankruptcy shakes you to your core, questioning your decisions and worth. I had to remind myself daily that my past failures didn't define me. I'd built something great once, and I could do it again.

## The Anchor of Family

Through it all, my family became my anchor. Rachel and the kids were the reason I got out of bed every morning and pushed forward, even when it felt like the weight of the world was crushing me. No matter how bad things got, I was determined to shield them from the worst of it.

I promised myself my family would never feel the full brunt of this financial chaos. They would never miss a meal or go without what they needed. That promise became my North Star, guiding me through the darkest days. There were nights when I'd sit at the kitchen table after everyone had gone to bed, running through the numbers, searching for ways to stretch every dollar. The overhead light buzzed faintly—the only sound in an otherwise silent house—as I strategized and planned, determined to hold it all together for them.

## Wrestling with Doubt

Still, there were moments of crushing doubt. There were nights when the weight of it all felt unbearable, and I couldn't see a way out. I wondered if I'd ever recover. The shame and regret crept in like shadows, whispering that I wasn't good enough and didn't have what it took to climb out of this hole.

But I've been in the darkness before. I've stared down impossible situations and clawed my way forward. I reminded myself that survival is in my DNA. If I could endure the hardships of my childhood, the grind of building a business from scratch, and the betrayals and setbacks that brought me to this point, I could survive this, too.

## Hard Lessons and Harder Truths

The road back has been challenging, but it's been full of lessons I never wanted to learn but desperately needed. Bankruptcy taught me to be more cautious, to value stability over speed, and never to let pride stop me from asking for help. It taught me to appreciate minor victories, to lean on the people who genuinely care about me, and never to stop fighting for the future I want for my family.

This experience also forced me to redefine what success means. It's not just about the numbers in a bank account or the size of a business. True success is about resilience—recovering after life knocks you down. It's about creating a life filled with purpose, love, and determination, no matter the circumstances.

## A New Beginning

Starting over has been the hardest thing I've ever done, but it's also been the most transformative. It's taught me that even in the face of devastation, there's always a way forward if you're willing to fight for it. I've come to see this chapter not as an ending but as the beginning of something new.

The work of rebuilding continues one step at a time. And while the path ahead is still uncertain, I'm walking it with a renewed sense of purpose. My family, my future, and my faith are worth every ounce of effort I can give. Starting over isn't just about survival—it's about proving to myself that I can still build something great. And this time, I'll do it with the hard-earned wisdom gained from weathering the storm.

## Trust, But Verify: A Lesson Paid in Betrayal

One of the most painful lessons I learned during my journey was the difference between trust and blind trust. In business, trust is essential, but when it's misplaced, the consequences can be devastating. I've always believed in the good intentions of others, often giving people the benefit of the doubt. However, I learned that not everyone operates with integrity, and trusting without verifying can lead to disaster.

Whether it was the crooked insurance agent who forged my documents or the tough choices I faced, I learned an important lesson: trust has to be earned, not assumed. Now, I approach trust like a contract. I don't take anyone at their word without evidence to back it up. I ask hard questions, dig into the details, and only sign something after fully understanding the fine print. It's not about being cynical—it's about being wise.

For others, this lesson is just as vital. Whether hiring a new employee, partnering with a vendor, or signing any agreement, take the time to verify everything. Check references, ask questions, and get a second opinion if you need further clarification. Trust is an invaluable currency in business, but when misplaced, it can cost you far more than you realize. By making trust something you verify, not just assume, you protect yourself, your business, and your future.

Trust is invaluable, but so is vigilance. That lesson didn't just save me from future disasters—it empowered me to rebuild with wisdom and confidence. By making trust something I verify, I've gained the clarity and strength to create a stronger foundation for the future.

## Prepare for the Unexpected

If there's one thing the COVID crash taught me, it's that certainty is an illusion. I once thought I was prepared for the difficulties and trials of running a business. I had a healthy savings account, reliable contracts, and a thriving company. But I didn't have a contingency plan for a global pandemic that would turn the industry upside down.

The supply chain disruptions, the used truck market grinding to a halt, and the skyrocketing diesel prices hit like a tidal wave I couldn't outrun. The situation caught me entirely off guard. Financial reserves aren't just nice to have—they're a lifeline. Proper risk management isn't just a strategy—it's survival.

Now, I approach every decision with a mindset of "What if?" Not out of fear but out of respect for the unpredictable nature of life. What if the market crashes again? What if my primary income stream disappears? What then? What if the worst-case scenario becomes reality? These questions don't paralyze me—they prepare me. Today, I've prioritized diversifying my income streams so no disruption can topple everything I've built again. Building resilience against future downturns is now as integral to my life as building the business itself.

## Never Stop Adapting

Adaptability isn't just a skill—it's a mindset. When COVID hit, I pivoted from hauling trucks to owning equipment and hauling sand to frac sites. None of those pivots worked out in the long run, but I'm proud that I kept trying.

My decisions didn't always lead to success, but they kept me moving forward when fear could have stopped me. Those failures taught me an important lesson: taking calculated risks separates those who survive from those who fail. Adapting doesn't always guarantee success, but refusing to adapt almost always leads to failure.

Now, every challenge is an opportunity to think creatively, to step back and assess, and to find a new way forward. It's not about being fearless—it's about being resourceful. I've learned to move forward anyway, even when fear whispers that the next move might fail.

## Resilience is Everything

Above all, I've learned that resilience isn't just a quality—it's the backbone of true success. There were moments in this journey when I felt like giving up—moments when the weight of failure felt like it would crush me. I questioned whether I had the strength to keep going, whether it was worth trying.

But resilience isn't about ignoring the pain. It's about facing it head-on. It's about acknowledging heartbreak, fear, and regret, and choosing to move forward. Resilience doesn't mean you don't break; it means you get back up after falling.

Those dark moments have been a crucible where I forged strength. I grew every time I pushed through the doubt and found the courage to try again. And that growth has become a deeper form of success than I ever imagined.

## The Bigger Picture

The lessons I've learned—trust, preparation, adaptability, resilience—are no longer just business strategies. They've become guiding principles in every area of my life. They shape how I raise my children, approach relationships, and view challenges.

Looking back, I wouldn't have chosen the struggles I faced, but I wouldn't trade the person they've made me for anything. The hardships didn't just challenge me—they transformed me. They taught me that success isn't about avoiding failure but about what you do after failure. It's about the person you become.

## Moving Forward

Today, I'm rebuilding—not just my business but my life. The road ahead is steep, and there are still days when the weight of past failures feels like it's dragging me down. But I'm more determined than ever to move forward.

Starting over isn't about recreating what I had before—it's about building something more substantial, something wiser. The setbacks I've faced have reshaped my understanding of success. It's no longer about the size of the paycheck or the accolades. True success is about resilience, creating a life that aligns with your values, and building something meaningful using the lessons you've learned.

I'm driven now by a new vision—not just for myself, but for my family. They've stood by me through the darkest days, offering unwavering support and love. My wife and children are my reason for pushing forward, my reminder that setbacks are not the end of the story. I want to show my kids that failure isn't something to fear—it's something to learn from. It's a stepping stone, not a roadblock.

This time, I'm building with intention. The hard-earned lessons from the past inform every decision I make. I'm focusing on long-term stability rather than short-term gains, surrounding myself with people and opportunities that reflect my values. The road ahead is uncertain, but I'm no longer afraid of uncertainty. I've faced it before, and I'll face it again.

The most important thing I've realized is this: I'm not starting from scratch—I'm starting from experience. Each failure and setback has equipped me with the tools necessary for success. They've given me wisdom, perspective, and strength.

As I rebuild, I often think back to the promise I made to myself all those years ago—to rise above my circumstances and create a life defined not by struggle but by purpose. That promise carried me through sleepless nights, endless sacrifices, and moments of despair. And even now, as I start over, that promise remains my anchor. It reminds me that no matter how many times I fall, I owe it to myself and the younger version of me who dared to dream to keep rising. Dreams might fade, despair might come, but the promise I made to myself endures. It's my commitment to never give up, no matter how steep the climb.

### Moving Forward: Reinvention and Legacy

Moving forward is about more than just recovery—it's about reinvention. It's about creating a legacy of resilience and determination for my children. It's about proving that no matter how often life knocks me down, I will always find the strength to get back up.

The journey isn't over, and the challenges haven't disappeared. But what has changed is me. I'm stronger, more thoughtful, and more determined than ever. The road ahead may still be long, but it's filled with possibility—and I'm ready for it.

My hardships have reshaped my outlook on success and life. The lessons I've learned—about trust, adaptability, resilience, and preparation—have prepared me for whatever comes next. And while I can't predict the future, I know one thing for sure: I won't give up.

Every step I take now is a testament to the grit and determination that carried me through the darkest times. Each move forward is a declaration that failure will not define me—it will shape me into someone stronger.

I've learned that success isn't measured by how high you rise, but by how many times you find the strength to rise again. Starting over isn't failure—it's proof of resilience. And as I rebuild, I'm not just creating a business—I'm building a legacy of perseverance for my children.

I want my kids to know that resilience isn't just about reacting to tough times—it's a mindset. It's about-facing challenges, learning from them, and pushing forward no matter what. That's the legacy I hope to leave: one of hope, strength, and the belief that setbacks don't define us—they prepare us for what's ahead.

No matter how often life knocks me down, I'll keep getting back up. That resilience is the ultimate measure of success. Resilience isn't about avoiding failure; it's about rising after every fall, stronger and wiser than before. And as I rebuild, I'm not just creating a business—I'm building a legacy of perseverance for my children.

# CHAPTER 13:

# BECOMING THE MAN I PRAYED TO BE

Now, onto the best chapters of my life. As an anonymous quote puts it, "If you want to get the woman of your dreams, become the man of hers." For years after graduating high school, I worked on becoming that man. I wanted to be ready for the woman I would one day meet, demonstrating that self-improvement and commitment to personal growth are essential for preparing for future opportunities.

"Luck happens when preparation meets opportunity" — Attributed to Seneca. In 2011, I had the opportunity to meet the most amazing woman. Rachel is not only intelligent and funny, but she also embodies compassion and has an infectious zest for life. She inspires everyone around her, and from the moment we connected, I knew I had found someone extraordinary.

I pursued Rachel for quite some time, dedicating myself to winning her heart with charm and unwavering determination. At first, winning her over seemed like an uphill battle, but I was undeterred. I made it my mission to show her my genuine interest and affection. Through subtle gestures—thoughtful messages, spontaneous outings, and sincere compliments—I aimed to break through her defenses.

Slowly but surely, my persistence paid off. Her walls began to crumble as she opened up to me, revealing glimpses of her true self behind that initial shyness. Each laugh we shared and every conversation brought us closer, solidifying the connection that had once felt so distant. Eventually, I won her over, not only with my charm but with my sincerity, showing her my genuine interest in her happiness. It was a rewarding journey that taught me the value of patience and the importance of truly understanding the person I was pursuing.

## Beyond Blood: Building a Bond with Gabriel

Rachel and I started dating on August 6, 2012. By the time I officially entered her life as more than just a friend, I had already met Gabriel. I had been introduced to him through Rachel before we started dating, and even though we were still finding our footing as a couple, Gabriel and I were already building a budding connection. He was an energetic, curious four-year-old, and though I hadn't yet cemented my place in his life, I knew I wanted to be more than just "Mom's boyfriend." I wanted to show him I wasn't going anywhere—that I was someone he could count on.

Mutual understanding has grounded our relationship. I've made the effort to listen to Gabriel's thoughts and dreams, emphasizing that his voice matters. We've shared countless conversations—some serious, others filled with laughter—creating a safe space where he can truly be himself. Whether we're diving into a discussion about basketball, MMA, or talking about life's challenges, I make it a priority to be present for him.

Shared experiences have brought us closer. Whether playing basketball, attending a WWE or MMA event, or watching a UFC fight or football game at home, each moment has strengthened our bond.

Most importantly, I strive to be a positive role model for him. I want to inspire him to pursue his passions and confidently navigate life's challenges. Watching him mature and come into his own has been one of the greatest joys of my life. We are creating a bond that transcends blood, built on love, respect, and our shared journey.

## Three Roses, One Wrestler, and a Bond Beyond Words

The night I met Rachel's mother and grandmother for the first time felt like a significant milestone. I'd already bonded with Gabriel in small, meaningful ways, but meeting the family felt like an official step forward in this relationship. I wanted to make a good impression—not just for Rachel, but for those who had helped shape her and Gabriel's world.

I arrived that evening clutching three single roses—one for Rachel, one for her mom, and one for her grandmother. The weight of the moment pressed on me as I rang the doorbell. This wasn't just about introductions; it was about showing them that I was serious about Rachel and Gabriel and ready to step into this role with intention and heart.

Rachel opened the door, her smile as radiant as ever, and immediately, some of my nerves melted away. I handed her the first rose, and she looked at me with that exceptional warmth that only Rachel can convey. "They're going to love you," she whispered as she pulled me inside.

Her mom and grandmother greeted me with kind eyes and warm smiles that did a lot to settle my nerves. I handed each of them their roses, their faces lighting up with genuine appreciation. But as we all exchanged pleasantries, there was one person I was still waiting to see—Gabriel.

He came running into the living room shortly after, clutching his ever-present stuffed wrestler. "Dustin!" he shouted, his voice full of excitement. He was already comfortable with me in a way that surprised and encouraged me, and my heart swelled at the sound of his greeting.

"Hey, buddy," I said, crouching down to his level. "What's up? You've been keeping that wrestler in shape, right?"

Gabriel's face lit up with a grin, and he nodded. "He's the best! You think you can beat him?"

"Beat him?" I said, raising an eyebrow and gesturing dramatically. "I don't know. He looks tough. But I can try!"

And just like that, I was in a full-blown living room wrestling match. Gabriel carefully set the stage, ensuring his stuffed wrestler had the upper hand in every round. I played along, groaning and falling dramatically to the floor as the stuffed champion hit me with "flying elbow drops" and "super slams."

The room filled with laughter—his giggles bouncing off the walls as I threw myself onto the carpet in exaggerated defeat. "Alright, alright, you win!" I cried, holding up my hands. "Your guy is unstoppable!"

Gabriel puffed out his chest with pride, holding his stuffed wrestler aloft like a trophy. "Told you he's the best!"

Rachel stood in the doorway, watching us with a smile that spoke volumes. Her mom and grandmother chuckled softly from the couch, sharing knowing looks. They said little, but their expressions told me everything I needed to know—they saw I wasn't just here for Rachel. I was here for Gabriel, too.

## The Turning Point

That night was more than just meeting Rachel's family—it was the night Gabriel and I took a big step forward in our bond. Until then, I think he'd enjoyed having me around, but this felt like the first time we connected on a deeper level. It wasn't about grand gestures or forced conversations. It was about rolling on the floor, pretending to lose to a stuffed wrestler, and letting him know that his world mattered to me.

After the wrestling match, Gabriel plopped down next to me on the carpet, his stuffed wrestler still in hand. "You're coming back tomorrow, right?" he asked, looking at me with the wide-eyed sincerity only a child can manage.

I glanced at Rachel, who smiled softly at the exchange, then looked back at Gabriel. "I'll be back," I said, my voice steady with the weight of my promise. "You can count on it."

## Building a Bond That Lasts

That night, I didn't just make a good impression on Rachel's mom and grandmother—I laid the foundation for something much more profound with Gabriel. From then on, every interaction with him became an opportunity to strengthen our bond. Whether playing hide-and-seek, watching wrestling on TV, or sitting down to talk about his day, I made it my mission to show up for him in ways that truly mattered.

Being a stepfather isn't about replacing anyone or forcing a connection. It's about being present, consistent, and open. That night with the stuffed wrestler showed me that the ordinary moments—the ones filled with laughter and play—are often the ones that matter most. Gabriel didn't need grand gestures or perfect words. He needed someone to step into his world, roll around on the carpet, and let him win.

My bond with Gabriel became a reflection of my own journey—a reminder that love is a choice we make every day and that becoming the man I prayed to be wasn't just about me but about the family I was building. His trust in me pushed me to grow, show up with integrity, and become the role model he deserved.

## A Bond Beyond Blood

Meeting Rachel's family that night was a significant moment, but the memory of wrestling Gabriel's stuffed champion stays with me the most. It marked the beginning of a bond that transcends blood—a bond built on trust, shared laughter, and the unspoken promise that I would always be there for him.

Gabriel became a mirror of my journey—showing me the man I prayed to God I would become. Through him, I learned that family isn't defined by biology, but by the love, we choose to give. It's about showing up, embracing the ordinary moments, and proving through action that love is a daily choice. Together, we've created a relationship that isn't just about roles or titles. It's about being there every day for the moments that matter most.

## From Hesitation to Harmony: The Day I Married My Dream Woman

On August 6, 2016, I stood in the castle courtyard, the grandeur of its stone walls and soaring towers mirroring the monumental moment unfolding in my life. This wasn't just a wedding—it was the realization of a dream I had long carried in my heart, built not on fleeting romance but on a foundation of love, faith, and unwavering commitment. Rachel, the woman of my dreams, stood just a few feet away, radiant in her gown, the soft August sun catching in her hair like a halo. Together, we were about to exchange vows that would forever change our lives. By the grace of God, we were building something extraordinary: a home that would become a sanctuary of love, laughter, and purpose.

The castle embodied everything I felt at that moment. Its timeless beauty and strength mirrored the marriage I had prayed for—a union that would endure, weathering storms and standing tall against the tests of time. Yet, as magical as that day was, the journey wasn't without struggles. It was a journey that required facing my deepest fears, reckoning with the scars of my past, and ultimately trusting that true love was worth the risk.

### Witnessing Broken Vows

My hesitation to propose didn't come from a lack of love for Rachel. If anything, my love for her was so deep, so all-consuming, that it terrified me. My parents' history of broken vows loomed large over me, casting long shadows I couldn't seem to outrun. Between them, my parents had been married seven times, six of those ending in painful divorces. Each failed marriage felt like another brick in the wall I was building around my heart, a defense mechanism against the instability and heartache I had grown up with. My mother, who passed away while still married to her last husband, had lived through more broken commitments than I cared to count. I witnessed firsthand how the unraveling of promises could tear people apart, leaving behind emotional wreckage that wasn't easy to rebuild.

Those experiences shaped my deepest fears. They made me cautious, even skeptical, about marriage. I didn't want to repeat the patterns I'd seen, nor did I want to hurt someone as incredible as Rachel. For years, I carried the belief that marriage was something fragile, something that could shatter under the weight of human imperfection. And yet, as much as I feared failure, I wanted to break the cycle. I wanted to be the husband who honored his vows and fought for his marriage instead of abandoning it at the first sign of trouble. But to do that, I needed to be sure: Rachel was the one and that I was ready to be the man she deserved.

## Turning to Beverly's Wisdom

When indecision became too much to bear, I turned to my Aunt Beverly. Beverly had always been my rock—wise, grounded, and unshakable in her sense of clarity and inner strength. If anyone could help me untangle the knot of emotions I was feeling, it was her. Sitting across from her at the kitchen table, I finally admitted my fears.

"What if I lose Rachel because I'm too afraid to ask her to marry me?" I asked, my voice barely above a whisper. The thought of losing Rachel felt like losing a part of me, but the idea of stepping into marriage with all my doubts felt just as overwhelming.

Beverly didn't hesitate. She looked me straight in the eye and asked the most straightforward, profound question: "Is she the one?"

I didn't have to think about it. "Yes," I said, the word spilling out of me like a truth I'd been holding onto for years. "She's the most amazing woman I've ever met. I'd rather marry her than risk losing her, even if I'm scared and unprepared."

Beverly smiled, her expression both reassuring and challenging. "Then what are you waiting for? Love isn't about waiting until you feel completely prepared. It's about taking a leap and trusting your heart."

Her words stayed with me, echoing as I wrestled with my doubts. I realized that love, like faith, requires a leap. It's not about eliminating fear—it's about choosing to trust, even when fear is present. And so, I made my decision. I was going to ask Rachel to marry me.

## The Proposal and God's Perfect Timing

I proposed to Rachel on December 22, 2014, just a few days before Christmas. Proposing to Rachel felt like a significant step toward becoming the man I prayed to God I wanted to be. In her, I saw the future I had dreamed of—one filled with love, faith, and a sense of purpose. Originally, I planned to ask on Christmas Day, but with her sister Michele in town, I wanted her mother and Michele to be there as well. It felt right—intimate, surrounded by the people who meant the most to her. I remember my palms sweating as I held the ring, my heart racing as I dropped to one knee. But the look on Rachel's face—the surprise, the joy, the giggle, and the love—made every ounce of nervousness worth it. She said yes, and at that moment, I felt the weight of the world lift off my shoulders.

A few weeks later, we discovered Rachel was pregnant with our daughter, Iona. The timing couldn't have been more perfect. If I had waited to propose until after we learned about the pregnancy, Rachel might have thought my proposal was out of obligation. Instead, we knew our commitment was built on love, not circumstance, and that knowledge helped guide us through that season of life. It felt as though God Himself had orchestrated the timing, aligning everything just as it was meant to be.

I must admit that during this period, I had drifted away from my faith—not entirely, as I still prayed, but I wasn't actively attending church. It wasn't until years later, when my wife was invited to a service by her friend Sara while I was away on the road, that we began attending church regularly as a family.

## A Castle Wedding and a Darling Flower Girl

Fast-forward to August 6, 2016. We stood in a castle courtyard, ready to say, "I do." The setting felt like something out of a fairy tale—the stone walls rising high around us, ivy creeping along the edges, and distant birdsong carried on the warm summer breeze. I could feel the weight of history in the air, the echoes of vows exchanged in that place over centuries. And now, it was our turn.

Our daughter, Iona, was our flower girl, just shy of one year old. Barely able to walk, she shuffled down the aisle with the help of our friend Shelia, clutching a tiny basket of petals. She was the most precious flower girl we could have asked for, her rosy cheeks and wide eyes full of curiosity as she took in the spectacle around her. Watching her brought tears to my eyes—a living reminder of everything Rachel and I had built together. She was a symbol of our love, our faith, and the family we were creating.

When Rachel walked down the aisle, my breath caught in my throat. Her gown flowed around her like something from a dream, her smile illuminating the courtyard. As she reached me and we joined hands, all the fear and hesitation I had ever felt melted away. At that moment, I knew with complete clarity that I was exactly where I was meant to be—standing beside the woman God had chosen for me.

As I stood beside Rachel, I felt the weight of those prayers I'd whispered as a boy. I was stepping into the role I had always hoped to fill: a husband, a protector, and a man of faith.

## A Covenant of Forever

Our wedding wasn't just a celebration—it was a covenant. We made promises to each other and to God to honor and cherish one another through every season of life. Standing outside that castle, surrounded by the people we loved most, I felt an overwhelming sense of peace. This was the life I had prayed for, the woman I had dreamed of, and the future I was ready to build.

Looking back, I'm filled with gratitude for the journey that brought us here—the doubts, the lessons, the leap of faith. Each step, though challenging, was necessary to bring us to this moment. By the grace of God, Rachel and I have built a home filled with love and laughter—a sanctuary where our family can thrive.

Reflecting on that day in the castle, I remember something Beverly said: "Love isn't about waiting until you feel completely prepared. It's about taking a leap and trusting your heart." She was right, and I thank God every day that I took that step.

## The Heart of a Father: Cherishing Iona's Spirit and Strength

My daughter, Iona Beverly, is not just my little girl—she is my greatest blessing, my fiercest supporter, and a constant source of joy and inspiration. Since the moment she entered my life, she has been my ride-or-die, the person I can always count on, no matter the task or occasion. Whether we're trekking through the woods as a family on a crisp fall day or distributing food in our pantry to help those in need, she's right there by my side, her small but mighty presence unwavering. Even the most ordinary moments become extraordinary just by having her there.

Iona is pure, unfiltered energy—a radiant bundle of light who seems to carry joy wherever she goes. The moment she steps into a room, the air shifts. There's a warmth, a spark, and an undeniable sense of possibility. Her laughter is infectious, so pure it can lift even the heaviest of hearts. It starts deep in her belly, bubbling up and spilling out in waves, pulling you into her world of happiness. She has a way of making you believe, if only for a moment, that life is as simple and wonderful as she sees it.

Her love for life is unmatched, and her adventurous spirit knows no bounds. Watching her play is like witnessing a work of art come to life. Whether she's racing through the backyard in a game of tag, her hair flying like a banner of freedom, or creating imaginary worlds with her friends, she brings so much energy that it's impossible not to smile. Even a simple game of hide-and-seek becomes an epic adventure, filled with giggles, whispers, and dramatic "Gotcha!" moments.

But it's not just Iona's energy that makes her special—it's her heart. She has a deep compassion and a rare, beautiful ability to see beyond the surface to recognize the needs of others. She notices when someone is feeling down, even if they try to hide it. And when she does, her response is always thoughtful and sincere. Whether it's sharing her favorite toy, writing a heartfelt note, or simply sitting quietly beside someone who needs comfort, she gives herself freely and without hesitation.

I've seen her pick flowers for her mom "just because" or craft little bracelets for her friends, each one personalized with care and intention. She treasures the small things, and in doing so, she makes others feel seen and valued in a way that's both rare and profoundly moving.

As her father, I have the honor of witnessing her spirit up close and helping shape the young woman she is becoming. One of my favorite traditions is our daddy-daughter dates. These outings aren't just about spending time together—they're lessons in how she deserves to be treated. When I pick her up for our dates, I make it a point to arrive with flowers and hold the car door open as she hops in, her grin lighting up her face. Even at this young age, I want her to know that she should always expect to be treated with kindness, respect, and care in every relationship she builds.

During these dates, I give Iona my full attention—no distractions, no phones, just the two of us. Whether we're sharing a milkshake at her favorite diner, wandering through a park with the leaves crunching under our feet, or watching a movie together, I make sure she feels cherished. I listen attentively as she shares her latest school adventures, dreams, or even the small dramas of her day, laughing and nodding along with her animated storytelling. These moments aren't just about making memories—they're about showing her that she matters deeply, that her voice is important, and that she is worthy of love and respect.

Rachel and I work hard to create a home filled with love and respect. Having grown up in homes where arguments and instability were constant, we knew we wanted something different for our family. We've made it a priority to keep our home peaceful, nurturing, and full of warmth. When we disagree, we handle it calmly and respectfully, always away from the kids. There are no yelling, cursing, or slamming doors. We want Iona and Gabriel to grow up knowing that love is about listening, understanding, and working together—not shouting over each other.

Watching Iona grow has been one of the greatest joys of my life. She teaches me something new every day—about love, resilience, and the beauty of seeing the world through fresh, hopeful eyes. When she wraps her little arms around my neck and whispers, "I love you, Daddy," it feels like the rest of the world fades away, leaving just the two of us in that perfect moment.

Iona reminds me of all the best parts of life—kindness, joy, compassion, and connection. She inspires me to be a better man every day. I strive to be the father she can look up to, someone who supports her dreams, guides her through life's challenges, and stands beside her, cheering her on as she grows into the incredible person I know she will be. She is my daughter, my sunshine, my little fighter with a big heart—and I thank God every day for the privilege of being her dad.

## From Broken to Blessed: Embracing Faith and Personal Transformation

When I close my eyes, the boy I see is almost unrecognizable—hungry, hollow-eyed, his clothes mismatched and threadbare. His shoulders slump under the invisible weight of fear, sadness, and neglect. I can still feel the ache in his chest, the sting of tears he refused to shed in front of anyone, and the hollow pit in his stomach that no amount of dreaming could fill. That boy was me—a fragile child navigating a world that often felt cold, unkind, and unforgiving.

But when I open my eyes now, I'm greeted by a completely different reflection. The man staring back at me is strong. He squares his shoulders purposefully, his gaze steady and filled with gratitude. The contrast between that broken boy and the man I've become is undeniable. This isn't arrogance—it's a quiet acknowledgment of the journey I've been on, the growth that's taken place, and the countless prayers whispered into the void. It's the realization that I am now the man I prayed to God I would one day be.

This transformation didn't happen overnight. There wasn't a single defining moment when everything clicked into place. It was a slow, deliberate process—like building a house brick by brick, each piece shaped by pain, hope, and an unrelenting desire for something better. I'm still a work in progress, chipping away at the rough edges, striving to be a better husband, father, and man. But every step forward reminds me that growth is not a destination—it's a commitment to the process.

## Faith as the Foundation

For me, the foundation of that transformation is faith. Faith isn't just an abstract idea or something I picked up because it seemed convenient—it's the bedrock on which I've rebuilt my life. The dictionary defines faith as "complete trust or confidence in someone or something." For me, that someone is my Lord Jesus Christ.

It wasn't always this way. Growing up, faith felt like a distant concept—something other people discussed, but I never truly understood. I didn't grow up in the church; there were no Sunday mornings spent in pews or afternoons learning stories of David, Moses, or Jonah. My childhood was too chaotic for that, filled with instability and survival. So, when my daughter comes home from Sunday school, excitedly recounting the stories she's learned, I hear most of them for the first time.

When I was younger, I blamed God many times. I cursed Him in moments of anger and despair, shaking my fists at the heavens and demanding to know why life was so hard, so unfair. Why did I have to go hungry? Why was love so conditional? Why did loneliness feel like my closest companion? But through it all—whether I was blaming or ignoring Him—He was there, patiently waiting.

And I understand now, whether you blame Him—God knows I've blamed Him—or if you praise Him, one day, we will all have to face Him.

I am deeply humbled by the sacrifice that Jesus Christ made. His willingness to bear the weight of humanity's sins opened the door for grace and redemption. Through that grace, I've found the strength to transform my life. Now, I believe that life is happening for me, not to me. This shift in perspective has been one of the greatest blessings of all.

## A New Perspective on Challenges

The road to transformation has not been easy. There have been moments that tested my resolve, times when it would have been easier to fall back into old patterns of doubt and defeat. But faith has taught me something powerful: challenges aren't roadblocks—they're stepping stones. They're opportunities to grow, to learn, and to become stronger.

One thing I've learned is to face challenges with humility and openness. Instead of asking, 'Why is this happening to me?' I now ask, 'What is this teaching me?' This shift in mindset has been transformative, helping me find purpose even in the most challenging moments.

Embracing this mindset wasn't easy at first. When you've spent years feeling like life is just one hardship after another, it's hard to see those struggles as anything but punishment. But I've come to realize that every trial has a purpose. Every moment of pain, setback, and unanswered prayer is part of a bigger plan.

There's a quiet strength that comes with this perspective. It doesn't mean I don't feel fear or frustration; it means I face those emotions with resilience. When I'm having a bad day, I think back to what a bad day used to look like and remind myself that this, too, shall pass. And on the other side of that struggle, growth awaits me.

## The Little Boy Who Prayed

One of the most profound moments in my journey of faith comes when I reflect on the prayers of my younger self. Scared, lonely, and lost, that little boy prayed for someone to save him. But he didn't realize then that he was praying for himself—praying for the man he would one day become.

It's a humbling thought. All those nights when I felt like no one was listening, when I cried into my pillow and begged for relief, God wasn't ignoring me. He was preparing me. He was shaping me into someone who could endure hardship, break the cycle of pain, and build something beautiful in its place.

I look at my life now and see the answers to those prayers. I see them in my wife, Rachel, whose love and unwavering support have been a guiding light. I see them in my children, whose laughter fills our home with a warmth I never knew as a child. I see them in my work, in the people I serve, and in the small, everyday moments that remind me how far I've come.

## Grace and Gratitude

When I think about the boy I once was, my heart aches for him. But it also swells with pride because even in his darkest moments, he never gave up. He kept praying, hoping, and believing—sometimes quietly, sometimes angrily—but always holding on to the possibility of something better. And now, here I am—the man I prayed to God I would one day be.

I'm not perfect. I still stumble and have moments of doubt. But every day, I wake up filled with gratitude—for the love of my wife, the laughter of my children, and the faith that sustains me. Life isn't without its challenges, but I now see them as opportunities to grow, to love more deeply, and to live with purpose.

Life has taught me that every trial shapes us, every setback prepares us, and every prayer strengthens us. I've come a long way, but I know there will be more challenges ahead. Still, I'm ready to face them—with faith, love, and the determination to keep growing into the man God has called me to be. The best chapters of my life are still ahead, and I can't wait to see where this journey leads next.

To anyone feeling broken, lost, or afraid, you are not alone. Transformation is possible. Take that first step, trust in God's plan, and lean into the challenges. Every struggle can shape you, every prayer can strengthen you, and every day offers a chance to grow. Believe in the best chapters yet to come—they're waiting for you.

If I could overcome my past to become the man I am today, so can you. This is not the end of my story—it's just the beginning of the best chapters yet to come.

# ACKNOWLEDGMENTS

First and foremost, I want to thank God for the grace, strength, and direction that has carried me through every chapter of my life. This book is a testament to your faithfulness, even in my darkest moments. Without You, none of this would have been possible.

To my incredible wife, Rachel—thank you for being my partner, anchor, and greatest cheerleader. Your unwavering love, faith, and belief in me have given me the courage to write this book and share my story with the world. You've stood by me through the trials and triumphs, and your encouragement has made all the difference. This book is as much yours as it is mine.

To my children, Gabriel and Iona—thank you for inspiring me every single day. Gabriel, you've shown me the joy of connection and the meaning of family beyond blood. Iona, you are my bright light, laughter, and endless motivation. You both remind me what's truly important in life and why I strive to be the best man I can be.

To my brothers, David and Jesse—thank you for being my companions through it all. Despite the hardships we faced, we found ways to support each other and grow together. The bond we share has been a constant source of strength, and I'm grateful for the moments we've shared and the lessons we've learned along the way.

To my father—this isn't easy, but I forgive you. I forgive you for the neglect, the pain, and the choices you made that left me feeling abandoned. I forgive you because I've learned that holding on to resentment only keeps me stuck in the past. In forgiving you, I free myself to move forward, to heal, and to be the person I was always meant to be. While our relationship will never be what I once hoped, I choose peace over bitterness.

To Uncle Kelly—thank you for being a steady and positive influence in my life. You've shown me what it means to lead with humility and wisdom. Your example has helped shape my understanding of what it means to be a man of character, and I will always be grateful for your guidance and presence in my life.

To my Aunt Beverly—I carry your memory with me every day. I am forever grateful for your guidance with Rachel. I will always cherish our time together, the endless laughs at the simplest things, and our hard-fought euchre games.

To Uncle Mike—whose life and struggles inspired a fire in me to push through my challenges—I carry your memory with me every day, and your story continues to fuel my determination to break the cycles of pain and hardship.

To my grandparents, Karl and June—There are no words vast enough to capture the depth of my gratitude for you. You have endured unimaginable loss, outliving all three of your children, yet you continue to stand with grace, love, and quiet strength. Your resilience has been a guiding light in my life, showing me that even in the face of sorrow, love remains steadfast.

Thank you for being my anchor when the world felt unsteady. For the warmth, wisdom, and unwavering support you have given me, I am endlessly grateful.

To my foster parents, Keith and Theresa—thank you for stepping into my life when I needed stability and love the most. You didn't just provide a roof over my head; you gave me hope, structure, and the foundation I needed to believe in a better future. Your compassion and generosity shaped me profoundly, and I will forever be grateful for your impact on my life.

To Lori Hale—thank you for opening your heart and home to me during one of the most pivotal times in my life. In my twenties, when I was still finding my way, you gave me a place to belong. Your warmth, love, and steady presence gave me the space to grow and heal; for that, I'll always be grateful. You treated me like family and helped me believe in myself when I needed it most.

To the Bellinger family— who introduced me to the world of piggyback trucking and shared your wisdom, I am forever grateful for your generosity and guidance. Your lessons extended beyond trucking and shaped my approach to hard work and perseverance.

To my sister-in-law, Shell Bell—We've been through our share of difficult times, but no matter what, I want you to know that I love you and will always be here for you. Family isn't about perfection—it's about standing by each other through the highs and lows, and I wouldn't trade our bond for anything. You mean so much to me, and I am grateful for every moment we've shared, the laughter, the tears, and everything in between.

To my closest friends and extended family— Brandon, Neil, Larry, Nicholas, Jason, Elizabeth, Brandon, Ben, Brian, Cody, Jermaine, thank you for the love, support, and encouragement you've shown me throughout my life. You've celebrated my victories and stood with me in my struggles; I am eternally grateful.

Lastly, to anyone who reads this book—thank you for allowing me to share my journey with you. I hope my story will inspire, encourage, and remind you that faith, perseverance, and love can carry you through, no matter how difficult the road ahead may seem.

With deep gratitude,
Dustin Bryan

www.ingramcontent.com/pod-product-compliance
Lightning Source LLC
Chambersburg PA
CBHW070641160426
43194CB00009B/1536